Macmillan Building and Surveying Series

(*continued overleaf*)

Macmillan Building and Surveying Series
Series Standing Order ISBN 0–333–69333–7

You can receive future titles in this series as they are published by placing a standing order. Please contact your bookseller or, in case of difficulty, write to us at the address below with your name and address, the title of the series and the ISBN quoted above.

Customer Services Department, Macmillan Distribution Ltd
Houndmills, Basingstoke, Hampshire RG21 6XS, England

Law and the Built Environment

Douglas Wood

Law School
Staffordshire University

MACMILLAN

First published 1999 by
MACMILLAN PRESS LTD
Houndmills, Basingstoke, Hampshire RG21 6XS
and London
Companies and representatives throughout the world

ISBN 0–333–67759–5

A catalogue record for this book is available from the British Library.

This book is printed on paper suitable for recycling and made from fully managed and sustained forest sources.

10   9   8   7   6   5   4   3   2   1
08   07   06   05   04   03   02   01   00   99

Printed in Great Britain
by Antony Rowe Ltd, Chippenham, Wiltshire

Contents

Introduction

This is a book for students. Its purpose is to provide an introduction to the legal aspects involved in property and construction based disciplines. This includes qualifications in Estate Management, Valuation Surveying and degrees in which property based studies represent a considerable element. It equally includes relevant materials for those studying for degrees in Architecture, Civil Engineering, and Quantity and Building Surveying. It is additionally appropriate for those studying for higher degrees in areas such as Facilities Management or Land Use and Planning. The book can also be used for examinations of relevant professional bodies.

This is primarily an introductory text. Its purpose is not to create pseudo-lawyers from those involved in construction and property. The hope is that it will help students to resolve law based problems and enable them to have a general idea of the legal position if they encounter relevant problems after finishing their studies. Hopefully, it will also make them realise when to seek specialist legal advice instead of relying solely on their own judgement. Those readers familiar with the subject matter covered by this book will be aware that there already exist a number of sound and well written books dealing with the legal aspects relating to both property and construction. These books are either orientated towards landed property or towards construction. This book attempts to marry the two aspects by providing a general introduction to both areas. The rationale behind such an approach is the close relationship which exists between the subject areas studied on the relevant courses and the fact that a building or property dispute often does not fit neatly into being land or building based. Indeed there is a considerable overlap where the knowledge acquired in one area is pertinent to the other.

Chapter 1 provides a general legal background which needs to be understood before progressing to the more specialist areas. The material on contracts in Chapter 2 attempts to consider the subject both from the view of a construction professional and from those involved with contracts relating to the sale and letting of land and buildings. Consequently the emphasis is on the principles which underlie all contracts. The chapter contains brief descriptions of a number of standard form contracts but there is no clause-by-clause discussion. A similar approach is taken in Chapter 3 as far as the tortious aspects are concerned. Relevant areas of the law of tort are considered from both the property and construction aspects, with appropriate case law by way of illustration. Although the property aspects in Chapter 4 are mainly of interest to estate management related students, those who are construction based should find much that is of interest to them. Building surveyors, in particular, need an understanding of landlord and tenant law, while there is reference to the relatively new party wall legislation. Chapters 5 and 6 contain a cross-section of subject areas. The highway, planning and environmental law aspects in Chapter 5 are equally useful for construction and property related students, as are the facilities management and disability aspects in Chapter 6.

Hopefully the text is sufficiently detailed for those studying at professional qualification level but readable and practical for those embarking on their studies. I have attempted to fix the law as at May 1st 1998.

Acknowledgements

I wish to express my thanks to the following for advice and help directly or indirectly: Julia Burden, Isobel Bowden, W.H. Rees, Jim Forster, Michael Haley, John Reyers, Ron Smith, Stuart Vesey and Chris Williams.

Any errors in the text are of course my responsibility.

Table of Cases

Table of Statutes

1 The Administration of Law

1.1 The Nature of Law

Any system of law is basically a method of trying to enforce order and a reasonable standard of fair play. In any community, rules will develop to control the relationships between individual members. The law acts as a set of rules which protect the rights of individuals and organisations while at the same time imposing obligations on the community at large. There must be some method of enforcing these rules and ensuring that the system is flexible enough to respond to the need for change where and when it is necessary. This book is concerned primarily with rights and duties which affect those in the landed and building professions. These are areas of life which have long had to comply with legal formalities and requirements. As society has evolved and become more complex, the laws governing such activities have increased and become more sophisticated. The aspects of law to be considered in this book have application in England and Wales. Some of the principles apply in Scotland and Northern Ireland as well, but in areas such as the organisation of the court system and the methods of transferring land there are significant differences.

1.2 Divisions of the Law

Civil and Criminal Law

A fundamental distinction is made in the English legal system between the criminal law and the civil law. Criminal law is the body of law made by the state to preserve society and uphold law and order. Its object is to punish conduct of which the state disapproves and to act as a deterrent. The punishment may take the form of a fine, imprisonment or some other form of penalty. A person or organisation who infringes these laws commits a criminal offence for which the consequence can be prosecution by the state.

Criminal cases are initiated by the state, via the police and the Crown Prosecution service, although occasionally private citizens bring such cases. The state (the *prosecution*) is responsible for bringing a case against the person alleged to be responsible for committing the criminal act (the *defendant* or *accused*). As the United Kingdom is a monarchy, proceedings are brought in the name of the Crown. Consequently, in England and Wales a criminal case is described in the following manner:

> *Regina* (latin for Queen) versus the person or organisation alleged to have carried out the criminal offence (for example, *Regina* v *Anthony Blair*). If the monarch is a king, the case will be described as *Rex* (latin for King) versus the person alleged to have committed the criminal offence (for example, *Rex* v *Frank Bruno*). In order to shorten the description of the case it may appear as *R* v *Anthony Blair* or *R* v *Frank Bruno*, as appropriate, when a record of the case is made.

Where the state is a major participant in the legal process, as in criminal cases, or the government is at the centre of such matters, the appropriate law is known as *Public Law*. Those who work in the professions relating to construction, and the management of land and buildings, should rarely encounter the operation of the criminal law in the course of their work. However, a property developer who constantly disobeys the rules relating to obtaining planning permission for a new building, or who contraves regulations relating to building activities, commits a criminal offence. Similar rules apply to a builder who allows an unsafe system of work to continue or disregards the law relating to health and safety. Those aspects of public law which are an integral part of the civil side of English law are encountered frequently by those involved in matters relating to land and buildings (see Chapter 5).

The civil law governs rights and obligations between individuals. Individuals may include a business, trade union, company or other form of organisation. Private individuals and organisations initiate such cases because they have a dispute with another person or organisation. The civil law attempts to resolve disputes and to give a remedy to the person or organisation that has been wronged (the *injured party*). Money is the essence of civil cases. Such cases are initiated with the intention of compensating the injured party who has suffered some form of financial or physical loss because of the actions of the other person. The civil law does not insist that the case be brought and the person bringing it may discontinue the process at any time. In a civil action the *plaintiff* brings the action against the *defendant*. For example: *Blair* v *Bruno* would describe a civil case brought by Mr Blair against Mr Bruno while if Coslett Contractors Ltd brought a case against Mr Quinn it would be described as *Coslett Contractors Ltd* v *Quinn* (*Coslett Contractors* v *Quinn (1996) 3 WLR 299*). Because this area of law is concerned with relationships between citizens and organisations and disputes personal to themselves it is known as *Private Law*. This is because, in the main, such disputes only affect the individuals involved in the proceedings. The civil law comprises many different subject areas. Company law, Commercial law and Employment law are good examples. As a general rule, any area of law which does not come within the scope of the criminal law is categorised as being part of the civil law. Together with property law, the principal subject areas on which the civil law is based are the law of contract and the law of tort. Consequently, much of this book is devoted to a study of these areas in an appropriate context.

Sometimes the same events give rise to both criminal and civil proceedings. A prosecution in a criminal court may well be brought against the driver of a vehicle under the Road Traffic Acts while the compensation aspects will be determined in a separate action brought by the plaintiff in a civil court. A similar situation could arise where an employer has been negligent in looking after the safety of an employee and as a result there has been injury. The employee may wish to bring a claim for compensation (*damages*) against the employer, while out of the same set of facts the employer may be prosecuted for breaches of or non-compliance with the *Health and Safety at Work Act 1974* (see Chapter 6, section 6.2). Where this situation arises, the two sets of proceedings are kept separate and the matters are dealt with in different courts. There are numerous other situations where this dual liability arises. In practice, whether a case is a criminal or civil matter, an appeal may be made to a higher court against the decision of the original court. In such circumstances the person bringing the appeal is known as the *appellant* and the person against whom the appeal is brought is known as the *respondent*. It is common for legal systems to govern particular procedures which have to be carried out within a legal framework even though there is no dispute or any matter which is *contentious*. The transfer of a house, making of a will or drafting of a contract are all good examples. These *non-contentious* matters are governed by rules developed by the civil law, although there is no conflict between the parties.

1.3 Evidence in Civil and Criminal Cases

Whether a dispute is a civil or a criminal matter, the action will not succeed unless there is sufficent evidence to support the case. It is for the prosecution or the plaintiff, as appropriate, to substantiate the case and not for the defendant to disprove it. This obligation is known as the burden of proof. When a case is heard in a court of law, the judge must determine the correct facts of the case and then, if necessary, apply the law to those facts. The legal principles can be straightforward or complex. Often, it can be more difficult to ascertain what the correct facts are than to apply the relevant law. In a criminal case the standard of proof which is required is that the prosecution must put foward sufficent evidence to show that the accused committed the crime beyond all reasonable doubt. In a civil action the plaintiff must prove the facts relied upon and is required to prove the issues on the balance of probabilities. This means that it is likely, after reviewing the evidence, that the defendant did the act complained of. The outcome tends to reflect which party's evidence the judge believes to be true. The vast majority of civil actions are settled between the parties at some time before the judge's final decision. In a civil case there are a number of methods by which the facts may be proved. The plaintiff has to put forward sufficent evidence on all the relevant facts necessary for the case unless the other party has accepted the appropriate evidence. An established method of pursuing or defending a case is through the use of witnesses giving oral evidence at first hand on oath. This is in addition to any documentary evidence which may be available, or real evidence such as a mechanical device or a photograph of a building site where an accident has taken place. In civil cases, evidence is given by a sworn statement, made on oath, known as an *affidavit*. A witness must not give an opinion on the facts at issue unless he is an expert witness (see section 1.16). Hearsay evidence is not admissible. This is evidence which is not perceived by the witness but stated by some other person. There are a number of important exceptions to this rule (*Civil Evidence Act 1968 s2*).

1.4   The Common Law

Most legal systems in Europe are based upon Roman law but England and Wales are subject to the so-called common law. This expression is used to describe English law and the other legal systems, such as those of Australia or the United States of America, which adopted the type of law to be found in England. The expression 'common law' can also be used to describe the law made by judges in courts of law as opposed to that made by Act of Parliament. A third interpretation is that it means the body of law which became common or uniform to the whole of England and Wales after 1066. Up to that date, the laws of England and Wales varied from area to area as there was no unified legal system. Each court operated in isolation. There were no centralised institutions exercising either administrative or judicial control over the legal system. This changed with the Norman conquest in 1066 when William the Conqueror (William I) proclaimed himself King of England replacing the Saxon kings. The object of the Normans was to establish a national system of law which would apply to all persons alike, wherever they were situated geographically and whatever their status in society. This law became based on the law which they brought with them from France and on those English customs which were found to be widespread after the conquest.

One consequence of the Norman conquest was the introduction of the King's Council or *Curia Regis*. This was the central government of the Kingdom which exercised administrative (*executive*), law-making (*legislative*) and judge-like (*judicial*) functions without distinction. In the period immediately after the conquest, the common law developed on an *ad hoc* basis with each problem being settled as it arose. The Normans developed a strong central government and gradually the old local customs began to disappear, with their place being taken by the King's Court. From this court, special courts were instituted to deal with particular types of cases in which the King's justice was sought. As new courts developed, the *Curia Regis* diminished in importance. Three major common law courts administered the new common law:

1. The Court of King's Bench
2. The Court of Exchequer
3. The Court of Common Pleas.

These courts were able to compel the attendance of parties involved in the disputes, and also of witnesses. The process began whereby judges, appointed by the King, acted as Royal Commissioners throughout the country. These judges dealt with civil and criminal matters wherever they arose. This process was developed in the reign of Henry II (1154–89) and eventually it led to the development of the assize system whereby judges toured the country on regular circuits in an attempt to deal with civil and criminal disputes in the regions. This process existed until 1971 and in a modified form still exists today. From the reign of Henry II, civil actions in the common law courts had to be started by writ. This royal command had to be obtained from the King's Chancellor. For every civil case there had to be a separate writ, and the plaintiff had to select the particular writ which fitted the facts of the case. These original writs were simply documents containing an order from the King addressed to the defendant, the County Sheriff or the Lord of the Manor, requiring the defendant's attendance at court to answer allegations against him. The different types of writ were said to give rise to different forms of action. This meant that the method of trial and the procedural rules which were applicable depended upon the nature of the writ used to start the case. Much of the civil law was built up through defining the circumstances in which the various writs could be brought.

1.5 Equity

By the end of the reign of Edward I (1272–1307) the short comings of the common law were becoming apparent. The writ system had become very formalised. Writs were not available to cover every set of circumstances and the rule was that, unless there was an appropriate writ, there was no remedy. No action could succeed unless the correct court was chosen. Technicalities dominated common law procedures. These became very complex and an action might fail because of a slight error in the preparation of the documents required to start off a case. Another problem was the lack of appropriate remedies to fit every set of circumstances. A successful plaintiff in the common law courts had only the remedy of damages. Plaintiffs who were dissatisfied with the common law, if they needed to go to law, began to petition the king in an attempt to redress their grievances. By the end of the Fourteenth Century there were so many petitions that the King referred them to the Lord Chancellor. From this process, the courts of equity emerged, presided over by the Lord Chancellor. The Chancellor granted remedies which he thought were just and equitable depending on the circumstances of the case. This process became so popular that eventually other judges needed to be appointed. These Chancellor's Courts, or Courts of Chancery as they became known, provided an alternative set of courts to those of the common law.

Equity offered new remedies as an alternative to a claim for damages. Initially, the Chancellor was able to grant any remedy which was thought appropriate to fit the circumstances of the case. Eventually, the Courts of Equity became as formalised as the common law, with the availability only of certain specific remedies with guidance from previous cases. Equity offered new remedies such as *specific performance* (a court order to compel the performance of the contract), *injunction* (an order requiring a person to stop doing something they should not be doing in the first place) and *rescission* (the right to withdraw from a contract) (see Chapter 2, section 2.14). The basis upon which equitable remedies operate has always been different from the availability of damages as a remedy in the common law courts. Equity has never been a complete system of law. Instead, it has acted as a gloss on the common law by filling in gaps. Equitable remedies are discretionary and are not automatically granted even if the plaintiff has proved the case in issue. At common law, once the case is proved the plaintiff is automatically entitled to damages irrespective of any other aspects of the case. If an equitable remedy is sought, the so-called Maxims of Equity are applicable. These are a set of rules which regulate the basis upon which remedies are granted. The conduct of the plaintiff, in particular, is very important where an equitable remedy is claimed.

In the Nineteenth Century a number of reforms were effected to the legal system, resulting in the Judicature Acts 1873–75. These Acts set up, to a large extent, the system of courts as it is today. Existing court structures were reorganised while it was established that matters governed by the common law and equity could be dealt with in the same court. Even so, except in those areas of law where equity has never developed or where only equitable principles have any application, as in the case of trusts, a modern court will have to consider the common law position initially and then see if equity affects the position in any way. The Acts ordained that where the rules of common law and equity conflicted, the rules of equity would prevail *(Supreme Court Act 1981 s49)*. Although the common law and equity were fused for administrative purposes, they still retained their own individual characteristics and both aspects are present today in the same system.

1.6   The Sources of Law

Before the common law system can be properly understood it is necessary to consider the ways in which English law developed and to find out where the law actually comes from. Most continental European countries have a legal system whereby much of their law is contained in written codes which are amended as the need arises. The *Code Napolèon* in France is a good example. English law has been developed from a number of sources, each arising as the situation required. Although most new law is produced by Act of Parliament, to meet the complex requirements of contemporary society, the greater part of English law has developed from the rules and principles pronounced in the decisions of courts throughout the centuries. The other major domestic source of law which is referred to is 'custom'. This was originally a source of law of great importance. In fact this is where the common law originated. Its practical importance nowadays is slight, but on those occasions when a case does come to court questioning the legal validity of a custom it tends to concern rights over land or buildings, so it is appropriate to consider it here.

(A) Custom

A custom is a right or duty which has come to exist through the consent of the population. Traditionally, a custom could either be general (applicable to the whole country) or local (applicable to a particular area). Nowadays, only local customs are of any importance, as general customs have either fallen into disuse or have become incorporated into the general law. Such rights are exercisable by members of a particular community such as a parish (*Brocklebank* v *Thomson [1903] 2 Ch 344*) or a town *(New Windsor Corporation* v *Mellor [1974] 1 WLR 504)*. A person who wishes to prove the existence of a custom never previously recognised by the courts, must satisfy a number of tests relating to the alleged right.

Time Immemorial

The custom must have existed since 'time immemorial'. This is historically fixed as 1189. In most cases it is impossible for those claiming the custom to show conclusively that it existed in 1189, so this requirement is satisfied by evidence that the custom has existed within living memory or at least without interruption for 20 years. This was shown in *Mercer* v *Denne [1905] 2 Ch 538*, where it was established that fishermen had the right to dry nets on a privately owned beach. The owner of the beach was restrained from building on the beach because to do so would interfere with the customary rights. If the custom could not have been exercised at some time since 1189, the claim will fail, as in *Simpson* v *Wells [1872] LR 7 QB 214,* where the holding of a stall on a highway was shown not to have been authorised before the Fourteenth Century.

Continuity

The custom must have been continuously in operation but it need not have been exercised throughout the required period as long as the right actually existed. It seems that a customary right cannot be lost by disuse once it is established, but failure to exercise the right may make it more difficult to prove in the first place. In *Wyld* v *Silver [1963] Ch 243* the rights of people in a parish to hold an annual fair on a specific piece of land were recognised as a custom, even though no such fair had been held within living memory. Consequently they were able to prevent the landowner from building on the land. Likewise in *New Windsor Corporation* v *Mellor [1974] 1 WLR 504*, mentioned previously, a local authority was prevented from utilising land where it was proved that for many centuries the land had been used for recreational purposes by the local inhabitants, even though such rights had not been exercised in recent times.

Peaceable Enjoyment

The basis of a custom is that it is exercised by common consent. If it is exercised with force or in secret there can be no custom (*nec per vim nec clam nec precario*). If the so-called custom is exercised by permission it cannot be as of right, and therefore it is impossible to establish as a local custom. In *Mills* v *Colchester Corporation [1867] LR 2 CP 567* a claim to a custom entitling the plaintiff to an annual licence to fish for oysters failed, as the existence of the licence prevented the fishing from being as of right.

Reasonableness and Certainty

The courts will not recognise any custom which is unreasonable. On that basis an attempt to claim the existence of a customary right enabling the Lord of the Manor to excavate on land without paying compensation for the damage to the owners of buildings on that land was deemed to be unreasonable *(Wolstanton Ltd* v *Newcastle-under-Lyme Borough Council*

[1940] AC 860). The custom must also be certain. Those obtaining the benefit of a customary right tend to be based on geographical location, while those who are to benefit from it must be capable of proper identification. In *Wilson* v *Wiles [1806] 7 East's Term Reports 121* a claim to a local custom to take turf failed because the extent of the 'right' could not be identified. The law is reluctant to recognise new customs which have not been previously established. The custom must be consistent with previously established customs and must not conflict with statute law or any basic principle of the common law.

(B) Case Law

Case law is the essence of the common law. The greater part of English law consists of rules and principles laid down by judges in courts of law, the more important of which are written down in law reports for future reference. When a judge makes a decision on a particular aspect of the law this will be recorded, and other judges are obliged to follow this decision in subsequent cases. When a judge is considering the facts of a case and applying the relevant law to the facts, it is necessary to look back to previous cases which have involved similar facts in the same area of law to see how those cases have been dealt with.

Law-Reporting

The importance of case law as a source of law depends upon the existence of law reports. Important cases which establish new principles of law are published in the law reports. The report contains details of the facts of the case together with the decision of the judge, known as the judgement, and the reasons for that decision. By no means are all cases of interest reported. There is no official law report and most court decisions are left unreported. Even so, an unreported case may be taken into account by a judge when coming to a decision in a later case. There is an element of chance as to whether a case is reported or not. The history of law reports goes back to the Year Books. These were manuscripts which referred to cases which had been dealt with in a particular locality. After the demise of the Year Books the practice grew up, in the first part of the Sixteenth Century, whereby a number of private reports were separately published. These were compiled primarily by lawyers for their own personal use, and their standard and quality varied greatly. Good examples include those of Coke, Dyer and Burrow, who all established a reputation for reporting cases accurately. All the available reports of the private reporters have been reprinted in what is known as 'The English Reports'. These are sometimes referred to by judges in the course of their decisions, while in The English Reports there is an index showing in which volume the reports of individual reporters are contained.

Modern law-reporting dates from 1865 with the creation of the Council of Law Reporting. In 1870 the Council was incorporated as the Incorporated Council of Law Reporting for England and Wales. The 'Law Reports' comprise four series of reports: Appeal Cases (AC), Queen's Bench (QB), Chancery (Ch) and Family (Fam). These reports are now supplemented by the Weekly Law Reports (WLR) which contain a report of all the decisions which will eventually appear in the more official reports. In addition to these reports there are other transcripts which are published commercially. The best known of these are the All England Law Reports (AER) which are a general series of reports published weekly which appear now in three or four volumes each year. Although the courts have traditionally preferred to use the more official reports, the importance of the commercially produced reports has increased in recent years. In construction matters and disputes concerning land and buildings it is common to encounter the Local Government Reports (LGR), Property and Compensation Reports (PCR), Building Law Reports (BLR), Housing Law Reports (HLR) and Rydes Rating Cases (RRC) among others. *The Times* newspaper carries daily reports of leading cases while periodicals such as the *Estates Gazette* and *The Journal of Planning and Environmental Law* publish reports of interest to their readers. Many cases are recorded in various reports and reference is made to them in a cross-section of journals. When a case is reported, after the names of the parties involved and the year it was decided, the name of the report is stated and the page where the case is to be found. For example, *Murphy* v *Brentwood District Council (1991) 1 AC 398* indicates that the first volume of the Appeal Cases reports for 1991 must be consulted, and on page 398 details of the case are reported. One other relevant factor which needs to be mentioned here is the appearance of computerised databases such as LEXIS, which has meant that practitioners and other interested parties now have easier access to unreported cases and the decisions in cases decided in foreign countries. Other technical aids are now much in use to find relevant information. The LAWTEL system comprises a variety of databases including case law, statute summaries, commencements and repeals, and statutory instruments, while information is available on CD-ROM to enable users to keep up with relevant data and specialist subject areas.

Judicial Precedent

After the reorganisation of the courts implemented by the Judicature Acts (1873–75) and the emergence of good law-reporting in the latter part of the Nineteenth Century, judicial precedent became an integral aspect of case law. By this doctrine of *stare decisis* (to stand upon decisions), as it is sometimes known, whenever a judge reaches a decision on a particular point the rules of law contained in previous decisions which deal with

similar issues must be applied. Not every judicial decision makes a precedent, as some courts are more important than others and not every case is
important enough to make new law. A distinction is made between the principle forming the decision, called the *ratio decidendi*, and other comments
made by a judge which are not strictly relevant to the decision, known as the
obiter dicta. The *ratio* is the binding precedent which must be followed in
future cases. The *dicta*, which is not material to the case, or does not form
the basis of the decision, need not be followed in subsequent cases. Even so,
dicta of an appellate court (see sections 1.10 and 1.11) may carry considerable weight. The doctrine is applied on a hierarchal basis. The rule is that
the lower courts are bound by decisions of the higher courts. The County
Court and the Magistrates Court, at the bottom of the court hierarchy (inferior courts), are bound by the decisions of the courts above them (superior
courts) but are not themselves bound by their own decisions. The High
Court is bound by a decision of the Court of Appeal and the House of
Lords, while the Court of Appeal is bound by a decision of the House of
Lords which is the supreme appeal court in the United Kingdom (including
Scotland and Northern Ireland) in both civil and criminal matters.
Decisions of this court are binding on all lower courts. Since 1966, the
House of Lords has been able to depart from its previous decisions.
Instances of this have been rare. The decision in *Murphy v Brentwood DC
[1991] 1 AC 398* is a good example of this process, where the Law Lords
overruled the previous decision in *Anns v Merton London Borough Council
[1978] AC 728*. The European Court (see section 1.8), whose major jurisdiction is concerned with the Treaties and institutions of the European
Union, is not bound by its previous decisions. By joining the European
Community, Parliament accepted that in the interpretation of the various
treaties between the member states of the Community, the supreme court
would be the European Court of Justice.

Interpretation of Judicial Precedent

The importance of a precedent tends to grow with age, but that does not
mean that a precedent must be followed regardless of the consequences.
Despite the importance of precedent in English law, a court will sometimes
refuse to follow an earlier decision. It is the *ratio decidendi* of a case which is
binding on subsequent courts, subject to the hierarchy rules. Before the
precedent has a binding effect it must be shown to be a decision of a court
in the English hierarchy. *Obiter dicta* of a court, particularly the House of
Lords, is of weight but need not be followed by a court in subsequent cases.
Similar considerations apply to the decisions of Scottish, Irish and particularly Commonwealth cases, which in recent years have been frequently cited
in building disputes. Decisions of the Privy Council (see section 1.12) also
come into this category. If there are grounds for distinguishing a case from

an earlier decision, the latter will not be followed. A court may overrule a legal rule in a decision which it considers to be obviously wrong, while the decision of a lower court may be reversed on appeal if the higher court disapproves of the previous case.

The Merits of the System

The following are considered to be *advantages* of the system of judicial precedent:

1. *Certainty*
It is suggested that precedent gives at least some degree of certainty and consistency to the law so that the probable outcome of a case can be predicted.

2. *Detail*
Case law has many detailed rules. The law reports provide full information relating to decided cases and it is argued that a code could never furnish similar precision.

3. *Practical aspects*
It is more useful to have a precedent than to argue a case on each occasion that a legal issue arises.

4. *Flexibility*
Where appropriate, a court is able to avoid an unsatisfactory precedent by distinguishing or overruling a decision, although the opportunities for this are limited.

The following are put foward as *disadvantages* of the system:

1. *Rigidity*
The process gives little scope for manoeuvre (at least in theory). Parliament can legislate for a change.

2. *Technicalities*
The sophisticated methods of avoiding a precedent tend to confuse the law and produce a degree of uncertainty.

3. *Bulk*
Because of the volume of cases it is increasingly difficult to refer to every appropriate authority. Sometimes cases go unreported but they still remain as precedents.

(C) Legislation

Although the bulk of English law is derived from case law, governed by the system of judicial precedent, the supremacy of legislation over all other sources of law means that law made by Parliament, or derived from it, is the most important source of law in the United Kingdom today. A statute, or Act of Parliament, is the quickest and clearest method of adding to the law or changing it to meet current social requirements. Such an Act overrules any existing custom, case law or earlier Act with which it is in conflict, and the only external factor which can affect this parliament-made law is a decision of the European Community (see section 1.8). This supremacy of legislation over other sources of law is known as the Sovereignty of Parliament. The effect of this is that Parliament, comprising the House of Commons and the House of Lords together with the reigning monarch, is sovereign and the legality of Parliament to make a specific law cannot be challenged. The courts must apply the Act once it becomes law, although it is a matter for the judges to ascertain what the Acts actually mean.

The Making of a Statute

In the United Kingdom, Parliament consists of two different legislative institutions known as the House of Commons and the House of Lords. Ideas for new laws are put forward by both the government in power and by private members of Parliament. The former are far more numerous and the latter stand little chance of success unless they are adopted by the government. The idea is put into technical language in a Bill. Government Bills are prepared by lawyers known as Parliamentary Draftmen and they can be introduced by the government in either House of Parliament. The normal practice is to introduce Bills in the House of Commons. A Bill has to pass through several stages in both the Commons and the Lords before it receives the Royal Assent (the Queen's approval) and becomes an Act. Once a Bill becomes an Act it will remain law unless it is repealed. It is presumed not to be retrospective (back-dated) in effect. A statute does not become obsolete simply by the passing of time. There are many Acts on the statute book which are antiquated and of no practical use. As a consequence there are now Statute Law (Repeals) Acts which repeal obsolete enactments on a regular basis. Occasionally an Act is only operative for a limited period, but as a general rule a statute ceases to have effect only when it is repealed by another statute.

Types of Legislation

Public Acts
These are Acts which affect the community generally. They are the most common types of Acts which are promulgated (brought into effect)

Private Acts
These do not alter the general law but confer special or local powers. They are often promoted by local authorities.

Consolidating Acts

Such an Act is a statute which gathers together several Acts on one area of the law and re-enacts them so that all the statute law on a particular topic can be found in the same Act. This is periodically done with tax legislation and Town Planning Acts.

Codifying Acts

A codification takes place when the whole of the law on a particular topic is enacted in one statute. It includes all previous case law, established customs and legislation. The law of most continental European countries is codified but in the United Kingdom and other Common law countries there is little codification. The classic example of codification in English law is the *Sale of Goods Act 1893* (now 1979) (see Chapter 2, section 2.7), which reduced all the law on the subject into a single code.

Delegated Legislation

Parliament frequently passes on responsibility for enacting legislation to others. In this way the framework of an Act can be laid down while the delegated body can fill in the detail required. This subordinate legislation appears in the form of rules, regulations and orders, while the legislators range from the government (the Queen in Council) to local authorities. Much of the law relating to building matters and the transfer of land is to be found in this form. Examples include the Building Regulations, and many aspects of Planning law and Health and Safety legislation. Delegated legislation is made by ministerial orders known as statutory instruments, which since 1946 have had to be published or 'laid' before Parliament before they become effective. A Statutory instrument can be recognised in that instead of having the word Act at the end of the name of the instrument (document), the order, rules or regulations will be cited (recorded) by reference to year and number with the letters SI indicating its status. Two other forms of delegated legislation are bye-laws and the regulations of professional bodies and trade unions. Bye-laws are local laws which regulate aspects of life. So-called autonomic legislation regulates the conduct of the members of professional associations such as the Royal Institution of Chartered Surveyors and The Royal Institute of British Architects, and provides for sanctions where appropriate.

Control of Delegated Legislation

Control over delegated legislation is exercised by Parliament and the courts.

Parliament

Committees of the House of Commons review statutory instruments and decide which of them should be brought to the attention of Parliament. The enabling Act (the individual Act which grants power to make particular regulations) sometimes requires that the instrument be brought to the notice of Parliament. Appropriate government ministers are answerable to Parliament in respect of regulations made by their own departments, while bye-laws must be confirmed by a Government department before they become law. Parliament also has the overall safeguard in that it may withdraw the delegated power if it so wishes.

The courts
Although the courts cannot challenge the validity of an Act of Parliament, they can challenge delegated legislation on the basis that the sub-legislator has exceeded the powers which Parliament has conferred upon him. In this case, the statutory instrument will be held to be *ultra vires* (beyond the power) and the rules rendered void. Many statutes, those dealing with compulsory purchase of land and planning law for example, contain provisions whereby delegated legislation can be challenged on the basis that it is *ultra vires*. Also, before certain types of delegated legislation are effected, a public enquiry is held so that the views of the public may be made known on the particular issues.

The Advantages of Delegated Legislation

1. *Speed*
In an emergency, Parliament may not have time to deal with every problem which arises.

2. *Volume*
It saves time for Parliament to deal with general aspects of policy and then to delegate the detail to the sub-legislators.

3. *Flexibility*
A flexible legislative process confers obvious advantages. The rules can be quickly altered and amended as necessary.

4. *Technicality*
Modern day statute law, such as environmental and safety legislation, is highly technical in nature and better dealt with by experts than by members of Parliament.

The Disadvantages of Delegated Legislation

1. *Bulk*
Over 3000 statutory instruments come into force each year, creating new law.

2. *Consultation and control*
With the widespread use of delegated legislation, law-making moves out of the control of elected representatives of the people and more into the hands

of civil servants. Because this type of legislation need not be mentioned in Parliament, there is a danger of insuffcient publicity and consultation with interested parties.

Statutory Interpretation

Although the courts are denied the opportunity of challenging the supremacy of Parliament, because of the concept of Parliamentary Sovereignty, it is a matter for the courts to determine the meaning of a particular section of an Act or statutory instrument and to attempt to discover Parliament's intentions from the language used in the provision. The rule is that judges must not imply words into a statute but must interpret the provision from what the enactment says. It is not possible, as in the case of most systems of law in Europe, to look at extrinsic material such as debates in Parliament to help interpret the provision. Rules have been formulated to deal with the interpretation of statutes by the courts. Many Acts contain an interpretation section dealing with the words and phrases used in it. A good example of this is section 205 of the Law of Property Act 1925. Parliament has also helped the courts, to some extent, by passing the Interpretation Act 1978 which defines many expressions used in legislation unless a contrary intention is apparent. The task of the courts is to 'interpret the will of parliament' as expressed in the statute. To help the judges in that task of interpretation the courts have developed a number of rules. It is for the judge to decide which is the appropriate rule in a particular case:

The literal rule
The basis of this rule is that if the words of the statute are clear and unambiguous they will be applied as they stand.

The golden rule
Where application of the literal rule results in an absurdity or is inconsistent, the meaning to be given is that which expresses best the intention of Parliament from reading the Act in full.

The mischief rule
Here the court attempts to find out the mischief which the Act is attempting to remedy and interprets the Act accordingly (*Heydon's Case [1584] 3 Co Rep 7a*; *Gorris* v *Scott [1874] LR Exch 125*).

These issues do not tend to arise in continental European systems of law or in the interpretation of European Community legislation (see section 1.8). In Civil systems of law the overall intention or purpose of the legislation is paramount. The background to the legislation is considered as an essential part of the process. Legislation must be interpreted 'purposively' to give effect to the broad intentions of Parliament (*Lister* v *Forth Dry Dock Co Ltd [1989] 1 All*

ER 1134; *H P Bulmer Ltd* v *J Bollinger SA [1974] Ch 401; Pickstone* v *Freemans [1987] 3 All ER 756*).

(D) Law Reform and the Law Commission

It is important that any legal system should be continually assessed in order that its principles do not become out of date. Statute law is the principal method by which the law is changed, but there are also pressure groups who inquire into the state of the law and where appropriate make proposals for amendment. In addition to professional bodies such as the Law Society and the Bar Council, external associations such as the National Council for Civil Liberties and the lawyers' political groups (for instance, the Society of Labour Lawyers and its Conservative equivalent) seek to influence the present state of the legal system. There are also a number of standing committees of lawyers who advise the Lord Chancellor (see section 1.16) on matters of law reform. At times the Government appoints a Royal Commission to research a particular topic. The Beeching Commission, which led to the Courts Act 1971 bringing about a fundamental change in the system of courts, is a good example.

The Law Commission Act 1965 established the Law Commission. This is a permanent organisation consisting of full time Commissioners, who are lawyers appointed by the Lord Chancellor to recommend changes which should be made to the law. It is an advisory body given the task of modernising the legal system. Its recommendations only become law if they are adopted by Parliament. It can claim considerable success in bringing about law reform, particularly changes in the criminal law. A good example of the Law Commission's work is the Latent Defects Act 1985 (see Chapter 3, section 3.4) which attempted to clarify the law on limitation periods (the length of time a plaintiff has in which to bring a case against a defendant). In 1993, Sir Michael Latham was commissioned by the Department of the Environment and other bodies connected with the construction industry to suggest a number of mechanisms for improving co-operation and productivity. Although the report 'Constructing the Team' has not been acted upon as yet in every aspect, The Housing Grants, Construction and Regeneration Act 1996 (see Chapter 2, section 2.16) has been passed as a partial implementation of the report. This Act, which provides for a new system of dispute adjudication and the outlawing of 'pay when paid' contracts, is a good example of a report leading to the enactment of legislation.

1.7 'Access to Justice'

As a response to the considerable criticism which has been levelled at the conduct of civil litigation in England and Wales, Lord Woolf, the Master of the Rolls (see section 1.15) was asked by the Lord Chancellor in 1995 to conduct a review of the system of civil litigation in England and Wales. The major object of the review was to make the system as accessible as possible to all. In his interim report 'Access to Justice' issued in summer 1995, Lord Woolf stressed the following underlying themes:

(1) Procedures should be as simple as possible and comprehensive to layman and lawyer alike.
(2) The underlying philosophy behind litigation should be to encourage the early settlement of disputes.
(3) The parties to proceedings and their lawyers are obliged to prosecute and defend proceedings with speed and efficency. Lord Woolf emphasised the shortcomings of the present system whereby lawyers are trained to win cases rather than to resolve disputes. A 'sea change' was perceived to be required placing greater emphasis on alternative forms of dispute resolution (see section 1.16).

1.8   European Community Law

The European Economic Community (EEC) was set up by the first Treaty of Rome in 1957. Its aim was to merge the interests of its member states into a common market of Europe whereby persons, goods, capital and services could circulate freely in order to create stability among its members and improve standards of living. After the merger of the EEC with the European Coal and Steel Community (ECSC) and the European Atomic Energy Authority (EURATOM) these three bodies became known as the European Community or 'EC'. The Treaty of Rome was concerned with attempting to harmonise the economic policies of the member states through common policies in matters such as employment, fair competition, transport, social issues, agriculture and fisheries. In 1973, the United Kingdom became a full member of the Community, thereby agreeing to dilute its sovereign powers. Over the last twenty years, many other countries have joined the Community and this process is continuing. Many Eastern European countries are seeking to embrace the Union. In 1992, the Treaty on European Union (TEU) was signed at Maastrict in The Netherlands, attempting to resolve many areas of the Community's activities.

Community Institutions

The Commission

This is the executive body of the Community. It initiates and drafts community legislation. It also acts as the guardian of the Treaties and has a duty to investigate any infringements of EC law. There are 17 Commissioners from the member states (including two from the UK) who must act independently of their national status. The President holds office for a renewable term of 2 years.

The Council of Ministers

The Council is made up of representatives from the governments of each member state. It is a political body which reflects the national interests of member states in legislative matters. Although the final decision on any legislative proposal rests with the Council, it may only act on proposals put foward by the Commission.

The Parliament

Originally referred to as the Assembly, this body is based in Strasbourg in France. Since 1979, members have been elected from member states (MEPs). Representation varies depending upon the size of the member state. Members vote on a personal basis and do not receive any voting mandate from their home state. Parliament may question the Commission on its activities but still acts primarily as an advisory and consultative body, although in recent years it has managed to increase its legislative powers.

The Court of Justice (ECJ)

Based in Luxembourg and not to be confused with the European Court of Human Rights (see section 1.13), the Court of Justice is charged with ensuring that community law is enforced and to provide a forum for the resolution of disputes between member states and the EC. It is also concerned with disputes between the institutions of the community and protecting rights of the individual. Judges are appointed from member states and one of them acts as President for a three year term. The judges are assisted by Advocate Generals whose role is to assist the court by presenting reasoned submissions on the facts and also recommendations for a decision. These are purely objective in nature and are not binding on the judges. Procedures are derived from continental European systems of law, with much greater emphasis on written submissions and pleadings. Dissenting judgements are not expressed and there is no right of appeal. Since 1989, a new court of first instance (CFI) has been in place to ease the workload of the Court of Justice. The workload of the CFI is limited to disputes between the EC and its staff, competition issues and certain matters relating to the ECSM and EURATOM. Actions brought by member states or the EC institutions are specifically excluded from the court's jurisdiction. There is a right of appeal to the ECJ.

The Court of Auditors

This court was established at the inception of the Community in 1957 and carries out audits of all revenue and expenditure of the Community. It has to provide the Council and the Parliament with a statement that transactions have been legally made and that the accounts are accurate.

The Sources of European Community Law

(a) The Treaties

A Treaty is a written agreement concluded between two or more states. In a way it is like a Public Act of Parliament made between nation states, but instead of having effect in one particular country it applies to all the parties to the treaty. Treaties are the primary source of EC law and take priority over subsidiary treaties and provisions contained in secondary legislation. Major examples include the two Treaties of Rome (1957), the Single European Act 1986 and the Maastrict Treaty (Treaty of European Union 1992). Subsidiary treaties or conventions may also be a source of EC law. Trading agreements between the community and other states come into this category.

(b) Community Legislation

Both the Commission and the Council of Ministers have law-making powers delegated to them by Article 189 of the EC Treaty. Hence they are able to enact legislation in a number of ways.

(1) *Regulations*
These are of general application in all member states. They are binding and directly applicable, and take effect without further enactment.

(2) *Decisions*
A decision is addressed either to a specific state or individual and is legally binding on the addressee.

(3) *Directives*
A directive may be addressed to one or more of the member states and will normally require implementation by that state in order to be legally binding. Member states have a discretion as to how to effect this state of affairs.

The Problem of 'Direct Applicability' and 'Direct Effect'

The extent to which treaties between member states and community secondary legislation is binding on member states is closely bound up with the principles of direct applicability and direct effect. If a provision is directly applicable it means that it can take effect in the legal system of a member state without any further enactment. A provision which is directly effective is one which gives rise to rights or obligations on which individuals may rely before their own national courts. In the United Kingdom, provision is made for the principle of direct effect in S2 (*Case 26/62 [1963] ECR 1*) of the European Communities Act 1972. A treaty provision will be of direct effect so long as it is clear and unambiguous, is unconditional in nature and able to take effect without further action by the EC or member states. In the early case of *Van Gend En Loos*, a private firm sought to rely on EC law against the Netherlands customs authorities in proceedings before a Netherlands tribunal. The Court of Justice held that the appropiate provision (Article 12 prohibiting member states from introducing new customs duties between themselves) was directly effective and could be relied upon before the Netherlands courts.

Article 189 of the EC Treaty states that Regulations are directly applicable and consequently they take effect without further enactment. They may be invoked vertically or horizontally so long as they are clear and unambiguous. If an obligation is imposed on a member state it may create vertical direct effect, in which case the provision may only be enforced against the state, or an organ of the state, and not against specific individuals. This is contrasted with horizontal direct effect, where obligations are imposed on individuals reflecting the relationship between them.

Difficulties have arisen as far as the question of the direct effect and direct applicability of directives is concerned. In *Van Duyn* v *Home Office 41/74 [1975] ECR* a Netherlands national who was refused entry to the United Kingdom to take up a job with the Church of Scientology was entitled to rely on a directive even though the UK had not implemented it, in circumstances where the ECJ was satisfied that the time for implementation had passed. It has been held by the European Court of Justice (*Marshall* v *Southampton and South-West Hampshire Area Health Authority 152/84 [1986] ECR*) that directives and decisions can only have vertical effect and not horizontal effect. Cases before the ECJ have decided that the concept of direct effect can be relied upon where the claim is against an organisation or body providing a public service which is subject to the control and authority of the state. This has included The Royal Ulster Constabulary (*Johnston* v *RUC 224/84 [1986] ECR*), a local authority (*R* v *London Boroughs Transport Committee ex parte Freight Association Ltd 132/1990 [1991] ECR*), and British Gas while it was still under private ownership (*Foster* v *British Gas 188/89 [1989] ECR*). Much depends on the actual wording and intention of the provision as to whether or not direct effect will be imposed. In *Grad* v *Finanzami Traustein 9/70 [1970] ECR* it was held that if the criteria are met, both directives and decisions may be directly effective. One significant decision is *Francovitch 9/90 [1992] ECR*, where it was decided that a person may be able to claim damages from a member state for loss suffered as a result of its failure to implement a directive into its own domestic legal system. Article 173 of the EC Treaty gives the ECJ power to review the legality of acts of the Council and the Commission on grounds which include the infringement of the treaty or of any rule relating to its application. EC secondary legislation can be reviewed only by the ECJ, while in the UK such legislation is implemented in the form of statutory instrument. In *Factortame [1991] 1 All ER 70* the European Court laid down that Community Law must be fully applied in all member states and that a relevant Community Law rendered automatically inapplicable any conflicting provision of national law.

1.9   The Court System in England and Wales

The court system in England is still based on that which was put into place by the Judicature Acts 1873–75 although, of necessity, changes have been made since in an attempt to reflect contemporary needs. Although some courts have both civil and criminal jurisdiction, it is better to consider the jurisdictions separately. The system is essentially a hierarchical one and as a rule it is possible to appeal from a lower court to a higher court.

1.10   The Criminal Courts

(A) Magistrates Court

The vast majority of criminal cases start off in Magistrates Courts and over 95 per cent finish there as well. Every town of any size has at least one such court and there are approximately 600 such courts in England and Wales. The court is comprised of Lay Magistrates, sometimes known as Justices of the Peace (JP). These are part-time judges, not formally trained in the law, who in criminal matters decide the innocence or guilt of the defendant on the facts put before them. Such judges are unpaid but receive an attendance allowance and payment for loss of earnings. There are about 30,000 Lay Magistrates. Justices are appointed by the Lord Chancellor on the recommendation of Local Advisory Committees and all newly appointed magistrates have to undergo some initial training. On matters of law, procedure and sentencing, they are advised by the Clerk to the Magistrates who is legally qualified. The retiring age is 70. In London, and some of the larger cities in the provinces, Stipendary Magistrates supplement the work of Justices. These are paid full-time magistrates, being either solicitors or barristers (see section 1.16) who have had considerable experience of practising as lawyers in the criminal courts. They are allocated to the busier courts where the volume of work is greater and more complex. A Magistrates Court is comprised of three Lay Magistrates although two justices will sometimes suffice. A Stipendary Magistrate sits alone and has the powers equivalent to a bench of Lay Magistrates. In court a magistrate is addressed as 'your worship'.

Criminal offences fall into two main categories. These are classified as either summary or indictable offences. In the case of summary offences the magistrates decide the verdict and the sentence. This will also be the case if an offence is triable either summarily or on indictment and the defendant consents to it being heard in the Magistrates Court. The maximum fine where a case is dealt with summarily is £5000 although higher fines of up to £20,000 are available in cases relating to health and safety and pollution. The maximum custodial sentence which magistrates may impose for any offence is in most cases 6 months' imprisonment. If the defendant has been convicted of two or more offences at the same time, the maximum is 12 months. The Magistrates Court also deals with a large number of indictable offences. If the defendant pleads guilty in respect of an indictable offence, he may be sent to the Crown Court for consideration of a more severe sentence than can be imposed in the lower court. Where the defendant maintains that he is not guilty the matter will be dealt with in the Crown Court before a jury.

Indictable offences are so called because they may only be tried 'on indictment', which means by the Crown Court before judge and jury. Procedure relating to such cases, and those summary cases where the defendant has elected trial in the Crown Court or where the offence can be heard either way but it has been decided that the case is better dealt with in the Crown Court, is governed by the Criminal Justice and Public Order Act 1994. In such cases the court must proceed with transfer for trial proceedings to remove the case to the Crown Court.

Special conditions apply where the accused is under the age of 18. For this purpose the magistrates sit as a Youth Court. Proceedings must take place separately from the adult court and the public are not admitted. Reporting restrictions are also enforced. Magistrates dealing with these cases must have had training in dealing with young offenders and the panel must include at least one woman. In addition to the actual hearing of cases, the preliminaries relating to them and sentencing, magistrates have extensive powers in respect of granting bail to the defendant or remanding to prison to await trial. Where a defendant is not represented by a lawyer, local solicitors attend on a rota basis to advise the accused. This is known as the duty solicitor system. Since the enactment of the Police and Criminal Evidence Act 1984, persons held in custody at a police station have an automatic right of access to legal advice.

Appeals from the Magistrates Court

(a) *The Crown Court*: The accused may appeal against sentence or conviction as appropriate.
(b) *The Divisional Court of the Queen's Bench Division*: Any party to the proceedings (including the prosecution) may appeal on a point of law by way of 'case stated'. The Divisional Court also deals with applications for Judicial Review (see Chapter 5, section 5.2) where there is a defect in the decision which the court has reached.
(c) *The European Court*: Where appropriate, a matter may be referred to the European Court and a Magistrates Court may order legal aid for purposes of proceedings before the Court of Justice.

(B) The Crown Court

The Courts Act 1971 abolished the Courts of Assize and Quarter Sessions and established the Crown Court as the single first instance criminal court above the Magistrates Court. The Central Criminal Court (The 'Old Bailey') is the Crown Court for the City of London area. Although most cities and large towns are near to a Crown Court centre, they are not all of the same importance. There are three levels of courts. The first-tier courts deal with the most important criminal offences. The judges in first-tier courts are High Court Judges, sometimes known as Puisne judges, and also Circuit Judges (see section 1.16). The first-tier courts act also as regional centres for dealing with High Court civil actions as well as criminal cases. The second- and third-tier courts deal only with criminal cases. Circuit judges or Recorders (part-time judges) hear cases in these courts but High Court judges can hear cases in the second-tier courts. In addition to the classification of courts, Crown Court offences are also categorised into four groups, indicating the level of judge who may try a particular offence. Lay Magistrates are entitled to sit with the judge in the Crown Court. In fact they must form part of the Crown Court where it hears appeals from the magistrates court and when sentencing defendants who have pleaded guilty in the Magistrates Court but that court does not have jurisdiction to sentence them.

Appeals from the Crown Court

(a) The Court of Appeal (Criminal Division): the accused may appeal against sentence or conviction where appropriate.
(b) The Divisional Court of the Queen's Bench Division: an appeal by way of 'case stated' (see section 1.11) may be made from the Crown Court to this court.

(C) The Court of Appeal (Criminal Division)

This court will be considered with The Court of Appeal (Civil Division) – see section 1.11(E).

1.11   The Civil Courts

(A) The Magistrates Court

Although essentially a criminal court, this court has some civil jurisdiction, primarily in 'family proceedings'. This includes applications for custody of children, maintenence orders, and separation and adoption matters. As in the case of Youth Courts, the public is excluded from the proceedings, there are rules as to the composition of the 'bench' and strict limitations are imposed on press reports. There is no power to hear divorce cases. Magistrates are responsible for the granting or refusal of licences required for businesses which sell alcohol to the public, and those for betting shops and casinos where these are still required. There is also jurisdiction to recover unpaid council tax from debtors.

Appeals from the Magistrates Court

(a) The Crown Court: this is appropriate in licensing and debt collecting matters.
(b) The Divisional Court of the Queen's Bench Division: where appropriate, the 'case stated' procedure will apply on a point of law.
(c) The Divisional Court of the Family Division; this will apply in the case of 'family proceedings'.

(B) County Courts

County Courts were established in 1846 to deal with minor civil matters cheaply and on a local basis. The County Court is the major first-instance court in civil matters and its jurisdiction is exclusively civil. In recent years plaintiffs have been encouraged to use this court when initiating proceedings, in an attempt to cut costs. County Courts are presided over by Circuit Judges who are solicitors or barristers. In the major cities more than one judge is allocated to each court. The majority of Circuit Judges spend the balance of their time dealing with the less serious Crown Court criminal cases. Where appropriate, Deputy Circuit Judges may be appointed to reduce delays in the system. Much of the routine work involved in the County Court system is undertaken by District Judges. Like Circuit Judges, they are appointed by the Lord Chancellor. District Judges have responsibility for interlocutory matters (applications and preliminary matters prior to the court hearing before the judge) and the administrative running of the court. District Judges have the right to hear claims involving less than £5000 and in respect of higher amounts if both parties agree. An appeal from the finding of a District Judge is to the Circuit Judge. District Judges frequently act as arbitrators in defended actions where the sum involved is classed as a 'small claim'. In 1996 the small claims limit was increased from cases involving up to £1000 to £3000, except in personal injury cases where the maximum is £1000. There have been proposals to increase the £3000 limit to £5000 *(Lord Chancellor's Department and the Court Service; handling small claims in the county court. Consultation Paper 1996).* The majority of claims relate to defective goods and unsatisfactory services. The arbitrator's decision can be enforced in the same way as that of a court of law (see section 1.20). Such proceedings are of an informal nature and the rules of evidence are relaxed. In such cases the practice is that each party will pay its own costs.

Jurisdiction

The jurisdiction of the County Court is set out in the County Court Act 1984 as amended. The technical rules governing the procedures in the court are to be found in the *County Court Practice* (known as the 'Green Book'). Cases have to be started off in the County Court for the district in which the defendant lives, carries on business or where the reason for the action took place. If the plaintiff is attempting to obtain possession of land, the place of trial depends upon where the land is situated. In most cases the jurisdiction of the court is restricted by the size of the claim and these limits vary from time to time. In general terms, the following constitutes the bulk of County Court work:

(A) *Actions based on contract/tort*
(1) Actions in contract and tort not exceeding £25,000 (libel and slander are excluded unless the parties agree or the High Court transfers the case to the County Court).
(2) Claims for damages for personal injuries unless the claim is for £50,000 or more.

In an attempt to encourage greater use of the County Court over the High Court in civil actions, a degree of flexibility was introduced into the system in 1992 whose effect is as follows:

(a) Claims involving up to £25,000 must be tried in a County Court unless that court considers that the claim ought to be transferred to the High Court (and that court agrees). If one of a number of factors is satisfied, the case may be transferred. These factors are as follows:

(1) the case is too important to be dealt with in the County Court or it raises questions of importance relating to others who are not parties to the action;

(2) the action is too complex to be dealt with in the County Court;

(3) the financial substance of the action, including the value of any counter claim that the defendant may be making, makes it more appropriate to try the case in the High Court;

(4) whether a transfer to the High Court would result in a speedier trial (this ground will not suffice on its own).

(b) Claims involving between £25,000 and £50,000 are allocated between the County Court and the High Court in accordance with the relevant criteria above.

(c) An action whose value is £50,000 or more must be tried in the High Court unless:

(1) the action is commenced in the County Court and that court, taking into account the criteria above, considers that the case should not be dealt with in the High Court;

(2) the action is commenced in the High Court, and the High Court having regard to the above criteria considers that the case should be dealt with in the County Court.

(B) *Other jurisdication*

(1) Equity matters involving sums up to £30,000. This would include specific performance of contracts relating to the sale of land, and requests for repossession orders by building societies or banks against mortgage defaulters.

(2) Actions for the recovery of land.

(3) Probate matters where the deceased person's estate is valued at less than £30,000.

(4) The winding up of companies with a paid up capital of less than £120,000.

(5) Landlord and Tenant, Housing and consumer credit matters.

(6) Some courts also deal with the following matters:

(1) undefended divorce petitions and proceedings ancillary to them;

(2) Admiralty matters;

(3) bankruptcy matters.

Appeals from the County Court

(a) The Court of Appeal: subject to certain conditions, an appeal from a Circuit Judge in the County Court lies directly to the Court of Appeal.

(b) The Divisional Court of the Chancery Division: where the County Court has bankruptcy jurisdiction, appeal lies to a High Court judge.

(C) The High Court of Justice

The High Court was established by the Judicature Acts 1873–75, replacing the Common Law and Chancery Courts which existed previously. The work of the High Court is divided into three divisions, each of which has a separate jurisdiction. The court is staffed by High Court judges and their role is to try civil cases which involve some complexity and/or considerable sums of money. The Queen appoints High Court judges on the recommendation of the Lord Chancellor. Administrative matters in the High Court are dealt with by officials known as Masters who carry out the same types of tasks as District Judges in the County Courts. In London, cases are dealt with at the Royal Courts of Justice situated in the Strand. High Court civil cases in the provinces are heard at first-tier Crown Court centres. The majority of chancery matters are dealt with in London, but there are eight other regional centres where such matters can be dealt with. High Court civil cases can be started off in the provinces without the need to go to London. This is done by filing the appropriate documents at District Registries which exist in the larger cities in England and Wales (often in premises used primarily as County Courts). When this takes place, the District Judges are given the powers of Masters of the High Court.

(a) The Queen's Bench Division

This is by far the largest of the three divisions and it has the residual task of dealing with all matters not covered by the other divisions. It is presided over by the Lord Chief Justice and staffed by High Court judges. A large number of judges are required because the division also staffs the Crown Courts at those first-tier centres where serious criminal cases and High Court civil cases are heard. The majority of actions brought are claims in contract and tort outside the County Court limits. Many cases involving the construction industry are dealt with in this court. The judge hears the case alone without a jury. Where a person's character is in dispute, a jury is empanelled (formed) to sit with the judge. Two highly regarded specialist courts, The Commercial Court and the Admiralty Court, sit within this division. Disputes relating to building matters can be dealt with by Official Referees (see section 1.16) and are classed as Official Referees' business. Although it is classed as part of the High Court, and its rules of evidence and procedure tend to follow High Court practice, this court is staffed by designated Ciruit Judges. These cases are heard at the law courts in London but provision has been made for them to be dealt with at designated provincial centres. Although the bulk of their work comes within the ambit of the

Queen's Bench Division, they can also hear cases which, but for the nature of the dispute, would be dealt with in the Chancery Division.

One increasingly important aspect of the jurisdiction of the Queen's Bench Division is its supervisory jurisdiction. This is a process whereby the court has powers to challenge the decision of an inferior court, tribunal or other public body such as a local authority if it is acting in a judicial manner. The jurisdiction is exercised by use of the Prerogative Orders known as Certiorari, Prohibition and Mandamus, together with an alternative sets of remedies known as a declaration and an injunction. The Supreme Court Act 1981, together with Order 53 of the Rules of the Supreme Court, allows an aggrieved person to make a claim for Judicial Review and the court will decide whether or not any of these remedies are appropriate in the circumstances. A potential plaintiff must obtain permission from the court before the case can be proceeded with, and must have a sufficient interest in the proceedings. It is important to realise that Judicial Review is concerned with the manner in which the original decision of the court was made and not the actual substantive merits of the case.

(b) Chancery Division

This is the successor to the Courts of Equity and is the smallest in numbers of the three divisions. Its nominal head is the Lord Chancellor but in practice the senior judge is the Vice-Chancellor who with 15 other judges hears cases in London and the major cities in the provinces. Its jurisdiction involves the sale of land, mortgages, trusts, company and taxation matters. Where there is an overlap between the County Court and the Chancery Division in jurisdiction, the venue will be governed by the financial limits mentioned earlier.

(c) Family Division

Established in 1970, this is the most modern of the three divisions and deals with all aspects of family law. Defended divorce petitions, family property disputes, matters relating to children and wardship and adoption come within its scope.

(D) Divisional Courts

Each of the three divisions of the High Court have Divisional Courts which hear appeals from inferior courts. In the Queen's Bench Division the court hears 'case stated' appeals on points of law from the Magistrates Court or Crown Court, together with exercising supervisory jurisdiction over tribunals and inferior courts. In the Chancery Division, the Divisional Court hears bankruptcy appeals from County Courts, while in the Family Division the relevant court hears appeals from Magistrates Courts in family proceedings.

Appeals from Divisional Courts

(a) The Court of Appeal (Civil Division): there is an appeal to this court from any of the three divisions of the High Court on matters of law and fact. If there is an appeal against the finding of the Divisional Court of the Queen's Bench Division when hearing an appeal from a lower court in a criminal matter, the appeal will go directly to the House of Lords.
(b) The House of Lords: it is possible, by the Administration of Justice Act 1969, in some cases to by-pass the Court of Appeal and to 'leap frog' directly to the House of Lords. The parties to the dispute must agree to this course of action. The original trial judge has to grant a certificate that the matter should go directly to the Lords and that it involves a matter of statutory interpretation, or the first-instance judge is considered to be bound by a previous decision of a superior court. The point of law must be one of general public importance and the House of Lords, itself, must grant leave. Examples of this procedure being used are rare. In *National Carriers Ltd* v *Panalpina (Northern) Ltd [1981] AC 675* these conditions were satisfied where the issue was whether a lease was subject to the contractual rules relating to frustration.

(E) The Court of Appeal

Appeals from the High Court and the County Court are heard in this court. The appeal may be on a question of law or fact from a lower court and certain tribunals. The court is divided into a criminal and a civil division. It is staffed by Lords Justice of Appeal (see section 1.16) who have been promoted from High Court judges. The head of the Civil Division is the Master of the Rolls, while the head of the criminal division is the Lord Chief Justice (see section 1.16). Each court will consist of three judges.

Appeals from the Court of Appeal

The House of Lords: leave must be granted by that court or by the Court of Appeal.

(F) The House of Lords

In addition to being the second chamber of Parliament, through which proposed legislation must pass before enactment, the House of Lords has a major function as a court of law. The House of Lords when sitting as a court of law is the superior appellate court in the United Kingdom. In theory an appeal to the House of Lords is an appeal to the whole House and not simply to those members who are judges and who are sitting to hear the appeal. Appeals to the Lords are heard by the senior members of the judiciary. These are judges who are members of the Appellate Committee of the House of Lords. These Lords of Appeal in Ordinary (known as 'Law Lords') are judges who have been promoted from Lords Justice of Appeal and on appointment have become Peers of the Realm. Five judges will hear an appeal to this court. The Lord Chancellor sometimes sits as a judge together with the 'Law Lords', while retired judges who have held high judicial rank are also called upon to supplement the court. The Law Lords take no part in the political sittings of the House unless the matter concerns an issue which is pertinent to the judicial process. As the House is the final domestic appellate court in the United Kingdom it hears appeals not only from the English courts but also from those in Scotland and Northern Ireland.

1.12   The Judicial Committee of the Privy Council

This is the final court of appeal from a number of Commonwealth countries. It is staffed by Lords of Appeal in Ordinary and the Lord Chancellor may also hear these appeals. Procedure is similar to that of the House of Lords when sitting as a court of law. Instead of delivering a judgement it tenders advice to the Sovereign. The Committee is not bound by its previous decisions. It also deals with appeals from the disciplinary committees of a number of professions.

1.13   The European Court of Human Rights

This court (not to be confused with the European Court of Justice – see section 1.8) was established in 1959 and is based in Strasbourg. Judges are elected by the Parliamentary Assembly of the Council of Europe from a list of candidates nominated by member states. The court is concerned with the interpretation of the European Convention on Human Rights (in the process of incorporation into English law), and its cases involve basic rights and freedoms.

1.14   Tribunals

A major characteristic of the English legal system since the end of the Second World War has been the growth in importance of tribunals. A noticeable defect of the traditional court system is that it is unsuitable for dealing with the settlement of every type of dispute. A system has to be formulated whereby disputes dealing with specialist topics can be dealt with by experts instead of by judges. The increasing role of government in economic and social matters has brought about a proliferation of disputes between private individuals and government departments. Acts of Parliament have set up tribunals in an attempt to provide a speedy and cheap method of settling disputes as a supplement to the court system. There is a diversity of functions among these administrative tribunals and they vary from immigration appeals and employment matters to disputes concerning tenanted farms.

Many tribunals have a legally qualified person to chair the proceedings but frequently members are qualified in their own particular capacity. Surveyors, for example, deal with disputes relating to the value of land. Appointments are usually made for a fixed term but are frequently renewed. Composition varies from one to another. Many tribunals are made up of three members, with a lawyer acting as the chair together with two lay representatives. The government department regulating the matter in dispute will have responsibility for the appointments. In many cases before tribunals, legal representation is not necessary. A problem relating to tribunals is that the availability of legal aid varies greatly. On matters of fact there is usually no appeal from the decision of a tribunal. Appeals on points of law can be made to the High Court while tribunals must now give reasons for their decisions. The Council on Tribunals is responsible for the review and supervision of the system and reports to Parliament on these matters.

Specific Tribunals

The Lands Tribunal

This tribunal was established by The Lands Tribunal Act 1949 to settle disputes involving the valuation of land on compulsory purchase. Such disputes involve the property owner and the local authority. Other jurisdiction includes applications relating to the valuation or discharge of restrictive covenants (see Chapter 4, section 4.14) under the Law of Property Act 1925 and certain matters relating to Town Planning Law (Compensation for Planning Restrictions), but most of the tribunal's time is spent dealing with appeals from Local Valuation Courts in respect of assessments of the rateable valuation of land. The tribunal consists of a lawyer, who acts as President, and other members who are either leading barristers or Chartered Surveyors. Administration is the responsibility of the registrar. Only one member decides each dispute but cases are not confined to London and the members will travel wherever work demands. Appeal lies to the Court of Appeal (Civil Division). In procedure and atmosphere, the Lands Tribunal is more formal than most tribunals.

The Agricultural Lands Tribunal

The eight Agricultural Lands Tribunals are organised on a regional basis. Each tribunal is staffed by a lawyer and two lay representatives. Nominations for membership are considered from the Country Landowners Association and the National Farmers Union. This tribunal is concerned with tenanted farms and, in particular, with notices to quit and compensation for improvements. On average, 400–500 cases per year have been dealt with in the last few years.

Domestic Tribunals

Not all tribunals are administrative tribunals. In addition, there are domestic tribunals which have been established to resolve disputes within professional bodies and to exercise disciplinary control over their members. Doctors, lawyers, surveyors and architects are subject to such rules. Trade Associations and Trade Unions have similar machinery to ensure common standards and maintain discipline.

1.15   Arbitration

Where disputes arise of a specialist nature, the parties can agree to nominate a third party to resolve the matter. This process is known as arbitration and it should be contrasted with litigation, as the process of determining disputes in courts of law is known. It is a procedure which is appropriate where the issues involved are primarily of fact, and a degree of technical expertise combined with an understanding of the basis of the legal system are required. Advantages claimed for the system include speed, cheapness (sometimes), convenience and informality. One major advantage of the system is that the hearing is held in private at a time and place suitable to the requirements of the parties. It is not suitable where the issues are essentially points of law or the character and trustworthiness of the parties are in dispute. Most disputes referred to arbitration are of a commercial nature but arbitration is used in the construction industry and also in connection with certain types of disputes relating to commercial and industrial property. There have been instances of cases brought before the courts where a person appointed to undertake some form of professional task has sought the immunity that an arbitrator has from claims in negligence, but failed. Examples include valuations of property, certifying that a building contract is progressing satisfactorily and making a valuation of shares (*Palacath Ltd* v *Flanagan [1985] 2 All ER 161; Sutcliffe* v *Thackrah [1974] AC 727; Arenson* v *Casson, Beckman, Rutley & Co 1977 AC 405*). The principal Act is the Arbitration Act 1996 which governs all arbitration proceedings begun after that date, even if the arbitration agreement was made at an earlier date. The agreement to submit a matter to arbitration can take place after the dispute has arisen, although increasingly contracts provide that in the event of a dispute arising the matter will be resolved in this way. A clause in a standard form contract may provide that a professional body such as the Royal Institution of Chartered Surveyors or the Royal Institute of British Architects appoint the arbitrator. Sometimes the parties have no choice but to refer the matter to arbitration because statute requires it. Disputes relating to street works come into this category. In a similar way, a court will refer proceedings to arbitration where appropriate. An arbitration agreement may contain a provision that arbitration shall be a condition precedent to the dispute being referred to a court of law (known as a *Scott* v *Avery [1856] clause*).

It is common practice for the parties to the arbitration to hold a preliminary meeting to agree time and place of hearing, attendance of witnesses, legal representation and any issues relevant to the proceedings where the parties hold a common position. Some disputes are settled entirely at this stage. Both claimant and respondent (plaintiff and defendant) will have submitted pleadings (see section 1.19) outlining the basis of their case by this stage, but if there are any outstanding the arbitrator will require them to be served. The arbitrator may also order discovery (production) of relevant papers. A *Scott's Schedule* can be used in the proceedings by the arbitrator to summarise the conflicting views of the parties. Procedure is similar to that in a civil court of law but less formal. The basic rules of evidence tend to be adhered to. There has been an attempt in the 1996 Act to try and distance arbitration from the paraphernalia of court proceedings but as yet it has been difficult to discern any major changes. Those involved in the property and construction professions are used as expert witnesses in arbitration references. Unlike ordinary witnesses, whose role in court proceedings is to describe a series of events, an expert witness is entitled and paid to express an opinion about the matters in issue. Standard practice is for the expert witness to prepare a report which takes a particular view of the dispute. The report may be referred to during the course of the proceedings while it is common for the witness to indicate qualifications and experience at the outset to reinforce the validity of the evidence. Such a witness should give observations and express an honest opinion without appearing to be partisan about the matters in dispute. The judgement of the arbitrator is known as the award, while the case itself is referred to as a reference. As in a court of law, the decision may be made at the end of the proceedings or the arbitrator may 'reserve the award', in which case it is given at a later date. If the dispute involves a specific building, the arbitrator should make an appropriate inspection before giving the award. The arbitrator's decision must settle all matters submitted for arbitration and no more. Such an award must also be certain, final, written and signed by the arbitrator and witnessed. On receipt of fees the award is published by the arbitrator. Costs follow the same rules as in court – the loser pays the successful party's costs unless otherwise agreed. If the losing party fails to pay in accordance with the arbitration award, the winner can sue for the money owing or register the award as a judgement of the High Court. An award may be referred back (remitted) to the arbitrator for reconsideration, while it may be set aside completely if it is in some way invalid or there has been misconduct by the arbitrator. Misconduct covers a variety of circumstances but includes such matters as refusing to hear evidence, where appropriate, and deciding a case in obvious disregard of the law. It would not cover a simple mistake of law or fact. It is a question of degree whether or not the award is remitted or set aside, but a court will prefer to refer the matter back to the arbitrator than to have it set aside completely.

It is possible for an appeal to be made to the High Court on a point of law after the award has been made. An arbitrator may also seek the opinion of the court during the course of the proceedings. Permission to appeal must be given by the court unless all the parties to the reference agree to the appeal, while the grounds for a further appeal to the Court of Appeal and House of Lords are narrow. Since 1980 it has been possible for the parties to an arbitration to make an exclusion agreement preventing any of those involved in the arbitration from seeking a determination from a court of law on a point of law or making an appeal. These exclusion agreements are designed primarily to cover arbitration proceedings involving foreign nationals or organisations. Where there is a domestic arbitration agreement, as in the case of the majority of arbitrations in the construction industry or those which are property related, the exclusion is only permissible if entered into after the commencement of the relevant arbitration.

In a desire to try and find cheaper and less formal methods of solving disputes, but at the same time give an injured plaintiff a suitable remedy, the concept of Alternative Dispute Resolution (ADR) has been much discussed in recent years. Mediation, mini-trials and conciliation approaches have all been voiced in connection with this concept, while there has been experimentation in these areas in Australia, the USA and the Far East. A major development in the UK appears to be the enactment of The Housing Grants, Construction and Regeneration Act 1996 which imposes statutory adjudication in many construction contracts (see Chapter 2, section 2.16). A compulsory arbitration scheme was introduced in April 1998 which requires surveyors who are members of either the Royal Institution of Chartered Surveyors (RICS) or the Incorporated Society of Valuers and Auctioneers (ISVA) to be bound by arbitration as a condition of membership of the professional bodies. Firms of surveyors will be required to set up an initial internal complaints procedure. If the matter comes to a hearing, it will be dealt with on the basis of documents rather than oral evidence. Under the new scheme, each party to the dispute will pay a registration fee of £200 which is refundable to clients who win their case. The arbitrator's costs are met by the RICS or ISVA. This scheme has replaced the previous voluntary system operated by the Chartered Institute of Arbitrators. The majority of disputes under this scheme have related to structural defects. The new scheme will also cover disputes relating to the level of fees and cases involving valuations.

1.16   Personnel of the Law

As of necessity, those involved in property and construction matters are likely, during the course of their professional careers, to work together with those involved in the legal profession. A peculiarity of the English Legal profession is that it is divided into branches which have different functions. Solicitors give advice on legal problems to the general public and conduct legal proceedings on their behalf, whereas the primary function of a barrister is to act as an advocate and give advice to solicitors when requested. The expression 'lawyer' can be used to denote either a solicitor or a barrister. Apart from working in general practice and as salaried 'in house' lawyers, both solicitors and barristers are to be found in commerce, industry, the civil service and educational institutions.

Solicitors

The Law Society is the organisation responsible for the control of the solicitors' profession. In order to practise as such, a person must have been admitted as a solicitor and possess a current practising certificate. This can only be obtained by passing the professional examinations of the Law Society and completing a period of training with an established solicitor. Once qualified, if the solicitor enters general practice, he or she may deal with a wide range of legal work. This may involve giving general advice, conveyancing (transferring the ownership of land), preparing wills, appearing in the Magistrates or County Court, dealing with matrimonial disputes or preparing cases for trial. On the other hand, the solicitor may quickly become a specialist dealing only with cases involving one or two areas of law, such as taxation, town planning or construction law. Much depends on the type of practice and its locality. Some solicitors prefer to practise on their own, while others work in partnerships of varying sizes. A provision in The Administration of Justice Act 1985 gives solicitors the option of forming a company as an alternative to being a sole practitioner or in partnership with other solicitors, but as yet this provision has yet to become law. Traditionally, much of the work of solicitors has been involved with property transactions. At one time, only solicitors could undertake the transfer of land/buildings. This is no longer the case (see subsection on 'Licensed Conveyancers' below).

There are restrictions upon the right of solicitors to appear as advocates in courts of law. Solicitors have long had a right of appearance in the County Court and the Magistrates Court but until recently, if the matter proceeded to a superior court the solicitor had to instruct a barrister to appear on the client's behalf. Since 1994 it has been possible for solicitors to appear as advocates in the higher courts but only if they have completed the necesary Law Society advocacy courses or been exempted from them. Where a barrister is instructed by a solicitor, this is known as *briefing counsel*. These are written instructions sent to a barrister, relating to the representation of a client in legal proceedings. They include a narrative of the facts, copies of any documents, specifications and, where appropriate, plans. A solicitor may take counsel's opinion whereby the views of a barrister are obtained on the law which applies to the client's case. Although the normal rule is that a lay person can only instruct a barrister via a solicitor, thereby incurring two sets of fees, members of certain professions have 'direct access' to a barrister and may instruct counsel without the requirement of having to contact a solicitor first so long as only an opinion is sought (see the Direct Professional Access Rules). Unlike a barrister, a solicitor may sue the client for non-payment of fees. Solicitors may also be liable to their clients if they have acted negligently in the conduct of their case. Any allegation of professional misconduct against a solicitor is dealt with by the Disciplinary Committee of the Law Society and in appropriate cases a solicitor's name may be 'struck off' the professional roll.

Legal Executives

Much of the routine work in solicitors' offices is carried out by unadmitted personnel known as Legal Executives. They carry out a considerable amount of work on behalf of their firms and much conveyancing and litigation is undertaken by them. Training and qualifications are governed by the Institute of Legal Executives. The initial qualification is Associate Membership of the Institute; after a further qualifying period and an examination the Associate may become a Fellow. In turn, a Fellow who completes the legal practice course may become admitted as a solicitor.

Licensed Conveyancers

Until the enactment of The Administration of Justice Act 1985, only qualified solicitors had the legal right to engage in conveyancing (the legal process of buying and selling land/buildings). Since then, members of the Council for Licensed Conveyancers have also been able to engage in conveyancing work for profit. Members of the Council are required to satisfy educational requirements and practice rules. These rules have been supplemented by the creation of a new body known as the Authorised Conveyancing Practitioners Board, which in its role of developing competition in the provision of legal services is authorised to supervise the activities of those who legally offer conveyancing services. In particular, there are specific rules dealing with 'tied' arrangements relating to inclusive legal services. These latter provisions are not as yet in force.

Barristers

The Bar has long been considered the senior branch of the legal profession in England and Wales. The main functions of counsel are to act as advocates in the superior courts, to draft the pleadings which indicate the manner in which the case is to be brought, and to give their legal opinion when so required. In order to practise as a barrister, a person must have been called to the Bar by one of the Inns of Court (Lincolns Inn, Grays Inn, The Middle Temple or The Inner Temple). After satisfying the appropriate educational requirements and 'keeping term', a newly called barrister who wishes to practise must undergo a period of pupilage for 12 months. By this process an experienced barrister (known as a Pupil Master) will supervise the new entrant's work. A newly qualified practising barrister will join one of six circuits in England and Wales and, unless working primarily in London, will appear in cases in the circuit area. Practising barristers are self-employed. Partnerships are prohibited but for convenience a number of barristers share offices or chambers each contributing towards the overheads of the establishment. The majority of sets of chambers are administered by a clerk who deals with solicitors' firms and negotiates fees. Some sets now dispense with the need for a clerk while the previous restrictions on barristers advertising have been reversed. In the regions barristers' work is often varied and common law and crime orientated. The majority of specialists, especially in commercial, company and Chancery matters, are to be found in London.

Most barristers are known as junior counsel. After a period of successful practice a junior may apply to the Lord Chancellor to become a Queen's Counsel. If successful, the applicant is said to have taken silk which entitles the QC to wear a silk gown in court. Leading Counsel, as these barristers are called, do not draft pleadings. Instead, their work is confined to appearing as advocates in the more important cases or giving opinions. At one time, whenever a Queen's Counsel appeared in court, the QC had to be accompanied by a junior barrister. Leading counsel may appear on their own without assistance. Unlike solicitors, counsel may not sue for their fees. This rule has been modified by the Courts and Legal Services Act 1990 which allows a barrister to enter into a contract with a client for providing services and paying fees. As advocates, the prevailing view is that barristers are immune from claims against them based on professional negligence, as shown in *Rondel* v *Worsley [1969] 1 AC 191*. This immunity extends to the drafting of pleadings but it does not extend to advisory or drafting work.

1.17   Judicial Officers

The Lord Chancellor

Abbreviated to LC in the Law Reports, the holder of this office may exercise legislative, executive or judicial powers. This is the principal legal office in the United Kingdom. The appointment is a political one and the Lord Chancellor is a lawyer, a member of the cabinet and Speaker of the House of Lords. He is also the chief judge and controls the process of appointing judges and Justices of the Peace. On a change of government his appointment is automatically revoked.

The Attorney-General

Abbreviated to Att-Gen this title is given to the chief law officer of the Crown and head of the English Bar. The appointment is a political one chosen by the Lord Chancellor and the holder is a Queen's Counsel and Member of Parliament. The principal tasks of the office are to advise the government on legal matters and to represent the Crown in civil and criminal proceedings. Certain prosecutions may only be commenced with his consent. The Attorney can also sue on behalf of the public to enforce public rights. Examples include stopping a public nuisance (see Chapter 3, section 3.9) or enforcing a charitable trust. He can lend his name to such an action at the request of a private citizen and these proceedings are known as relator proceedings. If he refuses to consent to the bringing of an action, his refusal cannot be questioned in the courts.

The Solicitor-General

Abbreviated to Sol-Gen, the Attorney-General's deputy is known as Solicitor-General. The holder of the post is a Member of Parliament and a Queen's Counsel (never a solicitor). Duties are in general similar to those of the Attorney-General. The junior law officer will often become the Attorney when that post becomes vacant. The law officers are forbidden to engage in private practice but receive a salary inclusive of fees.

Director of Public Prosecutions and Crown Prosecution Service

Abbreviated to DPP, the Director of Public Prosecutions is appointed by the Home Secretary but is responsible to the Attorney-General for the exercise of his powers. To a large extent the Director controls the prosecution process and initiates and conducts proceedings in complex cases. The Director is also head of the Crown Prosecution Service which has prime responsibility for the conduct of criminal prosecutions in England and Wales. The service has regional offices throughout the country and its employees (solicitors or barristers) prosecute in criminal cases.

Master of the Rolls (abbreviated to MR)

The judge who presides over the Court of Appeal (Civil Division) is known as the Master of the Rolls. He decides the composition of the various appellate courts and organises the distribution of work. In addition, he admits newly qualified solicitors to the Roll of the Court, thereby enabling them to practise.

The Lord Chief Justice

Abbreviated to LCJ, the Lord Chief Justice ranks next to the Lord Chancellor in the legal hierarchy. Although the holder of the office presides over the Queen's Bench Division of the High Court, his principal duties are as head of the Court of Appeal (Criminal) Division and the Divisional Court of the Queen's Bench Division.

The Vice Chancellor

Abbreviated to VC, the Lord Chancellor is the nominal head of the Chancery Division, although the actual organisation and management of Chancery Division business rest with the Vice Chancellor.

The Lords of Appeal in Ordinary

Abbreviated to 'Lord' followed by surname and any additional title, these are the senior members of the judiciary appointed from the Court of Appeal. On becoming 'Law Lords' these judges become life peers, but in practice take little part in the non-judicial business of the House of Lords. As the House of Lords as a court of law is the final court of appeal for the whole of the United Kingdom and not just England and Wales, it is normal practice to also appoint judges from Scotland and Northern Ireland. The Law Lords also play an active role in hearing appeals dealt with by the Judicial Committee of the Privy Council.

The Lord Justices of Appeal

Abbreviated to LJ, this is the title given to the judges who hear cases in the Court of Appeal. They are appointed from judges of the High

Court. On appointment they are made Privy Councillors. As they hear only appeal cases, their work, like that of the Law Lords, is confined to London.

High Court Judges

Abbreviated to J after the surname of the judge in question, High Court or puisne judges are appointed by the Crown after recommendations from the Lord Chancellor. Appointments are made from the ranks of practising Queen's Counsel but nowadays existing Circuit Judges are also appointed. On appointment the judge will be knighted and assigned to one of the three divisions of the High Court. The Queen's Bench Division accounts for approximately two-thirds of the judges.

Circuit Judges

Circuit judges are referred to as Judge followed by their surnames. Most trials which are heard in the Crown Courts or County Courts are dealt with by Circuit Judges. Such judges are appointed by the Crown on the recommendation of the Lord Chancellor. Circuit Judges are normally barristers but it is possible for a suitably experienced solicitor to be appointed directly to the circuit bench. Judges are allocated to one of the circuits and hear cases in a group of centres. In court, Circuit Judges are addressed as 'your honour'. Mention should also be made here of the office of Recorder. These are part-time judges who hear cases in the Crown Courts to supplement the Circuit Judges. Recorders must make themselves available on a number of occasions to hear cases.

Masters

Interlocutory matters in the High Court in London are the responsibility of Masters assigned to the Queen's Bench and Chancery divisions of the court. The costs incurred in an action are fixed by Taxing Masters where they are in excess of £20, 000.

District Judges

Referred to previously in connection with the County Court (see section 1.11), District Judges have an extensive range of administrative and judicial roles. District Judges are drawn from the solicitors' profession, despite the fact that barristers are eligible as well. These judges are responsible for maintaining the records of the court and ensuring that documents have been served where appropriate. Moreover they have responsibility for money which has been paid into court. As far as judicial tasks are concerned these judges deal with interlocutory matters, taxation of costs and actions involving relatively small amounts of money.

Official Referees

Official Referees are Circuit Judges nominated by the Lord Chancellor to deal with cases involving a prolonged examination of documents. The majority of 'Official Referees business' concerns building disputes, civil engineering matters and claims against professionals working in the construction industry, such as surveyors, architects and engineers. Disputes concerning the implementation of the building regulations by local authorities also come under this heading. The so-called *Scott's Schedule* mentioned previously in connection with arbitration proceedings (see section 1.15) is commonly used in disputes heard by Official Referees.

1.18   Juries

One feature of common law based legal systems is trial by jury. A jury is a body of persons selected to give a verdict in a particular case. Although seldom used in civil actions today, except in defamation cases, they are always used in criminal trials held on indictment at the Crown Court where the accused pleads not guilty. In criminal cases and in the High Court, in civil actions, a jury will consist of 12 men or women randomly selected. In general the jury decides facts and it is left to the judge to decide questions of law. Juries have no place in the appeal courts. Any person on the electoral register aged between 18 and 70 who has been resident in the United Kingdom for at least 5 years since the age of 13 is eligible. Certain persons are disqualified, ineligible or disqualified from sitting on juries. Examples include members of the legal profession, police officers, the mentally ill and those who have been the subject of certain prison sentences. The deliberations of a jury are held in secret and investigations into their workings are treated as a contempt of court. At one time the verdict of a jury had to be unanimous but, if certain conditions are met, the court will accept a majority verdict where there is a majority of 10 (7 in the County Court where 8 members are empanelled).

1.19   Court Procedure

This is governed by the nature of the dispute. Just as the type of court is dependent upon the type of proceedings at issue, there is a considerable difference between criminal and civil proceedings. In the criminal courts much depends on whether the accused is being tried on indictment or is subject to summary proceedings. Choice of court on the civil side is determined primarily by the complexity of the issues involved and the sums of money in dispute. One fundamental distinction lies in the obligation of proving facts. This is the so-called burden of proof. In a civil case it is the responsibility of the plaintiff to prove the factual issues on the balance of probabilities. A more stringent test applies in criminal cases in that the prosecution must prove the facts at issue beyond all reasonable doubt. Another factor characteristic of court proceedings in the UK and other common law jurisdictions is the so-called accusatorial or adversarial system. This means that the parties to a dispute or criminal proceedings have primary responsibility for finding and presenting evidence. The judge does not investigate the facts as such but listens to the case as it is presented by each of the adversaries. This is to be contrasted with the inquisitorial system in force in many continental European countries whereby the judge searches for facts, listens to witnesses, examines documents and orders that evidence be taken, after which he makes further investigations if he considers them necessary.

1.20   Procedure in Civil Actions

Although it is possible for those involved in the construction process or in the landed property professions to incur criminal liability, it is more likely that any legal dispute in which they become involved will be of a civil nature. Where the parties to a civil dispute choose litigation instead of arbitration, they will either commence proceedings in the County Court or the High Court. The choice of court will depend primarily on the complexity of the case and the amount of money involved. In civil actions of any consequence there will have been considerable correspondence and bargaining between the parties before the action is commenced. In both sets of courts there is often considerable delay between the action being commenced and the hearing of the case. The vast majority of civil actions never come to trial but are settled before the hearing by the parties. The high cost of litigation acts as an incentive to settle the case.

(a) The County Court

The procedure for bringing a claim in the County Court is to be found in the so-called 'Green Book' or County Court Practice. The claim is essentially one for damages so the plaintiff, or his solicitors, will file at the appropriate County Court a request for a summons to be issued stating the name and address of the defendant and the sum claimed. This is known as a default action. It is normal practice to serve with the summons the particulars of the claim, setting out the circumstances in which the action arises and the relief sought. The Court will issue to the plaintiff a Plaint Note containing the details of the action and the time limit within which the claim must be answered by the defendant. The defendant is served with forms of admission, defence and counterclaim. The defendant may have a defence to the claim or wish to make a counterclaim. Sometimes the particulars of claim do not give sufficent detail about the basis of the dispute, in which case the defence can ask for 'further and better particulars'. The paper work involved in bringing the case and defending it is referred to as the Pleadings and is often drafted by a barrister. A defence answers the facts relied upon by the plaintiff and where appropriate denies assertions made on the plaintiff's behalf. A counterclaim is a reverse statement of claim which the defendant makes against the plaintiff, and although it need not be connected with the defendant's action it can be conveniently dealt with at the same time. Alternatively the defendant may have a right of set-off. This arises out of the same facts as the plaintiff's action and operates as a defence. So, if the plaintiff sues the defendant for goods sold and delivered, the defendant may plead that the goods were not fit for the purpose for which they were bought.

After service of the pleadings by the plaintiff and the defendant, either party may seek discovery of relevant documents. This consists of documentary evidence, in the possession of either side, which may help or hinder a case. Examples include such items as formal legal documents and invoices, while either side may ask questions of the other so long as they relate to the trial and are specifically within the knowledge of the other. These interrogataries may be required to be answered on oath. Such matters are known generally as interlocutory orders, meaning any preliminary or non-final stage in the proceedings. A date will be fixed for the pre-trial review. This is held before a District Judge who may hear evidence given by affidavit. If the defendant has filed no defence or admission of liability, judgement may be entered for the plaintiff. If there is a defence, the matter will go foward to trial and at the review a time and date will be given. The trial itself will be conducted by a Circuit Judge sitting in the capacity of a County Court Judge. There is a right under the County Courts Act 1984 to ask for a jury of eight persons in a County Court in cases involving matters such as fraud, malicious prosecution and false imprisonment, but this right is rarely exercised. If both parties consent, the court may accept a verdict by any majority in a civil case. Apart from dealing with interlocutory matters and taxation of costs, cases involving relatively small sums of money can be dealt with by the District Judge as mentioned earlier.

(b) The High Court

Procedure in the High Court depends upon the Division in which the case is brought. The rigid distinctions which until fairly recently separated County Court jurisdiction from that of the High Court, primarily on a financial basis, have now disappeared although the sums involved in a dispute can still be a relevant factor. It is often a tactical issue to decide whether or not a case be brought in the County Court or High Court. The majority of construction disputes of any substance are commenced in the Queen's Bench Division, while disputes involving the sale of land and relating to mortgages and deeds will be heard in the Chancery Division. Actions in the Queen's Bench Division are begun by issuing a writ against the defendant. In the High Court this will be accompanied by a statement of claim setting out the basis of the case. The writ will be issued from the Central Office of the Supreme Court if the proceedings are initiated in Central London, but in the regions it is more likely that it will emanate from a District Registry of the Supreme Court. If the defendant fails to acknowlege service as required by the writ or gives notice of intention to defend the action, the plaintiff can apply for judgement. The rules relating to interlocutory proceedings are similar to those in the County Court. A Summons for directions is the equivalent of the pre-trial review while a Master of the High Court takes the place of the District Judge.

Order 14 of the Rules of the Supreme Court (the 'White Book' which governs procedure in the High Court) makes provision for a plaintiff to obtain judgement in the vast majority of cases in the Queen's Bench Division or Chancery Division without the expense and delay of a trial, if he can prove to the satisfaction of the court that the case is unanswerable. Such a procedure is only used where these is no substantial dispute as to the facts and the defendant does not have a triable defence. In a civil trial at any time before the judge has commenced summing up, a payment may be made into court by a party to the action. Such a payment is made to put pressure on the defendant. The other party will have the choice of accepting the payment in settlement of the dispute or going to trial. If the other party elects trial and the judge awards a sum less than the amount paid in, the refusing party will have to pay his own costs and those incurred by the other party after the payment in. The judge is only informed of the payment in after the proceedings have come to an end and the damages have been determined.

At the trial, counsel will open the case on the plaintiff's behalf. After the examination in chief, the witnesses for the plaintiff may be cross-examined by the opposing side while the plaintiff's lawyer may then re-examine the witness if desired. A similar procedure is carried out by the defendant's representative. After the defendant's counsel has summarised the case, and made any submissions as to the law, the plaintiff's advocate will have the last word and conclude the proceedings with his view. In many actions the judge will deliver judgement immediately thereafter, although judgement may be reserved to a later date. The successful party is entitled to judgement and must decide which is the most suitable method of enforcing it. Costs 'follow the event' unless the judge pronounces otherwise. This means that the loser must pay the winner's costs.

Costs may be taxed. This is the procedure for examining, and altering where necessary, amounts paid by a party in an action. This will be conducted by a Taxing Master or by a District Judge. Where the judgement is to pay money, the plaintiff can ask the High Court to issue a writ authorising the Sheriff of the county to enter the defendant's property and remove goods to the value of the debt. Interest on the debt and the costs of the action can also be claimed. In the County Court there is a similar procedure based on a Warrant of Execution.

Other options available to the plaintiff include the following:

1. *Charging order*
    This can be made over the defendant's land/buildings or personal property on the application of a creditor who has judgement. If the debt is not paid, the plaintiff can have the property sold and recover his damages from the proceeds.
2. *Garnishee order*
    A creditor may attempt to recover a debt owed by applying to have a sum owed by a third party to the debtor used to satisfy the judgement debt.
3. *Attachment of earnings*
    Where the defendant has no capital but is in employment, an attachment of earnings order may be made. The order is made only in the County Court. The debtor must give particulars of earnings and attend the court hearing at which the deduction rate from earnings will be decided. The employer must then, under the court order, deduct the specified amounts from the debtor's wages or salary and pay them to the court. This procedure is not available where the debtor is self-employed.
4. *Receiver*
    If the debtor owns property, a person may be appointed to receive any rents or profits and account for them to the court. The receiver may also be appointed as a manager to run a business where appropriate.
5. *Insolvency*
    Another option is that the plaintiff may serve on the defendant a notice that if he does not pay the debt (at least £750) within a specified time, bankruptcy or insolvency proceedings will be instigated.

Where the remedy sought by the plaintiff is of a non-monetary nature, non-compliance is treated as being a disregard of the authority of the courts and is punishable either by fine or imprisonment. Failure to obey an injunction comes into this category.

1.21   Aspects of Constitutional Law

Before considering the main aspects of private law relevant to the work of property and construction professionals, some mention should be made of the nature of the British Constitution. The expression 'Constitution' is used to denote the manner in which a state or other body is organised. The Constitution of most countries is to be found in a documentary form which states the fundamental rights and rules of the country. From this stems the duties and powers of the Government and those of the people. The United Kingdom does not have a written Constitution and there is very little formal law governing the topic. Instead it is based on a number of elements comprising statute, the common law, the treaties of the European Union and so-called 'Conventions'. These are undertakings, tacitly agreed, resulting from long practice by which the conduct of Crown and Parliament is regulated in the absence of formal written rules. One example of an established Convention is that the party with a majority in the House of Commons is entitled to have its leader made Prime Minister.

Central Government

After a general election, the successful party with a majority in the House of Commons will form a Government. It is the task of the Government to formulate and carry out policy (the executive branch of Government) and to effect the process of making new laws (the legislative process). The Prime Minister will be chosen and a cabinet formed. This is a group of ministers, selected by and presided over by the Prime Minister, who are collectively responsible for the general character and policy of legislation. Ministers, sometimes called Secretaries of State, are appointed by the Monarch on the recommendation of the Prime Minister to head the various Government departments. The number and variety of departments will vary depending upon the government in power.

Central Government departments are staffed by civil servants who are full-time professional men and women. Their major role is to implement new and existing law which has been enacted by Parliament. The House of Commons is one of the three constituents of Parliament which comprises the Monarch, the House of Commons and the House of Lords. The second chamber of Parliament is the House of Lords which is not an elected assembly but instead consists of hereditary peers, life peers and the Lords of Appeal in Ordinary who hear appeals to the House of Lords when acting in its capacity as a court of law. In practice the 'Law Lords' play little part in the legislative process in the House of Lords. In addition, the senior clergy of the Church of England (the Lords Spiritual) are also entitled to take part in the business of the House. In practice it is difficult for the House of Lords to reject proposed legislation that has come from the House of Commons, but it is able to amend and refine such proposals.

Parliamentary Sovereignty

Legislation is the supreme source of legal authority. Parliament can pass Acts of Parliament on virtually any topic. Parliament is only supreme for the period of its existence and it cannot bind its successors or pass laws on matters outside its jurisdiction. Because of this concept of Parliamentary Sovereignty, judges in the United Kingdom have no powers to hold an Act invalid or to ignore it, however unreasonable or unconstitutional it may be considered to be. In this respect the United Kingdom differs from many countries which have a written constitution.

The Separation of Powers

It is traditional to separate the functions of government into three independent divisions. This is the doctrine of separation of powers which has been interpreted to mean that executive, legislative and judicial powers shall be in separate hands. The executive power is vested in the Crown and is exercised by Government departments and other bodies such as local authorities. Parliament is the principal legislative body as its main function is to pass Acts of Parliament in the Queen's name. Again, powers are delegated to other bodies to enact subordinate legislation. The judges comprise the third organ in the courts of law. In the United Kingdom there is no distinct separation of powers, unlike in the United States of America. Instead there is a blend of all three aspects and considerable overlap. For example, members of the Government are members of one or other of the Houses of Parliament, while the power to make delegated legislation is vested by Act of Parliament in the Government. Although the independence of the judiciary is in practice preserved, superior judges are appointed by the Crown or by the Lord Chancellor, while inferior judges are appointed and removable by the Lord Chancellor. The Lord Chancellor is vested with all three functions as a member of the cabinet, head of the judiciary and speaker of the House of Lords.

2 The Law of Contract

2.1 General Principles

The law of contract is frequently the first 'case law' subject to which students are introduced when they commence their legal studies. The main reason for this is that contracts affect the general public more than most areas of law and arise daily in business and commercial life. When land or buildings are transferred, the contract is the most important stage in the process. The sheer number of agreements entered into leads to disputes which need to be resolved by one means or another. The 'golden age' of the law of contract was in the Nineteenth Century when its major principles were evolved on free market ideologies.

A contract is a legally binding agreement. It is a bargain and each side, or party to the contract, must contribute something to it for it to be valid. Not every agreement is a contract and is not intended to be so. Before a valid contract can emerge, the legally binding element must be present to show that the parties intend to adhere to the agreement made. If the contract is broken by one party to it, the other party must be able to take the contract-breaker to court if desired. A distinction is made between a bilateral contract, where the parties exchange mutual promises, and a unilateral contract where one party promises to do something in return for the other party carrying out some task. When the task is completed the promise becomes enforceable.

2.2 Formalities

A contract may be made in any form that the parties wish. This is the case regardless of the sums involved or the complexity of the agreement. If a large sum of money is involved, or the matter is a complicated one, there are advantages in having the contract formally drafted. There is no essential requirement in English law that a contract should be in writing and as a

49

general rule the parties to a contract may insert whatever provisions they wish into the agreement. Despite the individualistic development of the law of contract it became clear, as the Nineteenth Century progressed, that there were problems relating to complete freedom of contract. However, it is only in relatively recent times that the law has placed restrictions on the extent to which contracting parties may exclude their liabilities (see the Unfair Contract Terms Act 1977 in section 2.10).

(a) Simple Contracts

These are contracts made by word of mouth or in writing or a combination of both. No particular form is required.

(b) Deeds

A contract made by deed is known as a Specialty Contract. Until 1990, certain contracts had to be made 'under seal' and delivered up 'as a deed'. The best examples of such contracts were the granting of a lease for more than 3 years in duration and most transfers of freehold land and buildings. A seal is no longer necessary but no estate will pass unless the instrument transferring the land (the conveyance or lease) says that the document is a deed. It states in the Act (*Law of Property [Miscellaneous Provisions] Act 1989 s2*) that a contract is not made by deed unless the document in which it is written:

(1) makes clear that it is intended to be a deed, and
(2) it is validly executed by the appropriate party or parties.

In those rare situations where no consideration passes between the parties under the contract, the agreement must be in the form of a deed to be valid, while there are additional statutory requirements governing the execution of a deed by a company. One practical advantage of a contract being made by deed is that the limitation period governing such contracts is twelve years, as opposed to six years in the case of a simple contract.

(c) Contracts Which Must Be Made In Writing or Evidenced In Writing

Certain types of contract cannot be enforced or are invalid unless they are in writing although they do not have to be made in the form of a deed. This is particularly true of consumer credit and hire agreements governed by the Consumer Credit Act 1974. Presumably, the purpose of these requirements is to ensure that the borrower is aware of the extent of his indebtedness to creditors.

Standard Form Contracts

Certain transactions are governed entirely by standard terms which are predetermined. An example is where one of the parties enjoys a monopolist position or particular types of business are in relatively few hands. Where this arises the customer is not in a position to negotiate over the terms of the contract. Instead the person requiring the goods or the services contracts on a standard form prepared in advance by the dominant organisation. Such a contract makes a mockery of the concept of freedom of contract whereby a person is free to contract or not and the selection of subject matter, terms and parties are a matter of choice. Apart from the so-called adhesion variety of standard form contract, whereby no opportunity exists for any negotiations and the weaker contracting party must 'take it' or 'leave it', there is the type of standard form of contract which is commonplace in construction and land transactions where standard clauses have been settled over the years by negotiation. The purpose of these forms is to facilitate the conduct of trade and this is the type of contract which is invariably used in large scale construction works. The Joint Contracts Tribunal (JCT) Standard Form of Building Contract (see section 2.16) and the Institution of Civil Engineers (ICE) form of engineering contract (also see section 2.16) tend to govern major works, while other contracts such as the standard form of management contract have come to play significant roles.

2.3   The Essential Elements of a Valid Contract

A simple contract has three essential elements:

(a) agreement (or at least the outward appearance of agreement);
(b) consideration;
(c) the intention to create legal relations.

2.4   Agreement

It is accepted that before a formal agreement can be reached there must be a valid offer made by the *offeror* and a valid acceptance of that offer by the *offeree*. If a contract is entered into solely on the basis of what is agreed in a standard form of contract, it may be possible to ascertain with relative ease whether or not a valid agreement has come into being. Where a contract is alleged to have come into being by a combination of statements made orally together with documents in writing, it may be considerably more difficult to ascertain whether or not an offer and acceptance have been made. Not all agreements can be so easily reduced and the real test is whether the parties have accepted obligations to one another. If that is established, a valid agreement may be inferred from the conduct of the parties even though it has been made simply on an oral basis (*Trentham [G Percy] Ltd* v *Archital Luxfer Ltd [1993] 1 Lloyd's Rep 25*). As a general rule, arrangements which are too vague, uncertain or are conditional will not take effect. The following are the major rules which attempt to ensure that before an agreement can exist there must be a clear and formal offer and an unequivocal acceptance of that offer.

Rules as to Offers

(a) *An offer must be distinguished from an invitation to treat*
This is a preliminary stage in proceedings which may or may not result in an offer being made. It is not possible to accept an invitation to treat and thereby create a valid agreement. Marked prices on articles for sale will amount to invitations to treat (*Fisher* v *Bell [1961] 1 QB 394; Pharmaceutical Society of Great Britain* v *Boots Cash Chemists [Southern] Ltd [1953] 1 QB 401*) while catalogues and circulars which offer goods for sale come into this category (*Grainger & Son* v *Gough [1896] AC 325*). Difficulties of classification can arise in connection with advertisements. It is a question of intention which decides whether these are offers or invitations to treat. The advertising of an auction sale is not an offer (*Harris* v *Nickerson [1873] 28 LT 410*) nor is the advertisement of goods for sale (*Partridge* v *Crittenden [1968] 1 WLR 1204*), but advertisements for rewards are considered to be offers (*Carlill* v *Carbolic Smokeball Co [1893] 1 QB 256*). Likewise, if goods are offered for sale in a trade magazine or periodical, the advertisement would be likely to be treated as a formal offer if the advertiser intends no further negotiations to take place, and all that is required of the other party is to send a cheque for the goods or give a credit card number. An invitation to tender to carry out works or supply goods is an invitation to treat (*Spencer* v *Harding [1870] 23 LT 237*). The submitted tender is a formal offer which may be accepted or not. Unusually, there have been situations where 'invitations' to tender have given rise to an enforceable contract where the facts have shown a clear intention to create contractual obligations (*Harvela Investments Ltd* v *Royal Trust Co of Canada Ltd and others [1985] 3 WLR 276; Blackpool and Fylde Aero Club Ltd* v *Blackpool Borough Council [1990] 3 All ER 25*).

(b) *Inquiries and replies to inquiries are not offers*
Statements of price or rates on their own are not formal offers. Most of the relevant case law is concerned with the purchase of land or buildings

(*Harvey* v *Facey [1893] AC 552; Clifton* v *Palumbo [1944] 2 All ER 497*) but similar rules would apply to monetary rates relating to a job of work. Such a price could constitute an element in a contract subsequently entered into. In *Gibson* v *Manchester City Council [1979] 1 All ER 972* it was decided that a statement made in a letter by the defendants that the council 'may be prepared to sell' and inviting the other party 'to make formal application to buy' a house was an invitation to treat.

(c) *Communication of the offer*

Communication of the offer to give the offeree an opportunity to accept or reject is essential, although it may be communicated in any manner whether expressly, impliedly or by a mixture of the two. Only an offeree can accept (*Boulton* v *Jones [1857] 6 WR 107; Powell* v *Lee [1908] 99 LT 284*), while if an offer is made to the world at large (*Carlill* v *Carbolic Smokeball Co* – see above), any person with notice of the offer may accept it.

(d) *An offer may be **revoked** (withdrawn) any time before acceptance*

Once a valid acceptance has been made, the offeror is bound by the terms of the offer. In an auction sale, each individual bid is an offer which can be accepted or rejected at any time before the auctioneer accepts it (*Payne* v *Cave [1789] 3 Term Rep 148*). If the offeror agrees to keep an offer open for a specific period, he is not bound by that stipulation unless the offeree has given consideration to have the offer kept open. In such circumstances there will be a breach of contract if there is an attempt to revoke the offer within that period (*Routledge* v *Grant [1828] 4 Bing 653*). Revocation of an offer only becomes effective when it is communicated to the offeree (*Byrne* v *Van Tinenhoven [1880] C P D 344*). This rule does not create a problem if the rovocation is instantaneous but if there is a delay, for instance by post, there may be a valid acceptance before the revocation has been communicated. Valid communication of revocation may be indirect if from a 'reliable source' (*Dickinson* v *Doods [1876] 2 Ch D 463*). A difficult area arises where an offer requires a certain act to be carried out but the offer is revoked after the act has been commenced but before it has been completed. The problem arises in the case of unilateral contracts and reward cases are a good example. In *Errington* v *Errington and Woods [1952] 1 All ER 149* it was decided that the offer could not be revoked once the appropriate party had begun the actual performance of the conduct required by the offer. This tends to be contrasted with the position where the offer, or circumstances surrounding it, give some indication that the offer could be revoked before completion of the envisaged act by the offeree (*Trentham [G Percy] Ltd* v *Archital Luxfer Ltd* – see above).

(e) *An offer remains open until it is accepted, revoked, rejected or lapses*
Only proper acceptance of an offer will result in a valid agreement. If there is a valid revocation of an offer or a rejection of that offer by the offeree, no contract can be formed. An offer may also lapse and become incapable of acceptance by passage of time. This occurs where there is a time limit within which acceptance may be made and that time has passed. It also occurs where no time limit is specified and there has been no acceptance within a reasonable period (*Chemco Leasing PpA* v *Rediffusion [1987] 1 FTLR 201*). The length of time is dependent upon the circumstances of the case and the question of reasonableness may vary depending upon the nature of the contract.

Rules as to Acceptance

Once the existence of an offer has been proved, the courts must be satisfied that a valid acceptance of that offer has taken place. Since contracts tend to arise as the result of long and complicated negotiations, it is often difficult to ascertain the exact moment when the contract was formed. In such cases the conduct of the parties and all their actions and statements will be considered, to see whether or not the parties intended to contract and if there is an actual contract when it was made. Many of these rules are centred around the proposition that the acceptance must be clear and comply exactly with the terms of the offer.

(a) *The acceptance must be in response to an offer and must correspond precisely with the terms of the offer*
In *Peter Lind Ltd* v *Mersey Docks and Harbour Board [1972] 2 Lloyd's Rep 234* alternative tenders were submitted for the construction of a freight terminal. The offeree accepted 'your tender' without specifying which one. Consequently there was no contract (see also *Tinn* v *Hoffman & Co [1873] 29 LT 271*).

(b) *Counter offers*
This is similar to the position in (a) above. The insertion of new terms (see section 2.7) into the agreement amounts to a counter offer by the person who makes it, rather than being a valid acceptance. In *Hyde* v *Wrench [1840] 3 Beav 334* an offer was made to sell a farm for £1000. A counter offer of £950 was made and refused, whereupon the buyer tried to accept the original offer of £1000. It was decided that the original offer had been rejected by the counter offer. In circumstances where the parties agree to accept the counter offer the terms of that offer become the terms of the contract (*Davies* v *William Old [1969] 67 LGR 395*). A counter offer must be contrasted with an inquiry or a request for information from the offeree which will not vary the terms of the original offer (*Stevenson* v *McClean [1880] 5 QB 346*).

(c) *The nature and time of acceptance*

Silence will not amount to a valid acceptance (*Felthouse* v *Bindley [1863] 1 New Rep 401*). A contract takes effect from the time that acceptance is communicated to the offeror. Where an offeror insists on a particular method of acceptance that method must be adopted and the offeror can refuse to recognise an acceptance made in any other manner (*Manchester Diocesan Council for Education* v *Commercial and General Investments Ltd [1969] 3 All ER 1593*). In the case of a unilateral contract, the offeror may dispense with the need to communicate acceptance because of the terms of the offer (*Carlill* v *Carbolic Smokeball Co* – see above). In such circumstances the necessary performance by the offeree will be suffcent acceptance. It is possible for an offer to be accepted by conduct if that conduct unequivocally relates to the offer (*Brogden* v *Metropolitan Rly Co [1877] 2 App Cas 666*). A contract can come into existence during performance even if it cannot be precisely analysed in terms of offer and acceptance (*Trentham [G Percy] Ltd* v *Archital Luxfer Ltd [1993]* – see above). A postal acceptance is effective when it is posted even if it is late or is never actually delivered, so long as there is proof of posting (*Adams* v *Lindsell [1818] 106 ER 250*). If the offeror specifies that acceptance must actually be communicated, the rule does not apply (*Hollwell Securities* v *Hughes [1973] 2 All ER 476*). The post rule will not apply if it would give rise to 'manifest inconvenience or absurdity' (*ibid*).

Instantaneous Communication

An oral acceptance needs to be communicated to the offeror. If a facsimile or telex message is sent during ordinary business hours, it is treated as being instantaneous and takes effect when printed out on the offeror's machines where the acceptance is received (*Entores* v *Miles Far East Corp [1955] 2 All ER 493; Brinkibon* v *Stahag Stahl GmbH [1983] AC 34*).

(d) *Letters of intent and pre-contract work*

Letters of intent are indications by a potential party to a contract of an intention to contract at a future date. The status of these letters depends on their wording but where appropriate they can constitute a valid acceptance of an offer. Such letters may make provision for goods to be delivered or rendered before the actual formation of the contract. When the contract is eventually signed it will 'relate back' so as to apply to what was done previously (*Trollope & Colls Ltd* v *Atomic Powers Constructions Ltd [1963] 1 WLR 119*). Even if no contract is ever reached, a party may claim for work carried out (*ibid*), even if what has been done is of no use to the other party (*British Steel Corpn* v *Cleveland Bridge and Engineering Co Ltd [1984] 1 All ER 504*).

2.5   Consideration

Unless a contract is made by deed it must be supported by consideration otherwise it will be unenforceable. The party who wishes to enforce a contract must show that consideration has been provided for the obligation which is sought to be enforced. A bare promise without consideration is not binding. A contract is essentially a bargain requiring reciprocal obligations between the parties. Sometimes consideration is known as value. It relates to payment of money, the provision of goods, the performance of services or the transfer of land, but it may consist of any benefit which accrues to one party or is to the detriment of the other. A distinction is made between executed consideration, where the price is paid for the other party's act, and executory consideration, where the parties exchange promises to carry out obligations in the future.

Rules

(a) *Consideration must have some value but need not be adequate*
    This means that the consideration must have some worth but the courts will not interfere with a bargain which has been made between the parties in the absence of fraud or other underhand dealings. In *Mountford* v *Scott [1975] 1 All ER 198* a token payment of £1 securing an option to purchase a house for £10,000 was adequate consideration, while in *Chappell Co Ltd* v *Nestle Ltd Co AC 87* the wrappers from bars of chocolate were held to constitute good consideration. Forbearance to sue (agreeing not to pursue a claim in return for a promise by the other party) may be adequate consideration.

(b) *Performance of an existing contractual duty is not good consideration*
    Where a party performs an act which is simply a discharge of an existing obligation owed by contract, this will not amount to consideration. A similar rule applies where the existing duty is owed by the general law. Consequently, in *Collins* v *Godefroy [1831] 1 Dowl 326*, where the defendant agreed to pay the plaintiff a sum of money if he gave evidence at a criminal trial, a claim for the sum promised failed because the plaintiff had an obligation imposed by law to give such evidence. If the obligation is a contractual one and a party does more than he was bound to do under the terms of the contract, that will amount to good consideration. Two examples of the rule in practice are the decisions in *Stilk* v *Myrick [1809] 2 Camp 317* and *Hartley* v *Ponsonby [1857] 7 E & B 872*. Both cases involve claims by seamen relating to work carried out under their contracts. In the former case, a claim relating to extra work carried out under a contract was dismissed because the crew were contractually bound to carry out any extra work by the terms of their

contracts. In the latter case, any extra work involved in the voyage was an addition to the crew's contractual obligations and a successful claim could be made in respect of the additional work which had been carried out. In *Williams* v *Roffey Bros Ltd [1990] 1 All ER 512* the defendants were contractors responsible for the refurbishment of a block of flats. Mr Williams, a joiner, contracted to carry out joinery work on the flats for the sum of £20,000. The contract contained a provision that if the work was not completed by a specific date, damages would be payable by the defendants. The plaintiff had contracted at a sum which was unprofitable to him and was in no hurry to complete the contract. Somewhat concerned that the contract might not be finalised on time, the defendant promised to pay the plaintiff, by word of mouth, an extra £10,300 in respect of the flats so long as the work was completed according to schedule. The joiner carried out the work and claimed the extra sums. The Court of Appeal decided that these amounts were payable. Consideration had been given for the contractor's promise to make the additional payment. The contract had been completed, the damages payable in respect of late completion had been avoided and it had not been necessary to employ others to finish off the joinery work. Performance of an existing contractual duty owed to a third party is dealt with differently. The discharge of an existing contractual obligation to a third party can be valid consideration for another's promise (*Scotson* v *Pegg [1861] 9 WR 280*).

(c) *Consideration must not be past*
If one party performs an act before any promise of reward is made by the other party, the act in question is regarded as past consideration and will not support a contractual claim. The practical effect of this rule is that it is not possible to develop a social arrangement into a contract by making a promise of consideration after the arrangement has been carried out. In *Re McArdle [1951] Ch 669*, alterations and improvements to a house were carried out and paid for before the other parties to the contract agreed to reimburse the cost. The consideration was past.

Exceptions to the rule
(1) Where there is an implied promise to pay. It is common practice to pay for certain transactions after completion of the event, such as a taxi journey or a meal in a restaraunt.
(2) Section 27 Bills of Exchange Act 1882. Cheques are frequently paid in connection with goods and services received in the past.

(d) *Payment of a lesser sum under a contract than the amount which is due will not discharge the debt for a greater sum*
Where a debtor pays a lesser sum to his creditor than that which is due, the debtor is not discharged from the obligation to pay the balance. The

creditor can go back on the agreement and sue for the balance (*Foakes* v *Beer [1884] 9 App Cas 605*). There is an important exception to this waiver rule and it arises if, at the creditor's request, some new element is introduced into the arrangement such as payment at a different time or place. Appropriate compliance with this request will amount to consideration for the waiver and the creditor will have no further claim (*D & C Builders Ltd* v *Rees [1965] 3 All ER 837; Stour Valley Builders* v *Stuart. The Times February 2nd 1993*).

(e) *Consideration must move from the promisee*
Only a party who gives consideration under a contract (or his agent) can sue in the event of a breach of contract. This rule is similar to but must be distinguished from the privity rule (see section 2.9).

(f) *Promissory estoppel*
If certain conditions are satisfied, where a party has waived rights under a contract and the other party has relied upon the promise not to enforce those rights, the promisor is estopped from going back on the promise even though no consideration has been given for the waiver. Although the doctrine has its roots in the Nineteenth Century (*Hughes* v *Metropolitan Rlw Co [1877] 2 App Cas 439*), its modern development dates from the 'High Trees' case (*Central London Property Trust Ltd* v *High Trees House Ltd [1947] KB 130*). This case concerns the lease of a block of flats in London which turned out to be unprofitable because of the threat of enemy bombing in the Second World War. The landlord made a written promise to reduce the rent for the duration of the war. In 1945, when circumstances had changed, the landlord changed his mind and started to charge the full rent. It was decided that he could do so for the future, but the full rent could not be obtained for the period between making the promise and the end of the war since the tenants had relied on his previous promise. Before the doctrine can come into being there must be an agreement between the parties, an unequivocal promise by one party to the other and, at least for the time being, an indication that those rights will be waived. The defendant must have given no consideration for the promise but acted upon that promise by relying upon it. The promisor is then estopped (prevented) from altering his position under the contract if to do so would cause harm to the other party. Estoppel can only be used as a defence to a claim and not as a cause of action (*Combe* v *Combe [1951] 2 KB 215*). Whether or not promissory estoppel merely suspends an obligation or discharges it completely is the subject of debate (*Tool Metal Manufacturing Co Ltd* v *Tungsten Electric Co Ltd [1955] 2 All ER 657; Brikom Investments* v *Carr [1979] 2 All ER 753*).

2.6 The Intention to Create Legal Relations

A contract is a legally binding agreement. Where no such intention can be shown there is no contract. Many agreements are never intended to be legally binding.

(a) *Business agreements*

In business and commercial agreements it is presumed that the parties intend to create legal relations. This includes an agreement to build or to transfer land or buildings (*Milner & Son* v *Percy Bilton Ltd [1966] 2 All ER 284*). This presumption can be challenged (rebutted) if there is evidence to the contrary. There must be strong evidence from the agreement that the parties do not intend to create legal relations. The parties are not bound where the agreement is expressed to be 'binding in honour only' or something similar (*Jones* v *Vernon Pools Ltd [1938] 2 All ER 626; Rose & Frank Co* v *Crompton Bros Ltd [1924] 2 All ER 245*).

(b) *Social and domestic agreements*

In agreements of this type it is presumed that the parties do not intend legal relations to arise (*Balfour* v *Balfour [1919] 2 KB 571; Jones* v *Padavatton [1969] 1 WLR 328*). This principle may also be rebutted. An agreement which appears on the face of it to be simply a domestic agreement may be enforceable between the parties (*Simpkins* v *Pays [1955] 3 All ER 10*). Much depends on the formality of the agreement, whether consideration has passed between the parties and the language used. In *Spelling* v *John Spelling Ltd [1973] QB 87*, mutual promises between co-directors, who were brothers, that they would not withdraw money from a family business were deemed to be binding. Similar problems have arisen in cases concerning proposals to share houses with relatives. In *Parker* v *Clark [1960] 1 All ER 93*, a married couple gave up their house in order to go and look after a family relative. This was in return for an assurance that the property would be left to them by will. The assurance was deemed to be legally binding.

2.7 Terms of a Contract

The terms of a contract are its contents. Terms may be express or implied. Express ones are stated while implied terms arise in other ways.

(a) *Express terms*

Where the contract has been made on a wholly oral basis, the meaning of the terms is a question of fact to be decided by the court from the evidence which is given to it. Where the contract has been reduced to writing, the 'parol evidence' rule prevents oral or other extrinsic evidence to be admitted to vary or contradict the terms of the written agreement. There are some exceptions to this rule, among the most important being:

(1) to prove a trade custom or usage;
(2) to indicate the existence of a vitiating factor (see section 2.8);
(3) where the written contract is not the whole contract.

(b) *Terms and representations*
It is important to distinguish between these two factors. A representation is a statement of fact which acts as an inducement to enter into a contract. It is not a contractual term but may give a potential plaintiff a right to claim on the basis of misrepresentation if it turns out to be false. If the misrepresentation is actionable the remedies are governed by the Misrepresentation Act 1967 and not by the rules relating to remedies for breach of contract. The intentions of the parties and what they have to say about the statement are important. If this is inconclusive the test is to consider what an intelligent bystander would infer from the words and behaviour of the parties.

(c) *Implied terms*
A contract may contain terms which are not express but which are implied by custom, the courts or by statute. A term will not be implied by custom if the express wording of the contract shows that the parties had a contrary intention. Where appropriate a term will be implied by the custom of a particular geographical area (*Hutton v Warren [1836] 1 M&W 466*).

1. The Courts

The courts will imply a term in the following sets of circumstances:

(a) *Where such a term is a necessary incident of the type of contract in question*
Reasonableness of the term and the nature of the subject matter are important here. In contracts to build where a builder constructs a house there is a term implied that the dwelling will be reasonably fit for habitation when completed. Similar terms are implied in respect of the quality of work and the time in which the contract will be completed. Likewise, on the employer's part, it is implied that the contractor will be given possession of the site on which the building works are to take place and that a reasonable sum shall be payable for the work. These terms may be rebutted where there are express terms dealing with these matters to the contrary

(b) *To give the contract 'business efficacy'*
This means to make it a workable agreement in such a manner as the parties would clearly have done if they had applied their minds to

the matter arising. It may be necessary to fill a gap in the contract and the term(s) must be formulated with a sufficient degree of precision. There must be no express term dealing with the same matter, while the stipulations must be so obvious that they go without saying. The principle comes from *The Moorcock [1889] 14 PD 164*, where a vessel was damaged unloading a cargo owing to the unevenness of the river bed which had not been maintained properly. It was decided that there was an implied term in the contract that the owners of the wharf had impliedly contracted to take reasonable care to see that ships unloading their cargos were safe.

(c) *Where a term is implied by the previous course of dealings between the parties*
Where the parties have previously entered into contracts of a particular variety containing express terms, those terms will be implied into a contract of a similar kind in the absence of express stipulation.

2. Statute

In some instances, statute will imply terms into a contract. Good examples are the Sale of Goods Acts 1979 and the Supply of Goods and Services Act 1982. The Sale and Supply of Goods Act 1994 has made amendments to this legislation.

The Sale of Goods Act 1979

Terminology
A contract for the sale of goods is one whereby the seller transfers or agrees to transfer the property in goods for a money consideration called the price. 'Goods' includes all personal chattels other than money and choses in action (see Chapter 4, section 4.1).

Terms implied by the Act
The Sale of Goods Act 1979 implies terms into contracts for the sale of goods as follows:
Title (section 12)
In every such contract there is an implied condition on the part of the seller that he has the right to sell the goods or that he will have the right at the time when the property is to pass. If this condition is broken the buyer may treat the contract as at an end even though he has done some act which would otherwise have amounted to acceptance. Section 12 also provides that there is an implied warranty that the goods are free and will remain free from any encumbrances not known to the buyer before the contract is made.

Description (section 13)

The vast majority of sales are by description and in such a case there is an implied condition that the goods will correspond with that description. It extends to matters such as measurements, quantity and methods of packing (*Moore & Co* v *Landauer & Co [1921] 2 KB 519*). It also applies to private sales.

Satisfactory quality (section 14)

The following provisions only apply where the goods are sold in the course of a business. By section 14[2] there is an implied condition of satisfactory quality except as regards defects specifically drawn to the buyer's attention before the contract is made or where the buyer examines the goods before the contract as regards defects which the examination ought to reveal. 'Satisfactory quality' means that the goods meet the standard that a reasonable person would regard as satisfactory having regard, *inter alia*, to their description and price. Section 14[3] relates to fitness. The implied condition is that the goods are reasonably fit for any purpose which the buyer makes known to the seller. This purpose will normally be implied but if goods have a number of purposes, the buyer must indicate the one required.

Sample (section 15)

Certain items such as tiles, carpets and wallpaper are bought on the basis of a sample inspected before the sale takes place. In such circumstances the following conditions are implied:

(1) that the bulk will correspond with the sample in quality;
(2) that the buyer will have a reasonable opportunity of comparing the bulk with the sample;
(3) that the goods shall be free from any defects rendering them unmerchantable which would not be apparent on reasonable examination of the sample.

The Supply of Goods and Services Act 1982

A contract for the sale of goods must be distinguished from a contract for the supply of services where goods are also being sold under the contract. A contract for work done and materials supplied comes into this category. The sale aspect of the contract is governed by sections 2–5 of the 1982 Act which contains implied terms similar to the Sale of Goods Act 1979 (sections 12–15) The works aspects are governed by Part 2 of the Act which imply terms relating to reasonable skill and care, reasonable time for completion, and reasonable charges for services where no price has been fixed at the outset. The supplier must be acting in the course of a business for the terms to apply.

Conditions and Warranties

Whether a contractual term is express or implied, it will either be a condition or a warranty. This distinction is important because there are different remedies if there is a breach of contract and things go wrong. There is no special test to determine into which category a term falls. Each situation has to be decided on its own merits.

Conditions
These are terms of the contract but for which the injured party would not have entered the contract. Breach of condition allows the injured party to treat the contract as finished whereupon he will be discharged from his obligations under the contract. In addition, the other party can be sued for damages. The contract is voidable (see section 2.8) and it is possible for the injured party to treat the breach of condition as a breach of warranty and simply bring an action for damages.

Warranties
These are terms which are secondary or ancillary to the main purpose of the contract. Breach of warranty allows the injured party to claim damages but not to repudiate the contract. The contract is not voidable. It is for a court and not for the parties to determine the category of term.

A problem which has arisen is that a stipulation in a contract may be classified as a term but is neither a condition nor a warranty. The difficulty which arises is then to determine whether or not the injured party can rescind (avoid) the contract. Such provisions have become known as intermediate or innominate terms. The consequences of the breach are important here. Unless the contract makes it clear, in one way or another, that the parties intended that no breach of the contract should entitle them to terminate the contract, the term will be classified as an intermediate term. The question is whether or not the nature and effect of the breach are to deprive the injured party of substantially the benefit which it is intended they should obtain under the contract. If so, the injured party is entitled to terminate the contract as well as claiming damages (*The Hansa Nord [1975] 3 All ER 739; Hong Kong Fir Shipping Co Ltd* v *Kawasaki Kisen Kaisha [1962] 2 QB 26*).

2.8 Vitiating Factors

These are factors which affect the validity of a contract. The three essentials are present but a state of affairs arises which may make the contract no longer enforceable. Depending upon the circumstances a vitiating factor will make the contract either:

(1) void (no contract);
(2) voidable (the contract exists but can be avoided);
(3) binding (an enforceable contract exists).

(a) Capacity of the Parties

The difficulty here is incapacity. A distinction is made in English law between natural persons and artificial persons. Natural persons have full capacity to enter contracts. There are exceptions to this rule in the case of minors (those under the age of 18) and, to a certain extent, in respect of those suffering from a mental disorder. As a general rule, contracts are not binding on minors. A practical exception to this rule is to be found in respect of contracts of employment which are benefical to the minor. Artificial persons are corporations, local authorities and companies registered under the Companies Acts (see Chapter 6, section 6.1).

(b) Mistake

This arises where the parties make a mistake as to a term of the contract. Mistake does not affect the validity of a contract unless the mistake is a fundamental one, sometimes called an operative mistake. Such a mistake will render the contract void. In a limited set of circumstances the contract will be voidable (this may be the position where these is a mistake as to the identity of the person contracted with). Special rules apply to documents. Where a person signs a document and by so doing enters a contract, the contract is binding. This is so even if the signatory has not read the document nor understands it. There is a very limited defence based on *Non Est Factum* (it is not my deed), where a person is induced by a fraud or a trick to sign a document. In practice, the defence is difficult to rely on because the signatory must show:

(1) that all reasonable precautions were taken when signing the document, and
(2) the document signed was radically different from the one the person thought they were signing, or
(3) the person signing the document was under some legal disability, such as being illiterate, blind or senile.

An example of (3) above occurred in *Lloyds Bank* v *Waterhouse [1991] 10 Trading LR 161*, where an illiterate person, who failed to inform the bank that she could not read, signed a bank guarantee form in reliance on the bank's misrepresentation as to its nature.

There are some circumstances where the equitable jurisdiction of the English legal system will intervene in the case of a mistake where the mistake is an non-operative one. This includes rescission of the contract (see below), a refusal of specific performance of the contract (see below) and possible rectification of a contract if it does not accurately express the agreement reached between the parties. In such circumstances, equity will rectify the agreement so as to make it conform with the original agreement. In *Craddock Bros* v *Hunt [1923] All ER 394* there was an oral agreement to sell land. This was put into writing but, by mistake, the document missed out any reference to part of the land which had been paid for. It was held that the agreement would be rectified. The rule does not apply if there is simply a mistake by one of the parties in expressing intention. In *W Higgins Ltd* v *Northampton Corpn [1927] 1 Ch 128* the plaintiff stated an incorrect price for work in connection with a tender relating to the building of houses. This was due to incorrect estimating on the plaintiff's part. The tender was accepted by the local authority without realising a mistake had been made but the contract could not be rectified.

(c) Misrepresentation

Misrepresentation is concerned with the effect of statements which are made before a contract is formed. A representation is a statement of fact which is made by one person to another with the object of persuading the other party to enter into a contract. Where that party relies upon the statement, a contract is formed and the statement turns out to be incorrect it will be a misrepresentation. Remedies are governed by the Misrepresentation Act 1967 and the tort of deceit. A misrepresentation can be fraudulent, innocent or negligent. A plaintiff in such circumstances will be able to claim damages and rescind the contract. In the case of a non-fraudulent misrepresentation, the court has power to refuse rescission and to award damages instead.

(d) Illegality

A contract containing an illegal element is void. The illegal aspect may be the contravention of a statute or it may be against public policy to allow certain types of contract to be enforced, such as defrauding the Inland Revenue or contracts involving the commission of a crime. Where a building contractor enters a contract knowingly in contravention of a law and the work is completed, the contract price will not be recoverable. In *Stevens* v *Gourley [1859] 7 CB NS 99* statutory provisions required buildings to be made of incombustible materials. When a builder erected a wooden building upon wooden foundations, the contract was illegal. If the contract appears to be perfectly valid at the outset and only becomes illegal while in the process of performance, the contractor may recover the price for the work depending upon the circumstances. In *Townshend Builders Ltd* v *Cinema News [1959] 1 WLR 119* specifications for work to be undertaken were in contravention of a statutory provision but the completed work was not. As the contract was not fundamentally illegal and the builder was unaware of the contravention until the work was well advanced payment could be claimed.

2.9   Privity of Contract

One fundamental aspect of the common law is the principle that no person can sue or be sued on a contract unless a party to it. This can cause particular problems in the construction industry where many parties are involved in a building project, some of whom have privity of contract between themselves while others have not. The rule does not mean that a person cannot receive a benefit under a contract, but a stranger to a contract cannot sue for the benefit in the event of not receiving it. The general aspects of the principle are illustrated by *Tweddle* v *Atkinson [1861] 1 Best & Smith 393* where a couple were about to marry. The bridegroom's father and the bride's father agreed between themselves that each would make payments to the couple. The husband sought to enforce the contract when the bride's father refused to pay, but as there was no privity of contract between the parties the claim could not be enforced. There are a number of exceptions to the rule.

Good examples are third party insurance policies, the agency relationship where a principal can sue and be sued in respect of a contract made by an agent, and another tripartite arrangement known as a trust (see Chapter 4, section 4.18). The privity rule has been criticised by the higher courts (*Beswick* v *Beswick [1968] AC 58*; *Woodar Investment Development Ltd* v *Wimpey Construction UK Ltd. [1980] 1 All ER 571*). A successful attack was made on the rule with the enactment of the Landlord and Tenant (Covenants) Act 1995 which has abolished the rule between a landlord and the assignee of an original tenant in a leasehold transaction.

Because of the difficulties which plaintiffs have in being able to successfully sue a defendant in the tort of negligence for financial losses it has become standard practice in large scale construction projects for those who finance such transactions to insist that all the parties involved enter into contractual warranties with each other, to ensure that in the event of default an injured party will have a potential defendant to sue and claim damages. It is probably the case that the doctrine of privity as it stands might not have a great deal of life in it. The Law Commission published a report on the doctrine of contract (Law Com No 242) in July 1996, which recommends primary legislation to enable contracting parties to confer on a third party a right to enforce their contractual obligations.

2.10   Exemption Clauses

Common Law

It is a common practice, when a contract is entered into, for a party to insert a clause when excludes liability completely under the contract, or limits that liability to a specific amount of money in the event of a breach. Such clauses are used by suppliers of goods and services in respect of potential problems such as defective materials and unsatisfactory work. The courts have always disliked exemption clauses and tend to lean against them if such a clause has to be interpreted. At common law an exemption clause is valid so long as certain basic requirements are satisfied. A person seeking to rely on such a clause must show that it is a term of the contract and that as a matter of construction it covers the damage in question (*Chappleton* v *Barry UDC [1949] 1 KB 532*; *Photo Production Ltd* v *Securicor Transport Ltd [1980] AC 827*). The clause will only be a contractual term if adequate notice is given of it or such a term is implied by a clause having been incorportaed into documents where there has been a previous course of dealings between the parties. A common practice is to print exemption clauses on order forms or on a notice. Notice of the clause must be given before, or at the time of the contract, and the exclusion will not be effective if the clause or the notice is contained in a document which the average person would not assume to contain contractual terms. As far as the construction of the clause is concerned liability can only be limited or excluded by clear words.

Statute

The principal statutory provision regulating unfair reliance on exemption clauses is the Unfair Contract Terms Act 1977 (UCTA). It covers liability in respect of a breach of contract and in respect of the tort of negligence. The Act only has application in respect of 'business liability' where the other party deals as a consumer. 'Business liability' relates to a transaction which emanates from business activities while the other party makes the contract in a domestic capacity. Any provision in a contract excluding or restricting liability for death or personal injury is void. In other cases based on negligence liability can only be excluded or limited if it is fair and reasonable to do so. The reasonableness provision also applies in contractual cases. Where a party to a contract deals as a consumer or contracts on the other party's standard business terms, the fair and reasonable provision will also apply. The Act does not apply to contracts of insurance and to contracts which contain a foreign element. The provision was considered by the House of Lords in *Smith* v *Eric S Bush [1990] 1 AC 831*, where a firm of general practice surveyors inserted an exemption clause into a valuation report for mortgage purposes which had been prepared for a building society. The report was shown to the purchasers. The Law Lords concluded that it would not in the circumstances be fair and reasonable to rely on the disclaimer. The factors to be considered when deciding whether a purported exclusion is fair and reasonable include:

(1) the practical consequences of exclusion – in particular, the cost and availability of insurance cover;
(2) equality of bargaining power between the parties;
(3) whether it is practicable for the relevant party (or parties) to seek advice from an alternative source;
(4) if the task is unusual or dangerous, then the exclusion could well be reasonable.

Similar provisions have been developed in connection with purported exclusions of liability in respect of contracts governed by the Sale of Goods Act 1979 and the Supply of Goods and Services Act 1982. Sections 6 and 7 of UCTA deal with these matters. Any of the terms implied by the Act may be excluded or varied subject to UCTA. The Act states that any clause purporting to exclude section 12 of the Act (title) is void. In a consumer sale, any term excluding sections 13, 14 or 15 (description, quality/fitness and sample) shall also be void. A consumer sale arises where:

(a) the seller is making a sale in the course of business;
(b) the goods are of a type ordinarily bought for private use or consumption;
(c) the buyer does not purchase the goods in the course of a business.

In a non-consumer sale which is made in the course of business, a seller may exclude liability under sections 13–15 if it can be shown that it is fair and reasonable to do so. The majority of sales in a construction context will be non-consumer in nature. UCTA lays down guide lines as to the factors to be taken into account when applying the reasonableness test. The principal ones are as follows:

(a) the relative strength of the bargaining position of the parties taking into account the availability of suitable alternative products and sources of supply;
(b) whether the buyer received an inducement to agree to the term;
(c) whether the buyer knew or ought reasonably to have known of the existence and extent of the term;
(d) the extent to which the goods were manufactured, processed or adapted to the special order of the buyer (*Unfair Contract Terms Act 1977 s11*).

An auction sale or a sale by tender is not a consumer sale. If a private buyer buys at auction, an exemption clause may be valid subject to the reasonableness test. It is presumed that a sale is a consumer sale, but once the seller has proved it is a non-consumer sale it is for the buyer to show that it would not be fair and reasonable to rely on the term.

2.11 Discharge of a Contract

Where a contract is at an end it is said to be discharged. The rule is that on discharge, the parties are freed from their obligations. Discharge must come about by an act of the parties, as the contract does not end automatically. It can come about in one of four ways:

(a) performance;
(b) agreement;
(c) frustration;
(d) breach of an appropriate term of the contract.

(a) Performance

Each party must perform precisely and completely what he has bargained to do. A person who claims to be discharged from obligations on the basis of performance must show that the work has been completed in full, the goods supplied or the land transferred as appropriate. A building or engineering contract will be discharged by performance when the contractor has completed all the work and the employer has paid all sums due. If there are hidden defects, the contract has not been performed. This common law rule is enshrined in *Cutter* v *Powell [1795] 6 Term 320,* where the defendant agreed to pay Cutter a sum of money for performing duties as a seaman on a ship during a ten-week voyage. Cutter died 7 weeks after the commencement of the voyage. His widow attempted to recover wages under the contract. The claim failed because the ten-week contract had not been performed. Similarly in *Sumpter* v *Hedges [1895] 1 QB 673* the plaintiff builder contracted to construct two buildings on the defendant's land for an agreed price. The buildings were half finished when the project was abandoned because of lack of funds. The plaintiff was unable to recover any money in respect of the work carried out. In order to avoid possible injustice and to prevent unfair manipulation of the common law rule, the courts have recognised certain exceptions where a person may claim a reasonable sum for the work carried out on the basis of a *quantum meruit* application. This means 'as much as it is worth'.

The exceptions are as follows:

(1) Severable contracts
If a contract is severable, sometimes described as divisible, payment can be claimed for work done on completion of each stage. On the other hand, if the contract is an entire one the work must be completed in full before the other party becomes liable to pay. The terms of the contract are important in this context and much will depend on the intention of the parties. The courts tend to lean against finding a contract entire. A severable contract will arise where payments are due from time to time and the other party's obligations are rendered in return.

(2) *Substantial performance*

This arises where performance under a contract, although not complete, is virtually exact. In such a case a claim may be made for the work completed subject to any counterclaim in respect of work remaining unperformed. The contract price can be claimed subject to a deduction equal to the cost of remedying any omissions or defects. In essence, the defects must be of a trifling nature before the exception can be claimed. In *Hoening* v *Isaacs [1952] 2 All ER 176* the doctrine was applied where the cost of remedying the defects amounted to £56 on a contract worth £750. In *Dakin* v *Lee Ltd [1916] 1 KB 566* the court stated that if a builder has done work under an entire contract, but the work has not been completed in accordance with the contract, a claim can be made on a *quantum meruit* unless the customer received no benefit from the work, the work was entirely different from that which was contracted for, or the contractor had abandoned the work. The exception will not apply if the contract has not been substantially completed. The actual cost of remedying the defects in relation to the contract price is a relevant factor. In *Bolton* v *Mahedeva [1972] 2 All ER 1322* a contract to install a central heating system for £560 resulted in £174 having to be spent to remedy the work. In practice, the principle tends to be invoked by a party who has carried out work in breach of contract where the employer correctly refuses to pay the price. In *Lawson* v *Supa-Sink [1982] 3 Tr L 37* the defendants contracted to install a new kitchen for the benefit of the plaintiffs. The cost of remedying the defects was substantial and the defendants were in breach of contract as the plaintiffs had not received what they had contracted for. The plaintiffs were entitled to rescind the contract.

(3) *Prevention of performance*

If a party to a contract is prevented from performing what he has agreed to do by the other party, a claim for damages can be made or a claim can be made on a *quantum meruit* for work carried out. In *Roberts* v *Bury Improvement Commissioners [1870] LR 5 CP 10* a contractor was not in default where an architect neglected to supply him with necessary plans, thereby preventing completion by the contract date.

(b) Agreement

As contracts are created by agreement, they may also be discharged in the same manner. If the parties agree to waive their obligations under a contract, they must enter into another contract for the waiver to be effective. This will be appropriate where neither of the parties has completed their obligations due under the contract. Where one of the parties has completed obligations due under the contract but the other party has not, the party to whom the obligation is owed may agree with the other party to accept something different in place of the former obligation. This is known as the doctrine of accord and satisfaction, with the subsequent agreement being the accord, and the new consideration which has been given being termed the satisfaction. Alternatively, an obligation under a contract may be discharged by the operation of one of the terms of the contract itself. Contracts of employment often contain provisions whereby the contract can be determined by either party giving a period of notice to the other. In building and engineering contracts it is common to find provisions whereby the contract can be determined before completion on the happening of specific events. The serious default of the other party is a common example.

(c) Frustration

'Frustration' here means impossibility. As a rule, contractual obligations are absolute in that a contract is not discharged simply because it is more difficult or expensive than expected to carry it out. As the law developed, it moved from this rigid position and now a contract may be discharged by frustration if supervening events arising after the contract was entered into make it impossible to carry out as envisaged. Modern-day examples of building contracts that have been frustrated are rare, and to succeed a plaintiff must show that the circumstances have changed to such an extent that the performance of the contractual obligation has become fundamentally different.

Specific Examples of Frustration

(1) *Destruction of the subject matter*
If the subject matter is destroyed and its existence is crucial to the performance of the contract the contract will be frustrated. In *Taylor* v *Caldwell [1863] 3 Best & Smith 826*, a building which was to be used for a series of concerts was destroyed by fire.

(2) *Changes in the law*
If a change in the law makes the contract impossible to carry out, the doctrine of frustration will apply. Many of the examples from case law relate to war-time regulations (*Denny Mott and Dickson Ltd* v *James B Fraser & Co Ltd [1944] AC 265*; *Metropolitan Water Board* v *Dick Kerr Ltd [1918] AC 119*: *Fibrosa Spolka Akcyjna* v *Fairbairn Lawson Coombe Balfour Ltd [1943] AC 32*).

(3) *Inability to achieve the main object of the contract*
If the basis on which both parties entered the contract has been destroyed, the contract will be frustrated. To succeed on this basis there has to be a complete non-occurrence (*Krell* v *Henry [1903] 2 KB 740; Herne Bay Steam Boat Co* v *Hutton [1903] 2 KB 683*).

(4) *Death, personal incapacity or illness*
Death or permanent incapacity will frustrate a contract for personal services. Likewise if a party is likely to be ill or incapacitated for a considerable period of time, that may make the contract fundamentally different
from that originally envisaged and it will be discharged (*Morgan* v *Manser
[1948] 1 KB 184*). Cancellation of one or a number of performances by
a person who later provides the service required will not amount to a
frustrating event.

Specific Examples of Where Frustration Will Not Apply

(1) *The contract becoming more onerous to perform or less financially rewarding*
The fact that a contract proves more difficult or expensive to perform will
not frustrate the contract unless the difficulty arises from some fundamental
change of circumstances. In *Thorn* v *London Corporation [1876] 1 App Cass
120* contractors were liable to construct a new bridge when their design for
the new bridge proved difficult to put into practice. In *Davis Contractors
Ltd* v *Fareham UDC [1956] AC 696* builders agreed to erect 78 houses in
6 months. Owing mainly to a lack of skilled labour and a shortage of materials, the period extended to twenty two months. Building costs in that period
had risen considerably and the builders contended that they should be entitled to claim on a *quantum meruit*. The House of Lords decided that the
contract was not frustrated as it was simply more difficult to carry out.
Likewise in *Amalgamated Investment and Property Co* v *John Walker [1977]
1 WLR 164* the plaintiffs attempted to frustrate a contract when after
exchange of contracts, but before completion of the purchase of industrial
premises, the Department of the Environment listed the property which was
the subject of the sale. The Court of Appeal held, rejecting the appeal, that
listing was an inherent risk in all property transactions relating to buildings
of historical and architectural interest and the transaction after listing was
not radically different than it was previously.

(2) *Self-induced frustration*
At common law, a frustrating event must not have been one which the
parties could have contemplated when making the contract. If express provision has been made in the contract for the contingency in question,
the courts will give effect to the intention of the parties as expressed in the
contract. The event causing the frustration must not have been due to the
conduct of the parties.

Effect of Frustration

At common law, a frustrating event only operates to discharge the contract
from the time of the frustrating event. It does not frustrate it from the

outset (*ab initio*). Where the common law rules still apply (mainly insurance and shipping contracts), it is not possible to recover money which has been paid before the frustrating event takes place, unless there has been a total failure of consideration (the other party failing to perform their part of the contract). Other contracts than those stated above are governed by the Law Reform (Frustrated Contracts) Act 1943 which allows:

(1) money that has been transferred before the frustrating event to be recovered, and money due is no longer due;
(2) expenses incurred prior to the frustrating event may be deducted from money due to be returned;
(3) a party who has carried out work or services prior to the frustrating event may claim compensation on a *quantum meruit* basis.

(d) Breach of an Appropriate Term of the Contract

Any failure by a party who contracts to fulfil obligations under the contract amounts to a breach. Subject to a valid exemption clause to the contrary, whenever a party to a contract is in breach this gives rise to an obligation on his part to pay damages to the person who has suffered loss. Any failure by a person who contracts to fulfil his obligations under the contract amounts to a breach. Unless the breach can be classified as a repudiatory breach, the obligations of the parties to perform the contract remain unchanged. In each case the issue as to whether the breach is to be taken as a repudiation depends upon the importance of the breach in relation to the contract as a whole. In a building contract, repudiation will assert itself where execution of the works is so unsatisfactory as to affect the very basis of the contract. In the case of a repudiatory breach, the injured party has the option either to terminate the contract or to affirm it. The appropriate test to ascertain whether or not a party has repudiated the contract is whether or not a reasonable person would believe that the other party did not intend to be bound by the contract. If that is satisfied, the injured party may treat the contract as at an end and is released from further performance. The plaintiff may rescind the contract but must act without delay to do so (the normal rules as to seeking equitable remedies will apply – see section 2.14). Unjustified rescission of a contract does not always amount to a repudiation.

Anticipatory Breach

Where a breach takes place before the time set for performance of the contract, the injured party need not wait for the date set for performance. A right of action exists immediately as if there were a breach, and the plaintiff may sue for breach of contract (*Lovelock* v *Franklyn [1846] 8 KB 371*).

2.12   Damages

(A) Unliquidated Damages

Where the parties to a contract make no pre-assessment of any damages payable in the event of a breach, the claim is one for unliquidated damages. The object of such a claim is to put the injured party in the same position as if the contract had been performed. Any loss suffered as a consequence of the breach, physical or financial in nature, can be claimed by a successful plaintiff, but it is against public policy to allow compensation for every consequence which might logically result from the defendant's breach or there could be no limit to potential liability.

Remoteness and Causation

The rule in *Hadley* v *Baxendale [1854] 9 Ex 341* states that the only losses which are recoverable are those which may fairly and reasonably be considered as arising naturally from the breach of the contract, or losses which may reasonably be supposed to have been in the contemplation of both parties at the time they made the contract in the event of a breach. A good example of the second 'limb' of the remoteness rule is the decision in *Victoria Laundry Ltd* v *Newman Industries Ltd [1949] 1 All ER 997* where the laundry ordered a new boiler for their business which arrived late. The plaintiffs were entitled to recover damages for normal loss of profits because the supplier should have anticipated them, but they were not entitled to recover for further losses due to the demise of a profitable government contract as the defendants were unaware of its existence. To succeed, the loss must have been suffered as a result of the defendant's breach. In *Quinn* v *Burch Bros Ltd [1966] 2 QB 370* the defendants failed to supply the plaintiff plasterer with a step ladder. As an alternative he used a trestle which he leant against a wall. The trestle slipped, causing injury to the plaintiff. The Court of Appeal took the view that the injury was the plaintiff's own fault and that the defendant's breach of contract did not cause the injury.

Classification of Damages

General Damages

The measure of damages awarded is usually the actual monetary loss. In cases of defective building work, the cost of reinstatement will constitute general damages (*East Ham Corporation* v *Bernard Sunley & Sons [1966] AC 406*). If this formula does not represent the actual loss, then the damages will amount to the decrease in the value of the property.

Consequential Loss Damage

These are additional losses suffered as a consequence of the defendant's breach of contract and can be awarded as a further 'head' of damages.

Damages for Mental Distress

The traditional rule was that damages for breach of contract should not take account of any mental distress and inconvenience suffered by the plaintiff (*Addis* v *Gramophone Co Ltd [1909] AC 488*). Deviation was made from that position in *Jarvis* v *Swan Tours Ltd [1973] 1 All ER 71*, where the Court of Appeal decided that in an appropriate case such damages could be an additional element in the sum awarded. In general a contract-breaker is not liable for any distress or aggravation which the breach causes to an innocent party. This appears to be a matter of policy (*Watts* v *Morrow [1991] 4 All ER 937*). Where the object of the contract is to give pleasure, relaxation, peace of mind or freedom from molestation (*Hayes* v *James & Charles Dodd [1990] 2 All ER 815*), such damages may be awarded. Commercial contracts do not come within this exception (*Victor Jack Michael* v *Ensoncraft Ltd [1991] CILL 533*). This would include a contract to survey and to undertake building works (*Watts* v *Morrow* – see above). Damages are available in respect of physical discomfort resulting from a breach of such a condition, and this can include damages for mental distress.

(B) Liquidated Damages

In some cases the parties to a contract make an attempt in the contract to assess in advance the damages which will be payable in the event of a breach. This provision for liquidated damages will be valid if it is a genuine attempt to pre-estimate the likely loss suffered as a consequence of the breach. There can be no inquiry into the actual loss suffered. If the clause is a valid liquidated damages clause, the sum stipulated is recoverable upon that breach even though the loss is less or even nil. Such as provision must be distinguished from a Penalty Clause. This is a stipulation which is inserted to frighten the potential defaulter and to compel performance of the contract. A Penalty Clause is invalid but the injured party may recover any actual loss. It is common practice to find a liquidated damages clause for delay coupled with an extension of time clause giving the contractor the right to extra time if he is delayed by matters outside the control of either party. Relevant matters would include industrial action, bad weather, or the employer delaying the execution of the works by failing to supply necessary plans or give possession of the site. If any delay in the performance of the contract is caused by the employer, any claim to liquidated damages will be lost. The question as to whether a clause is a penalty or liquidated damages depends upon its construction and the surrounding circumstances at the time of making the contract. It is often difficult to estimate with accuracy the status of such a clause, as a breach of contract may result in a variety of consequences resulting in differing amounts of losses. The leading case is *Dunlop Pneumatic Tyre Co Ltd v New Garage Ltd [1915] AC 79*, where a number of propositions were put foward to determine whether a provision is a liquidated damages clause or a penalty:

(a) The name which the parties give to the clause is not conclusive and it is the task of the court to decide the category.
(b) The essence of liquidated damages is that the sum stated is a genuine pre-estimate of the probable loss, while the essence of a penalty is that it is a threat to carry out the contract.
(c) It is presumed to be a penalty clause if the sum stated is extravagant compared with the greatest possible loss.
(d) It is a penalty if the breach consists only in not paying a sum of money by a certain date and the sum fixed is greater than the sum which was originally to be paid. For example, X agrees to pay Y £5000 on January 1 and if he fails to pay at the contract time Y must pay £10,000 as 'liquidated damages'.
(e) There is a presumption that where a single sum is made payable on the happening of one or more events, some of which are serious and some of which are of little consequence, the sum is likely to be a penalty. There is a likelihood of greater losses emanating from a major breach than from a minor one. In *Law v Redditch Local Board [1892] 1 QB 127* the sum stated in the relevant clause was to be paid on the happening of a single event only. Therefore, it was deemed to be a valid pre-estimate of likely loss and was considered to be a liquidated damages clause.

Mitigation of Loss

The injured party has a duty to mitigate any losses suffered. This means that reasonable steps must be taken to minimise damage. An employee who is wrongly dismissed must attempt to find alternative employment, while a buyer of goods which are not delivered must try to buy as cheaply elsewhere. Failure to do so will be taken into account when assessing damages. Only reasonable steps to mitigate need be taken. The plaintiff is not expected to incur great expenditure or undertake great risks.

2.13   Limitation of Actions

Limitation periods are the time periods within which a plaintiff must commence an action for damages. It is recognised that a plaintiff must pursue a claim with due diligence while potential defendants should not have the threat of litigation pending indefinitely. Specific time periods are laid down by statute within which actions for damages must be brought. The reliability of evidence is an important factor here. Claims that have been in circulation for a considerable period of time make bad law and the eventual outcome of a case unreliable.

Limitation in Contract

The law is statute based and governed by the Limitation Act 1980. By section 5 of the Act, if the claim for breach of contract is based on a simple contract the action must be brought before the expiration of 6 years from the date on which the cause of action accrued. In the case of a deed, by section 8 of the Act the action must be brought within 12 years from that date. If the claim is not commenced within these time limits, it is statute-barred and cannot be pursued. In contract claims, the date when the cause of action accrued is the date when the breach of contract occurred. If the breach is a continuing one, a plaintiff can choose the last date that the defendant was in breach before the time period begins to run.

Limitation periods have to provide for the possibility of a defendant acting fraudulently or concealing the true state of affairs from a potential plaintiff. The current provisions are to be found in sections 31 and 32 of the 1980 Act. Section 32 provides that where the plaintiff is unaware of the true state of affairs because of the defendant's fraud or deliberate concealment of a breach of contract, the limitation period does not begin to run until the plaintiff has discovered the fraud or concealment, or could with reasonable diligence have discovered it. A good example of the rule is *Clark v Woor [1965] 2 All ER 353*, where the plaintiff commissioned the defendant builder to construct a bungalow, specifying the materials to be used and giving detailed instructions. The defendant knowingly used inferior facing bricks from those specified, concealing the true state of affairs from the plaintiff. No supervising architect or surveyor was involved in the contract. Some 8 years after construction of the bungalow, the plaintiff became aware of the defects. The claim was held, by the Court of Appeal, not to be statute-barred. Not surprisingly, cases concerning defective foundations have been covered by sections 31 and 32 of the 1980 Act. In *Applegate v Moss [1971] 1 KB 406* the defendant builders agreed in 1957 to build houses on a raft foundation supported by specified steel network. Eight years after their completion, cracks appeared beneath the houses. On inspection it was revealed that there was no raft and the reinforcement was inferior to that specified. The plaintiffs succeeded in their action, taking advantage of the concealment provisions. A similar result was reached in *King v Victor Parsons and Co [1973] 1 WLR 29*, where the defendants concealed the fact that a house had been built on a tip that had been filled in and did not have any proper foundations. When cracks appeared outside the limitation period, the plaintiff's claim was not deemed to be statute-barred (see also *Peco Arts Inv* v *Hazlitt Gallery [1983] 1 WLR 1315*).

2.14   Equitable Remedies

These may be available to an injured party where the common law remedy of damages is inadequate or inappropriate. They comprise the remedies which before the Judicature Acts 1873–75 were only available in the courts of equity. Since the fusion of the common law and equity, any civil court is able to grant these remedies if thought appropriate. They are discretionary and not automatically available in the event of winning a case. Certain principles apply generally to the grant of equitable remedies while others apply, in addition, to individual remedies. In all cases the conduct of the parties is taken into account, while no equitable remedy will be available if damages are considered to be an adequate remedy in the circumstances of the case. Limitation periods are not relevant to equitable remedies. Time is of the essence in such circumstances and each equitable remedy must be sought with reasonable promptness.

(a) Specific Performance

This is a court order directing the defendant to carry out a promise according to the terms of the contract. It is appropriate where the subject matter of the contract is not freely available, such as a rare painting or antique. In such cases the payment of a sum of money would not be adequate compensation in the event of a breach of contract. It is mainly used as a threatened remedy where contracts for the sale or lettings of land are broken (see Chapter 4, section 4.4). Apart from the normal conditions required before equitable remedies will be granted, specific performance will not be awarded to enforce a contract for personal services or where the contract requires supervision to ensure that it is being enforced properly (*Wolverhampton Corpn* v *Emmons [1901] KB 515*). Consequently it is not available to enforce a contract to build, as a claim for damages is more appropriate. Specific performance of a building contract will be awarded where:

(a)   the building work to be carried out is clearly specified in the contract;
(b)   the plaintiff has a special interest in having the work done which cannot be satisfied by an award of damages;
(c)   the builder is in possession of the land, so it is not practicable to employ another builder.

(b) Injunction

This equitable remedy restrains a person from continuing a wrong or alternatively can be used to order a party to do something to remedy a breach. Unlike specific performance it applies to contracts containing a personal services element. The usual rules as to equitable remedies apply and an injunction will not be granted if damages are an adequate remedy. It has been held to be appropriate to restrain a contractor from continuing work after a breach of contract has taken place, entitling the employer to determine the contract. Failure to obey an injunction is a contempt of court and may result in the imposition of a fine or imprisonment.

2.15   Agency

An agent is a person who acts on behalf of another who is known as a principal. Such an agent may conduct the principal's affairs in many ways but the primary function is to create a contractual relationship between the principal and a third party. Where the agent contracts with such a party, he is doing so on behalf of the principal. The effect of this arrangement is to create an enforceable contract between principal and third party with the agent dropping out of the transaction. This relationship is a familiar characteristic of business life. Companies will often contract through their directors and managers, while partners will act on behalf of their firms (see Chapter 6, secction 6.1). The self-employed and employees can act in this capacity. Auctioneers, estate agents, architects and engineers are all examples of agents.

Creation

Express Authority

The agent may be expressly appointed by word of mouth or in writing. Familiar appointments include estate agents to find prospective purchasers for residential and commercial properties, an engineer appointed to administer a contract on behalf of an employer, site agents acting as an employer's agent on site, and a sales representative selling goods on behalf of a company. No particular form of appointment is required unless the agent is empowered to execute deeds, in which case the authority must be given by power of attorney.

Implied Authority

Where, by their conduct, the parties have acted in such a manner so as to infer the relationship of principal and agent, it will be deemed to exist. This may occur where one party receives a commission, accepts goods, or pays for items ordered by another person. In *Ryan* v *Pilkington [1959] 1 WLR 402* an estate agent was instructed by owners of property to find a purchaser. The estate agent accepted a deposit from a prospective purchaser 'as agent' of the owners. Although not expressly authorised to accept deposits, he was deemed to have acted as an agent. The owner was liable for the deposit when it was misappropriated by the estate agent.

Necessity

An agency of necessity arises in an emergency where a carrier of goods needs to take immediate action to protect them. If the carrier cannot obtain instructions from the person on behalf of whom the goods are being carried, the carrier may deal with the goods as is considered appropriate either by sale or by storage in order to preserve them. The agent must act in good faith and in the interests of the parties concerned. The implication of an agency of necessity will result in the carrier being able to claim payment in respect of his efforts to preserve the goods.

Ratification

If an agent has no authority to act on his principal's behalf in any particular set of circumstances, or he exceeds his authority, the principal is not bound. As an exception to this rule the principal has the option of confirming transactions which were made without his authority. The effect is to legitimise the agent's acts from the outset, and the principal can adopt the transaction so as to obtain the benefit and undertake the obligations agreed. If the principal does not ratify the transaction, the agent is personally liable. Certain conditions apply:

(a) the principal must have existed and the third party must have been informed by the agent that the agent was acting on behalf of the principal;
(b) the principal must have had capacity to contract when the agent acted;
(c) ratification must take place within a reasonable time;
(d) the contract must be capable of ratification.

Estoppel

If a 'principal' by conduct or acquiescence allows third parties to believe that somebody is acting as their authorised agent, the 'principal' will be estopped from denying the existence of the agency where the third party relies on such conduct or representation to their detriment. This is the case even though the 'principal' had no intention of creating the principal/agent relationship or the agent has no authority of any sort. Where a 'principal' becomes aware of the likelihood of this problem arising, appropriate third parties whom the agent has been dealing with should be informed that the 'principal' will not be bound by the agent's acts. Such an agency will only apply if the person dealing with the alleged agent has no notice of the lack of authority.

The Scope of an Agent's Authority

To a large extent, an agent's authority will depend on what has been agreed between the principal and agent. This is the agent's actual author- ity, which has been specifically granted or is implied by the nature of the job, task or particular business. In some cases an agent acquires status from the authority and powers which third parties assume an agent to possess. This is known as the ostensible or apparent authority of an agent. A principal will be liable in respect of those acts which are usually under- taken by an agent in respect of a particular job. An engineer, architect or site agent will bind the principal when carrying out the normal tasks associ- ated with these professions under a contract, even though the specific indi- viduals do not have express authority to act in a particular way. Any agent signing a cheque or a contract on behalf of a principal should make it abundantly clear that the transaction is being carried out on behalf of the principal and should qualify any signature as such. Failure to do so will make the agent personally liable on the cheque or contract. A person who is not an agent but holds themself out to be so is personally liable on a contract. A problem which can arise is that of the undisclosed principal. It may be that a agent, when dealing with a third party, fails to disclose the nature of his position and the third party takes the agent to be a principal. In such circumstances the third party may elect to sue the agent or the principal on the contract so long as the principal can be identified. Where the agent discloses his position but refuses to identify the principal, the agent will not be liable on the contract. Another factor is the extent of the agent's implied authority to the third party so far as his power to contract is concerned. An auctioneer has implied authority to make statements rele- vant to individual properties. An estate agent has no implied authority to give a warranty that premises can be used for a specific purpose. In *Hill* v *Harris [1965] 2 WLR 133*, such an agent was deemed to have no authority to warrant that premises used for boot and shoe making could be occupied for a confectionery and tobacco business.

The Agency Relationship

The existence of the relationship of principal and agent imposes certain duties and obligations upon both parties. The concept is primarily based on contract. A principal may sue on a contract made by an agent, making agency a major exception to the privity rule. In addition to the contractual aspects there is also a fiduciary element of trust underlying the obligations between the parties.

Duties of an Agent

(1) Skill and Care

An agent must exercise skill and care in the performance of his duties. If engaged in a profession, the standard expected is that of a reasonably experienced member of that profession. Where an agent hold himself out as having special skills he must be able to apply them. If an agent is employed to sell, there is a duty to obtain the best price possible. In *Keppel* v *Webster [1927] 1 KB 527* estate agents were liable when they omitted to inform their client that they had received a higher offer for his property.

(2) Accounts

An agent must account to his principal in respect of all transactions connected with the agency. Accounts should be rendered to the principal when requested. All sums received on the principal's behalf should be handed over, even if the agreement under which the money was received was illegal. The agent must not mix up the principal's property with his own.

(3) Delegation

An agent cannot further delegate duties to another except in the usual course of business by employing assistants and secretarial staff, unless it is standard practice in a particular type of agency to delegate duties. Some delegation may be required for the proper performance of work. It is not normal in the construction industry for delegation to be allowed unless there is express authority to that effect.

(4) Obedience

The agent is under a duty to obey the lawful instructions of the principal unless they are illegal. If not, the agent could well be in breach of contract.

(5) Good Faith

This is the very essence of the agency relationship. As an agent must disclose anything which might affect the principal's position under the contract, he must not act for both sides in a transaction. In *Fullwood* v *Hurley [1928] 1 KB 498* an agent acted for both sides in the purchase of a hotel without the knowledge of the respective parties. He was only entitled to commission from the vendor who instructed him. The agent must not take a secret profit from his position nor must he take bribes. Instead the agent is entitled to commission or other agreed remuneration. In *Mahesan* v *Malaysia Officers Housing Association [1970] 1 WLR 241*, both the amount of the bribe and the secret profit were recovered by the principal where the agent had accepted money allowing a third party to make a secret profit. The agent is accountable to his principal in respect of any benefit received from the unauthorised use of his position. If the obligation is broken, the principal may dismiss the agent without notice, recover the secret profit and withhold any commission payable. In the event of bribery, both the agent and the person paying the bribe may be guilty of a criminal offence.

Duties of the Principal

(1) Payment

Any agreed amount of commission may be claimed by the agent. Payment can only be effectively claimed if there is an express or implied provision to that effect. The amount depends upon the contract or the custom in a particular trade or business.

(2) Indemnity

The agent must be reimbursed for expenses properly incurred in carrying out his duties. Entitlement may be lost if the agent acts beyond the authority given to him or he performs his duties negligently.

(3) Lien

Any agent has a right to retain possession of goods where the principal has not paid his proper remuneration or reimbursed him.

Termination of Agency

The agency relationship may be determined by an act of the parties themselves or by operation of law. A professional person will cease, in the ordinary course of events, to act as an agent on completion of the contract which he was engaged upon. In construction projects, appointment as an agent may be limited to one or various stages of the work. If the contract is for a fixed term the relationship may terminate by expiration of time, although a principal may revoke an agency at any time for good reason but will be subject to a claim for damages by the agent if the revocation was not justified. Death or insanity of either of the parties will terminate the relationship. Bankruptcy of either party will also bring the agency to an end.

2.16   Forms of Contract in the Construction Industry

As mentioned at the beginning of this chapter, it is a widespread practice in contemporary commercial life to use standard forms of contract. Contracts involving the sale of land and buildings are notable examples while in a construction context there are a plethora of standard forms. In fact, in 1964, the Banwell Committee recommended the use of one single standard form of contract in the construction industry but the reality has been an upsurge in the varying types of forms used. Although not essential, where the contract is complex and expensive, it is more convenient and safer to use a standard form. In many cases a contracting party has little option other than to be a party to such an arrangement. Such a form does give the professional and industry parties to a contract a degree of certainty as to their likely obligations under the contract, while constant use in practice means that its users should be well versed in the form's application and how it distributes risk among those contracting. Moreover, it is open to the parties to agree among themselves to modify the forms where appropriate. Simply because a standard form of contract is used does not mean that the ordinary rules of contract law can be avoided.

(a) The Standard Form of Building Contract, JCT 80

In 1931 the Joint Contracts Tribunal (JCT) was set up, consisting of representatives from the construction industry and the professions involved in major building works. The best known form of contract issued by the JCT is the JCT 80 Standard Form of Building Contract, which is intended for use in connection with all types of building works. This form comes in six versions, catering for local authorities and private employers, with or without reference to quantities, and also for use with approximate quantities. The latest edition was published in 1980 with amendments made in 1987, 1992 and 1994. The 1980 form consists of three sections. These are the articles of agreement, the contract conditions and the appendix. There is also a provision dealing with VAT.

The articles are primarily concerned with definitions. Apart from setting out the names of the employer (the client) and the contractor (the builder) they deal with the contractor's obligations, the contract price and the identity of the architect. The appointment of an architect or 'contract administrator' is a fundamental feature of this traditional method of procurement. The architect is responsible for supervision of the works. It is normal practice to name the quantity surveyor engaged by the employer. Such a person has responsibility for the valuation of work. The contract conditions, together with the contract bills and drawings form the substance of the contract. The conditions are divided into three parts. The first is of a general nature while the second deals with nominated sub-contractors.

A common feature of the traditional method of executing building works is for the main contractor to appoint independent sub-contractors to carry out specialist tasks, designs or supply materials. The sub-contractor is liable to the main contractor in the event of any default. In contracts to build employers regularly nominate sub-contractors with whom the main contractor is obliged to contract. The third part of the conditions is concerned with fluctuations. As the name suggests, this aspect is concerned with any changes which have come about in the amounts paid for labour and in the price of materials since the contract was entered into. The conditions deal at length with matters such as the contractor's obligations and the architect's powers, particularly in respect of ordering variations, provisions for certification and payment, and the methods of dealing with any disputes.

(b) ICE Conditions of Contract

The 6th edition of the Institution of Civil Engineers' Contract is the current established contract for use in connection with major civil engineering construction works. The form dates from 1945 and unlike JCT 80 the same form is used by private and public employers. Under the ICE contract the engineer has extensive powers of supervision and control. The engineer is not, as such, a party to the contract. The contract is made between the promoter/employer and the contractor. The engineer acts as an agent of the employer and in accordance with normal agency rules must act in the best interests of the employer. The engineer will have a contract with the employer based on the appropriate conditions of engagement. In contrast to JCT 80 the contractor is not paid on the basis of a 'contract sum'. Instead the contractor is paid on a 'measure and value' basis calculated on the basis of contract rates for the actual work carried out. This is sometimes known as 'admeasurement' or a 'remeasurement' contract. The basis of the contract will be found in the tender which has been accepted. The conditions envisage that the contract will be accompanied by drawings, together with a specification describing the proposed works and appropriate bills of quantities, measuring and costing the works in question. The main provisions of the contract cover the engineer's control of the works, the obligations of the contractor, the powers of the promoter and the engineer, certification and payment, and mechanisms for dispute resolution. Where a contract for civil engineering works is of less that 6 months' duration and the contract price is less than £100,000, the ICE Minor Works Contract based on ICE conditions may be an appropriate option.

(c) JCT Small Works Contracts

Just as there is an ICE based contract for more minor works, the JCT publishes a contract for use in connection with minor and intermediate works. Although based on the main JCT form, the small works document is somewhat basic and is not appropriate in respect of contracts involving more than £50,000 to £60,000. The Intermediate form is becoming increasingly common and is reasonably flexible in operation. It can be used in both the public and private sectors and allows sub-contract work to be placed with a 'named person', which has approximately the same effect as the nomination of a sub-contractor in the main form.

Other Forms of Main Contract

(a) FIDIC International Conditions

Since 1956, civil engineering contracts containing an international element have been able to take advantage of this form which is based on ICE conditions. The national law governing the contract must be stated in part 2. The engineer is appointed to act as representative and agent for the client. The contract contains the normal provisions to be found in standard forms relating to building works and provides for settlement of disputes by arbitration under the International Chamber of Commerce rules (ICC).

(b) GC/Works/1

These are encountered on government based and what were PSA (Property Services Agency) projects. A major characteristic of this form is the extensive powers of the employer, who is referred to as 'the authority'. The form provides for the appointment of a project manager who has similar powers to those of the engineer under the ICE conditions. There is provision for arbitration but, as an alternative, disputes arising during the course of the works may be referred to the adjudication of a person appointed to that task.

Sub-contracts

Sub-contracting is a major feature of the UK construction industry, with a considerable proportion of the work undertaken being carried out by specialists responsible for certain aspects of the contract. The practice of the employer making individual agreements with sub-contractors is not common in England and Wales and the standard procedure is for the work to be originally let out 'en bloc' to the main contractor who then sub-lets aspects of it but is responsible for the overall work completed. Standard forms are available to cover the situation whether the sub-contractor is 'domestic', in which case the employer plays no part in selection, or is 'nominated', where the employer reserves the right to choose the sub-contractor. Where there has been a nomination, JCT Form NSC/4 may be used. Domestic sub-contractors are now covered by a procedure laid down in clause 19 JCT 80.

The NSC/4 form is drafted on a similar basis to the main contract. It is available for sub-contractors who have tendered on the appropriate NSC/1 document and executed NSC/2 which creates contractual obligations between employer and sub-contractor. NSC/3 specifies the sub-contractor nominated for the particular works under JCT 80. After setting out the articles, the relevant clauses deal with documentation, state the sub-contract sum and then deal with the sub-contractor's position under the contract. Determination of employment under the sub-contract and the termination of the main contractor's employment under the main contract are also dealt with. As in the main contract, there is a choice of fluctuation provisions.

Management Contracts

The essence of a management contract is that the main contractor does not actually undertake any of the building work involved. Instead, the actual physical work is carried out by 'works contractors' (sub-contractors) and the main contractor manages the operations. The advantage to the management contractor is that contractual liability is diminished because, as a general course, the management contractor is only liable if the sub-contractor can also be held responsible. There are indirect economies of scale in that the main contractor can reduce operating costs by not having to keep a large workforce, with appropriate reductions in equipment and plant. The Joint Contracts Tribunal has issued the JCT Standard Form of Management Contract 1987 (MC 871). Management contracts should not be confused with construction management, which is a new concept where there is no main contractor in the scenario at all and where individual contracts are made directly between the developer and the works contractors.

Design and Build Contracts

In a traditional construction contract the task of design is essentially a matter for the design team comprising the architect/engineer as appropriate. It is becoming increasingly common to find contracts where the contractor has partial or complete responsibility for design matters. A number of design and build contracts in standard form are now available. Probably the best known of these 'package deal' or 'turnkey' contracts is the 'Building Contract with Contractor's Design' 1981. The procedure for determining the design in such contracts is made up of the 'Employer's Requirements' and the 'Contractor's Proposals' which will become incorporated into the contract. An employer who enters a design and build project on the basis of lower costs might find difficulties if he wishes to vary it at a later stage because these types of package deals tend to allow the contractor to object to a variation which will affect his responsibility for design. It is common practice for design and build contracts to be sub-contracted.

NHBC Schemes

The National Housebuilding Council (NHBC) has been in existence since 1936 and now operates under the trademark of 'Buildmark'. This body was established by leading builders on a voluntary basis to encourage consistant high standards in house building. The system operates by the maintenance of a register of builders and developers whose work adheres to the standards prescribed by the Council. Those builders on the register enter into a standard form agreement with the first purchaser and with the NHBC. After stating that he is a party to the scheme, the builder warrants that the property has been built properly and that it complies with the Council's requirements. By registration on the scheme, the builder authorises the building council to issue the appropriate Buildmark documents. An insurance system operates to cover any defects arising in dwellings covered by the scheme. To apply, the defects must become apparent and be notified to the council within the first 10 years of construction. It is only in the 'initial guarantee period' of 2 years that full cover is given to the purchaser, dependent on notice being given by the purchaser. During the remaining 8 year 'structural guarantee period', the NHBC agrees to cover defects but is limited to major damage covered by structural defects or settlement/subsidence problems. Subsequent purchasers may also obtain the benefit of the scheme. The Council employs officers to inspect work completed and in the event of non-compliance a builder may be removed from the register. The contract specifies the obligations of the Council to satisfy any judgement obtained by the purchaser against the builder relating to defects in the construction of a dwelling. In practice, disputes are dealt with by conciliation and arbitration. The NHBC is one of the few regular users of the 'approved inspector' system in the building regulation process (see Chapter 5, section 5.6).

New Engineering and Construction Contract

Primarily because of its adjudication provisions and its praise in the Latham Report, the NECC has received a considerable amount of attention in the construction press, but as yet its benefits have not been apparent. It dates from 1991 and can be used in conjunction with various types of contract either in traditional form or in one of the more innovative contractual arrangements. It has the flexibility of using core clauses which can be adapted to various types of projects.

Because of its implications for the resolution of construction contract disputes, generally some reference should be made to the Housing Grants, Construction and Regeneration Act 1996.

Background

This Act is the result of a number of the recommendations made in the Latham Report and subsequent Department of the Environment Consultation papers. It is also consistent with the obvious desire of the Woolf Report to promote ADR as a means of resolving disputes. It received the Royal Assent in July 1996 but there was considerable delay in the Act becoming implemented.

The Act can be divided into three main areas:

(a) definitions and scope;
(b) adjudication;
(c) payment.

(a) *Definitions and scope*

The Act applies to 'Construction Contracts' which are defined as agreements with any person for the carrying out of construction operations. It extends to sub-contracts and management contracts. It also covers agreements for the provision of architectural design or surveying work, and advice on building, engineering, interior work and exterior decoration or landscaping work in relation to construction operations. The contract must be in writing or evidenced in writing. The Act has application to contracts in England, Wales and Scotland.

Exceptions

The following are not covered by the Act:

(1) contracts with residential occupiers;
(2) contracts relating to drilling for or the extraction of oil or natural gas;
(3) contracts relating to the extraction of minerals and certain nuclear work;
(4) contracts relating to the manufacture or delivery of building or engineering components, materials or plant (if there is an installation of these items, that aspect will be covered);
(5) purely artistic work.

(b) *Adjudication*

Section 108 of the Act provides that a Construction Contract must contain certain provisions relating to adjudication otherwise the provisions of the

'Scheme' will apply. The 'Scheme' is the crucial aspect in this legislation. The Secretary of State has the responsibility of issuing the 'Scheme'. Much will depend on the extent of the Scheme so far as the effectiveness of the legislation is concerned, and the reason for the delay in implementing the Act is centred around the contents of the Scheme. The Scheme came into effect in May 1998. The right to adjudication arises in respect of any difference occurring between the parties to a construction contract.

Construction contracts must contain the following provisions:

(a) the right of any party to give notice of intention to submit a dispute to adjudication at any time;
(b) a timetable which provides for an adjudicator to be appointed and the dispute referred within 7 days of notice;
(c) the adjudicator shall reach a decision within 28 days of the matter being referred to him, this period to be extended by mutual consent of the parties;
(d) the 28-day period may be extended by another 14 days with the consent of the party who originally referred the matter;
(e) the adjudicator has a duty to act impartially;
(f) the adjudicator must take the initiative in ascertaining the facts and the law;
(g) the adjudicator's decision will be binding until the dispute is finally determined by arbitration or by a court of law;
(h) the adjudicator is not liable for acts or omissions in carrying out his functions unless he has acted in bad faith;
(i) the adjudicator's decision may be regarded by the parties as a final determination of the matter despite the interim nature of his decision.

(c) *Payment*
The payment sections of the Act (sections 109–112) operate in a similar way to the adjudication provisions. These sections provide for a system of stage payments. A construction contract must deal with payment in a specific way to prevent the provisions of the Act applying by default:

(a) If a construction contract is at least of 45 days' duration, any party to the contract is entitled to payments by instalments.
(b) The parties to the contract are free to agree the amounts of the payments and the stages when payable. If they do not, the provisions of the Scheme will apply.
(c) An adequate mechanism must be in place to determine what payments are due and the final date for payment must be specified.
(d) Every construction contract must contain provisions relating to the serving of notices by the payer and payee in respect of making payments and, where appropriate, notice of an intention to withhold payment.

Certain additional protection is given to the payee in the absence of an effective notice of intention to withhold payment.

(e) In the event of non-payment by the payer or there is no effective notice of withholding payment, the payee has the right to suspend performance of the contract. This may be effected by a notice to suspend the performance of the contract. This right ceases when the amount due is paid in full.

'Pay when Paid' Clauses

Provisions making any payment under a construction contract conditional upon the payer receiving payment from a third party are ineffective. The only exceptions arise in situations of insolvency.

3 The Law of Tort

3.1 The Nature of Tort

A tort is a civil wrong. The law of tort, like contract, is part of the civil law and has been developed from common law principles. Unlike the law of contract there is no complete body of rules which apply to all torts in the way that all contracts are governed by the same general principles. There are some similarities between contract and tort but also substantial differences. In civil jurisdictions, contract and tort tend to be grouped together as the Law of Obligations. A claim in tort is concerned with the adjustment of losses while the remedy sought is damages. The plaintiff is seeking compensation for loss to property, reputation, pocket, physical injury or some other interest protected by the law. This may be in the form of an act, omission or the giving of advice. There can be an overlap between tortious liability and other areas of law, while certain factual circumstances may result in a civil action in tort and also in criminal proceedings. Common examples include road traffic accidents and accidents at work. In such circumstances each set of proceedings is dealt with differently, one aiming to compensate the victim and the other to punish the wrongdoer. Liability in contract is dependent upon the existence of an agreement, while duties in tort are imposed automatically by the law. The same act may be a tort and a breach of contract. A person who commits a tort is known as a tortfeasor.

3.2 Liability in Tort

This has traditionally depended on fault. It amounts to the intentional or negligent causing of harm by one party to another. Torts vary in the mental elements required to incur liability on the defendant's behalf. Sometimes strict liability is imposed. This is where the defendant is liable for the consequences of his actions even though he neither desired them nor ought necessarily to have avoided them. Examples include the rule in

Rylands v *Fletcher [1868] LR 330* (see section 3.9), liability for dangerous animals and breaches of certain statutory duties. By and large the law of tort is not concerned with a person's motive. A malicious motive will not make an otherwise lawful act unlawful, and conversely a good motive cannot legitimise an otherwise wrongful act. The classic illustration of this principle is *Bradford Corporation* v *Pickles [1895] AC 587* (see section 3.5) where the defendant lawfully interrupted a supply of water to the corporation by sinking a shaft on his own land in order to influence the authority to buy land from him at his asking price. The court decided that the act was lawful and the defendant's motive was irrelevant. A similar position was reached in *Chapman* v *Honig [1963] AC 19* where a landlord maliciously served a valid notice to quit (see Chapter 4, section 4.27) on his tenants but was deemed to have committed no tort. In some circumstances a defendant's conduct may be actionable as a tort even though no damage or loss has been sustained by the plaintiff. These torts are said to be actionable *per se*.

3.3 Vicarious Liability

At times, a person is deemed to be legally responsible for torts committed by others. This liability arises because of the relationship between the parties and is known as vicarious liability. In practice, the only relationship which gives rise to this rule to any degree, in English law, is between employer and employee. This is the so-called master/servant relationship. The principle is that an employer is liable for any torts committed by employees in the course of their employment. A much more limited form of vicarious liability arises between principal and agent (see Chapter 2, section 2.15) and between partners in a firm, but these instances apart the law has been slow to develop the concept. Successive governments have intimated a desire to make parents vicariously liable for the criminal acts of their children but have shown little enthusiasm for implementing such policies in practice.

'Servants'

An employer will only incur liability for the acts of employees (servants) acting within the course of their employment. An employer is not liable for the torts of an independent contractor. Difficulties can arise in distinguishing between the two relationships and all the circumstances have to be considered to determine the category which the arrangement comes into. An important factor to be taken into account is the amount of control which the employer has over the employee, together with payment of wages and rights of dismissal and suspension.

'Course of Employment'

Once it has been determined that the employer/employee relationship exists, the courts must be satisfied that the employee was acting in the course of employment before the employer can be held liable in respect of his actions. This is a question of fact and it covers acts which have been authorised by the employer, and includes those which amount to an unauthorised manner of doing what the employer was employed to do. The question is whether the employer has prohibited the act itself, in which case the employee cannot be in the course of employment when performing it, or whether the employer has prohibited a particular method of carrying out the act, in which case the employee may be in the course of employment. In *Kooragang Investments Pty Ltd* v *Richardson & Wrench Ltd [1982] AC 462*, an Australian case, an employed valuer was deemed to have acted outside the course of his employment when carrying out valuations for a client whom his employers had black-listed. If the employee commits a tort outside the course of employment, the employee will be treated as being on 'a frolic of his own' and will be personally liable. In *Hilton* v *T Burton [Rhodes] Ltd [1961] 1 All ER 74* employers were not liable where four workmen, from a demolition site, left work to go to a cafe seven miles from the site. Shortly before reaching the cafe they decided to turn back and one of their number was killed due to the negligence of the driver.

'Joint Liability'

The vicarious liability of an employer in no way displaces the employee's own legal responsibility for the tort which has been committed. Both employer and employee are liable as joint tortfeasors. If the employer satisfies the judgement, he may be able to claim a contribution from the employee under the Civil Liability (Contribution) Act 1976.

'Independent Contractors'

An employer is not responsible, on a vicarious basis, for acts committed by an independent contractor which cause losses to an injured party in the law of tort. Nevertheless, there are a number of situations where an employer may be liable for the acts of an independent contractor.

(a) The Employer's Personal Negligence in Choosing, Selecting or Instructing the Independent Contractor

In *Kealey* v *Heard [1983] 1 WLR 573* the owner of a number of houses, who was having them converted into flats, was held liable where a plasterer was injured because of faulty scaffolding erected by another (unknown) independent contractor. The court considered that the employer should have supervised the works as he had overall control of the building works on the property. He had not discharged his duty by delegating the works to an independent contractor.

(b) Strict Liability

The law imposes strict liability on the employer in respect of the independent contractor's acts. Relevant examples include liability under the rule in *Rylands* v *Fletcher* (see section 3.9) and in respect of animals. See also *Cambridge Water Co* v *Eastern Counties Leather plc [1994] 2 AC 264.*

(c) 'Non-Delegable' Duties

There are a number of instances (mainly statutory) where there is an obligation upon a person to act in a particular way. In such circumstances the obligations cannot be delegated to another. Examples include operations on the highway (*Gray* v *Pullen [1864] 5 B & S 570*) and where, by its nature, a contractor's work involves a special danger to others.

3.4 Negligence

Negligence has become the most important independent tort. It covers wide areas of activity, resulting in more litigation than all the other aspects of the law of tort put together. As an independent tort it is of comparatively recent origin and it is concerned with conduct. Although the lay person tends to equate negligence with 'lack of attention' or 'carelessness', liability in negligence is dependent upon the plaintiff being able to prove that:

(a) the defendant owed the plaintiff a duty of care;
(b) the duty was broken by the defendant;
(c) the plaintiff suffered damage as a consequence of the breach.

(a) Duty of Care

This is a matter of law. Before 1932 there were situations where the courts recognised the existence of a legal duty of care and a plaintiff could recover damages in respect of a negligent act. Nevertheless, there was no firm principles relating to the duty of care. In *Donoghue* v *Stevenson [1932] AC 562* Lord Atkin, who delivered the leading judgement in the House of Lords, pronounced a general test and stated that a person owes a duty of care to his neighbour. He then defined a neighbour as a person who is 'so closely and directly affected by my acts that I ought reasonably to have him/her in contemplation as being so affected when I am directing my mind to the acts or omissions which are called in question'. In this case, a man bought a bottle of ginger beer for his girl friend. After drinking some of the ginger beer she discovered that the bottle contained a decomposed snail and became ill as a consequence. The design and materials from which the bottle was made prevented detection of the snail's presence until most of the liquid had been consumed. No claim in contract could be brought by the girl as she had not bought the drink. In the tort of negligence a claim succeeded against the manufacturer. A test of likely harm based on foreseeability is used to satisfy the existence of a duty of care, and in such cases the injured party must suffer personal injury or there must be damage to the plaintiff's property apart from the product itself.

A series of cases in the 1970s and early 1980s extended considerably the 'neighbour' test. In *Dutton* v *Bognor Regis UDC [1972] 1 All ER 462* a claim was brought against a local authority and a builder in respect of a house which had been built with inadequate foundations. The Court of Appeal decided that the local authority, through their building inspectors, owed a duty of care to the plaintiff and were liable in respect of the negligent inspection. The claim against the builder was settled before the trial but the court decided that where the seller of a house was also the builder, there could be liability in negligence for building the property in a defective manner. Moreover, a claim was not limited to physical injury but also covered damage in respect of the property itself. In *Anns* v *Merton LBC [1977] 2 All ER 492* (now overruled) there was an acceptance of the principles laid down in *Dutton*. In *Junior Books* v *Veitchi Ltd [1982] 3 WLR 477* flooring sub-contractors laid down a floor at the plaintiff's factory. The floor was laid negligently and required replacing. The plaintiff successfully argued that the defendants owed them a duty of care which had been breached. In addition to the replacement of the floor, damages were successfully claimed in respect of having to move machinery from the factory, the cost of new office furniture and loss of profits during the period while the floor was being relaid.

After *Junior Books*, the courts began to take a considerably more cautious approach to the question of tortious liability which has resulted in plaintiffs having considerable difficulty in sustaining successful claims in negligence. The core of these decisions has been to refuse to permit recovery for purely economic losses as a consequence of negligent acts. The trend began in a series of cases heard in 1985 (*Peabody Donation Fund [Governors]* v *Sir Lindsay Parkinson [1985] AC 210*) and reached refinement in *D & F Estates Ltd* v *Church Commissioners for England [1988] 2 All ER 992* and *Murphy* v *Brentwood DC [1991] AC 398*. *D & F* concerned defective plastering work in a block of flats which had been carried out by a sub-contractor for a main contractor. Some fifteen years after the work had been carried out the plaintiff company, who occupied one of the flats, sued the main contractor for the cost of remedial work. The plaster was considered to be the item which had been damaged but as it had not caused damage to persons or other property the claim failed. In *'Murphy'* the plaintiff bought a new semi-detached house from a development company. The house was built on a concrete raft foundation on an infilled site. The plans received building regulations approval but 11 years after construction the plaintiff discovered cracks in the property and realised that there were defects in the foundations. In 1986 the plaintiff sold the house on, subject to the defects. The sum paid was £30,000 less than its market value. A claim against the local authority in respect of negligent perform-ance of their building control responsibilities failed on the basis that the damage suffered was purely economic in nature. It was emphasised in the decision that a defect which does not render a building an immediate danger to the health or safety of its occupants is purely economic in nature and not foreseeable.

(b) Breach of the Duty of Care

Breach of the duty of care depends upon standards of 'reasonableness'. The existence of such a breach is a matter which is applied by an objective test. Many factors have to be taken into account. The courts evaluate the concept in terms of risk. Likelihood of harm is important. In *Bolton* v *Stone [1949] 1 All ER 237* the plaintiff was hit by a cricket ball. As it was improbable that the ball would be hit out of the ground, or cause injury if it did, the defendant was not liable. The seriousness of the injury risked is another factor. In *Paris* v *Stepney BC [1951] AC 367* the plaintiff, who had only one good eye, was blinded in that eye during the course of his employment. He contended that his employers were negligent because they had not provided him with goggles. His argument was upheld. The House of Lords emphasised that a higher degree of care is always required when dealing with persons suffering from a mental or physical disability, children (particularly young ones) and old people. In *Haley* v *London Electricity Board [1964] 3 WLR 479* the defend-ants were placed under a higher duty of care in circumstances where they knew of the existence of blind people in a particular locality and did not take adequate steps when fencing off excavation works on the highway. The utility of the defendant's act is also of importance. The risk must be balanced against the end to be achieved. In the situation where a person engages in an activity for which some measure of professional experience or skill is required, the degree of competence required is that of the reasonably compe-tent person exercising that skill or profession. This so called *'Bolam'* test has been given judicial approval in many cases (*Bolam* v *Friern Hospital Management Committee [1957] 1 WLR 582*). Inexperience in a particular pro-fession or type of work is no excuse. Although a professional person must be skilful and careful, it is not necessary that he or she be correct. An inaccurate valuation of premises or of the cost of executing building works is not necessarily negligence. The courts tend to rely heavily in these cases on expert evidence from practitioners and recognised codes of practice.

(c) Damage

Loss is a prerequisite to a successful claim in negligence. The tort is not actionable *per se* and therefore damage must be proved. For all practical purposes a plaintiff cannot claim successfully for economic losses caused as a result of a negligent act committed by the defendant. If the negligent act causes death or personal injury to the plaintiff a claim may be sustained. Any losses which might be potentially recoverable are subject to the rules relating to causation and remoteness of damage. The damage claimed for must relate back to the defendant's breach of duty, while there must be no intervening event which breaks the chain of causation. As in the case of claims based on contract, the damage must not be too remote (*Wagon Mound No 1 [1961] AC 388*).

The Burden of Proof

In civil cases, the burden rests upon the plaintiff to show that on the balance of probabilities the defendant was liable. In negligence cases, the burden of proving breach of duty of care and consequent damage falls upon the plaintiff. At times it is difficult to prove negligence because of an inability to show how the alleged events actually happened. To a considerable extent, the problem is overcome by the doctrine of *res ipsa loquitur* ('the facts speak for themselves'). This principle applies where the facts are so unusual that the defendant must have been negligent or the act would never have taken place. The circumstances are such that they raise the inference of the defendant's negligence so that a *prima faciae* case exists. Negligence is assumed simply because the event has taken place.

The leading case is *Scott v London and St Katherine's Docks Co [1865] 3 H & C 596* where a successful claim was brought by a customs officer who was injured when bags of sugar fell on him from the upper floor of a warehouse. Where the doctrine is raised, the burden of proof is reversed and the onus of disproving negligence is put upon the defendant. If the defendant offers a reasonable explanation, it is up to the plaintiff to prove the case in the normal way. Examples of the principle include a barrel falling from a building (*Byrne v Boadle [1865] 2 H & C 722*) and where a household gas system disintegrated (*Pearson v NW Gas Board [1968] 2 All ER 669*).

Negligent Advice

A significant development took place in 1964 with the decision in *Hedley Byrne & Co Ltd v Heller & Partners [1964] AC 465*. The plaintiff advertising agents acted on behalf of a client known as Easipower Ltd. In order to check the financial position of their client, who owed them money, the plaintiffs asked their bankers to find out from the defendants, who were Easipower's bankers, whether or not their client was financially sound. The defendants replied that the company was 'good for ordinary business arrangements'. Shortly after this correspondence, Easipower went into liquidation owing the plaintiffs a considerable sum of money. Although the defendants escaped liability by inserting a valid disclaimer of liability with their advice, '*Hedley Byrne*' is important because the House of Lords recognised that a duty of care would arise in certain situations where a person gives negligent advice which produces financial loss.

This decision, and the cases based on it, survives the decision in *Murphy* v *Brentwood DC* (see above). This means that economic losses can be recovered arising out of negligent mis-statements, in the law of tort, irrespective of whether or not there is a contract between the parties. In '*Hedley Byrne*' it was emphasised that a 'special relationship' needs to exist between the parties before any claim will be actionable. This will arise where the defendant knows or ought reasonably to foresee that the plaintiff will rely on his skill and judgement. The relationship between the parties must be one of close proximity, while the advice will be formally given in return for payment. Those who give professional advice may well fall into the scope of this principle. In *Yianni* v *Edwin Evans [1981] 3 WLR 143* a surveyor instructed by a building society to value a house for mortgage purposes was deemed to owe a duty to the house purchaser. Although this decision is a first-instance one it was approved by the House of Lords in *Smith* v *Eric Bush [1990] 1 AC 831* on similar facts.

Occupiers' Liability

This is negligence liability as far as dangerous premises are concerned and it is primarily governed by statute. The principal Act is the Occupiers Liability Act 1957 which provides that an occupier of premises or the landlord, if responsible for repair, owes a common duty of care to ensure that all lawful visitors will be reasonably safe when using the premises. 'Premises' includes any fixed or movable structure and will include cranes, ladders and scaffolding as well as vehicles, ships and aircraft. Liability rests with the occupier and not beyond. An occupier is one who has control over the premises and it is a question of fact in each case as to who has occupation. Premises may have more than one occupier. Where large scale building works are in progress, the site owner and the main contractor may be both in occupation (*AMF International Ltd* v *Magnet Bowling Ltd [1968] 1 WLR 1028*). Where a lease is entered into, liability rests in the majority of cases with the tenant. An empty building may be occupied. In *Harris* v *Birkenhead Corporation [1976] 1 All ER 341* a local authority failed to block up a derelict house which was subject to a compulsory purchase order and were held liable as occupiers. Again, in *Morrison Holdings Ltd* v *Manders Property Ltd [1976] 2 All ER 302* a tenant who had given up his tenancy but still retained the keys was held to be in occupation.

Lawful Visitors

Occupiers owe a common duty of care to lawful visitors. A lawful visitor is a person who expressly or by implication has been given the right to enter premises. This will include persons who have the right to enter premises under a contract after paying for entrance, those who have a licence to enter the premises and those who have the right to enter premises in the exercise of an authority imposed by the law, such as officials of the electricity and gas companies and VAT and Customs officials. While the visitor is on the premises the occupier must take care to see that the visitor will be reasonably safe in using the premises for the purpose for which he is invited or permitted to be there. An occupier may revoke the right of a lawful visitor to remain on the premises at any time. Any person entering premises 'in the exercise of their calling' must not exceed the purpose for which they are present or they will become trespassers. The degree of care owed depends upon the status of the visitor. A higher degree of care is owed to those under a disability. This is the case with children. Dangers to which children may be specially attracted or allured must be particularly guarded against, while hidden dangers which children may not understand should be made known. An occupier can expect very young children to be accompanied by an adult. Any limitation of liability by the occupier must be read subject to the Unfair Contract Terms Act 1977 in situations where there is 'business liability'. An attempt to exclude liability for death or personal injury will not be upheld, while in other cases the stipulation will not be upheld unless it is reasonable in the circumstances. If lawful visitors have little option other than to enter the premises, the occupier will find it difficult to exclude liability.

Independent Contractors

Where a person is injured because of the faulty work of an independent contractor, the occupier may be able to exclude liability if he can show that he took care in selecting the contractor and took reasonable steps to ensure that the work was carried out properly. He could be liable if the work could have been checked by the occupier with relative ease to ensure that it was satisfactory (*Kealey* v *Heard* – see above). In large scale construction projects, an occupier would be expected to have the contractor's work supervised by a surveyor/engineer or architect as appropriate (*AMF International Ltd* v *Magnet Bowling Ltd* – see above).

Trespassers

Trespassers are not governed by the 1957 Act. Historically, an occupier of premises owes no duty of care to trespassers and such people must take the consequences of their acts. The common law attitude was that an occupier must not intentionally harm a trespasser whom he knows to be present or create hidden dangers such as traps or manholes. Subject to that, an occupier would not be liable for a trespasser's injuries. In *Addie [R] & Sons* v *Dumbreck [1929] AC 358* the defendant colliery owner was held to owe no duty of care, as an occupier at common law, towards a child trespasser who was crushed by haulage gear at the mine. A significant development took place in 1972 when the House of Lords introduced the concept of a 'duty of common humanity' in the case of *British Railways Board* v *Herrington [1972] AC 877*. This case concerned a 6-year-old boy who was electrocuted on a railway line after climbing through a fence which had not been properly maintained. Children regularly played near the line and the local station master was aware that children had been seen on the track. Local inhabitants also crossed the line as a short-cut from one side of the railway embankment to the other. Although it was admitted that the boy was a trespasser, the House of Lords decided that the Board owed a duty to the child to act with 'common humanity', it had not done so and was consequently liable. The principle was subsequently applied in a number of cases (see *Pannett* v *McGuiness & Co [1972] 2 All ER 137*), but the legal position in such circumstances was not entirely clear. The issue was referred to the Law Commission (LW75), and as a result the liability of occupiers to trespassers is now governed by the Occupiers Liability Act 1984. The Act does not provide that an occupier automatically owes a duty of care to trespassers. It indicates the circumstances in which such a duty of care might be owed. It covers injury suffered by persons exercising private rights of way, but damage to property and injuries sustained by those using public rights of way are specifically excluded. An occupier is expected to take reasonable steps to ensure that the danger is avoided. As in the case of the 1957 Act an occupier can discharge the duty by putting up warning notices on the premises. Such notices will be subject to the same rules as those which apply in the case of the 1957 Act. Although much depends upon the individual circumstances of the case, the following will be important factors in determining whether or not a duty is owed to a trespasser:

(a) The nature of the trespass
Is the trespasser a rambler who has lost his way or a burglar?
(b) Where the trespass takes place
Construction sites or railway lines will require more supervision than an ordinary residence.
(c) The probability and extent of likely injury

The greater dangers involved in the activity, the greater the precautions that need to be taken.

(d) The defendants's knowledge and likelihood that trespassers are present on the property.

Specific Defences to Negligence

In addition to the general defences which may be raised in respect of a number of torts, there are also specific defences which have application in respect of individual torts. In negligence actions, apart from showing that one of the essential elements of the tort is missing, the defendant may allege the plaintiff's consent to run the risk of the damage caused as a bar to the action. Another specific defence which is frequently used is that of contributory negligence.

(a) Contributory Negligence

This is established where it is proved that an injured party failed to take reasonable care and thus contributed to his own injury. Before 1945 a sustained allegation of contributory negligence was a complete defence to the plaintiff's claim. Nowadays, the Law Reform (Contributory Negligence) Act 1945 regulates the position. The consequence of proving contributory negligence is to reduce the damages awarded to the plaintiff. In effect, the court makes an apportionment between the parties according to the degree of fault. A plaintiff's damages are reduced to the extent that the court considers him liable for the loss suffered. The defendant must show that the plaintiff failed to take reasonable care for his own safety and contributed to his own physical loss or damage to property. In *Wheeler v Copas [1981] 3 All ER 405*, a bricklayer's damages were reduced by 50 per cent when he was injured on a ladder, which had been lent to him, which broke under his weight.

(b) Consent ('Volenti Non Fit Injuria')

Voluntary assumption of risk is a complete bar to a plaintiff being able to claim successfully in the tort of negligence. It arises where the plaintiff knows of the risk involved, is aware that the defendant is being negligent, and suffers the type of injury which would be expected from the defendant's negligent act. Despite these circumstances, the plaintiff is still willing to continue co-operating with the defendant. The test is objective. The court approaches the question by asking whether a reasonable man in the circumstances who did what the plaintiff did and said what the plaintiff said would have done so because he consented to run the risk of injury himself. In *ICI v Shatwell [1965] AC 656* two shot-firers tested a firing circuit by applying a galvanometer to detonators. Both were injured when they failed to take cover. The men had been expressly told that this method of testing was unsafe. In a claim by one of the men based on breach of statutory duty, the employers were deemed not to be vicariously liable and were entitled to avoid liability on the basis of *Volenti*.

Limitation of Actions in Negligence Claims

As in the case of contractual claims, the Limitation Act 1980 governs claims in the law of tort. A claim in negligence is statute-barred unless brought within 6 years from the date on which the cause of action accrued. As an exception by section 11 of the 1980 Act a personal injury claim must, as a general rule, be brought within 3 years. One problem in this area of law is that of hidden or latent damage. This is damage which only manifests itself ·many years after the limitation period has expired. The modern law on limitation, in negligence cases, dates from *Cartledge* v *E Jopling and Sons Ltd [1963] AC 758*. This personal injury case established the principle that a cause of action in negligence accrued at the date when the injury or damage took place and not when it is discovered. This decision was not universally welcomed and as a consequence a Limitation Act was passed in 1963 to allow plaintiffs, in personal injury cases, additional time in which to bring their claims. It was not until the decision in *Sparham-Souter* v *Town and Country Developments [Essex] Ltd [1976] QB 858* that the courts began to deviate markedly from *Cartledge*. *Sparham-Souter* was concerned with defective foundations and involved claims against the builders of two houses together with the relevant local authority. The Court of Appeal decided that the cause of action accrued when the damage was discovered by the injured party, or it ought to have been if the plaintiff had acted with due diligence. These rules were developed by the House of Lords in *Anns* v *Merton LBC*. *Anns* was not a limitation case but the issue was taken up by the Law Lords. They considered that the cause of action accrued in such cases when the state of the building in question was such that there is present or imminent danger to the health or safety of persons occupying the building. This expression gave rise to problems of interpretation, while it was a matter of conjecture whether or not the rule appied solely to claims against local authorities or also covered claims against building contractors and members of the construction team (see *Percival* v *Walsall MBC [1986] 279 EG 218*).

In 1983 *Pirelli G C Works Ltd* v *Oscar Faber and Partners* came to the House of Lords. The case concerned a chimney made out of pre-cast concrete which developed cracks and had to be demolished in part and replaced. The chimney was built in 1969 and the plaintiff discovered the damage in 1977. The House of Lords considered that the plaintiff's cause of action accrued not later than 1970 while the writ was issued in 1978. The court decided that the cause of action accrues when damage occurs to the building, except in exceptional cases where the defect in a building is so great that the building is doomed from the start in which case the owner's cause of action will accrue immediately the building is constructed. *Pirelli* appeared to be in conflict with certain aspects of the *Anns* decision and as a consequence the Law Reform Committee published their report in 1984 titled 'Latent Damage'. The Latent Damage Act 1986 was the result. This Act is essentially a compromise between the positions taken in *Sparham-Souter* and *Pirelli*. The starting point is the primary limitation period which the Act states as being 6 years from the date when the cause of action accrued. This will be the date when the damage occurred. As an alternative, a plaintiff who cannot satisfy that provision has an alternative time period in which to bring the claim. The period is 3 years from the date when the damage was discovered or ought to have been discovered. This secondary limitation period is subject to an overriding time limit of 15 years, which provides that an action for damages for negligence cannot be brought more than 15 years from the date on which any act or omission alleged to constitute negligence occurred. This is known as the 'longstop' provision and it does not apply to personal injury claims. In *Murphy*, the *Pirelli* decision was treated as a *Hedley Byrne* case and was not overruled.

3.5   Breach of Statutory Duty

Where a defendant incurs liability in tort, it is not uncommon for there to be also a breach of an Act of Parliament or of Regulations made under a statute. The usual consequence of a breach of a statutory provision is a fine, while in tort a plaintiff will be looking for a sum of money by way of damages. One problem which arises is whether a breach of a statute can give rise to a civil action in tort as well as resulting in criminal liability. This is known as a breach of statutory duty. A number of hurdles must be cleared before a plaintiff can succeed in such an action.

(a) The first consideration is whether the statute confers a private right of action. The plaintiff must prove that the statute was intended by Parliament to confer a civil remedy for its breach and that the duty owed to the plaintiff was broken.

(b) The injury must be of a kind that the statute was intended to prevent. Moreover, the breach of duty must be the cause of the damage which must not be too remote. In *Ginty* v *Belmont Building Supplies Ltd [1959] 1 All ER 414* statutory regulations required those involved in the roofing business to use crawling boards when working. The defendants supplied the boards but the plaintiff, an experienced workman, failed to use them and fell through a roof. Although they were technically in breach of the statute, the defendants were acquitted because they had done everything that could be expected in the circumstances and the plaintiff's breach was the direct cause of the accident. Many, if not most, statutes fail to state whether or not damages are recoverable. The majority of actions commenced in this area of law are concerned with employer safety legislation.

3.6 Trespass

Although often associated with the criminal law trespass is a long established tort. It occurs where there is direct interference with the person, goods or land of another. Here we are concerned only with trespass to land where the trespasser interferes with the plaintiff's possession of land without justification. As trespass is actionable *per se*, there is no need for a plaintiff to prove damage as a consequence of the tort. The interference may be intentional at the outset or alternatively it may arise when a person's lawful right to remain on land has been revoked. The intrusion may come about in a number of ways. The slightest entry on to the land is suffcient to constitute the tort. Leaning a ladder against a wall on the plaintiff's land had been held to be a trespass (*Westripp* v *Baldock [1939] 1 All ER 279*). The trespasser must have meant to enter the land even if mistaken about some aspect relating to it such as ownership. The tort will arise by entering on to the land without express or implied consent. Also, the right of entry may be abused. A person who enters land for a specific purpose, even under statutory powers, will commit a trespass if the purpose for which they are there is exceeded. Hence, a person who uses the highway other than to pass or repass will become a trespasser (*Harrison* v *Duke of Rutland [1893] 1 KB 142*).

Rights in land are considered to extend upwards to infinity and downwards to the subsoil. An invasion of airspace is a trespass. Overhead cables, sign boards and advertisements have all been held to come into this category. In *Woollerton and Wilson Ltd* v *Richard Costain Ltd [1970] 1 WLR 411* (see also *Anchor Brewhouse Developments Ltd* v *Berkley House [Docklands Developments] Ltd [1987] 2 EG 625*), the swinging of the jib of a crane over other land was deemed to constitute a trespass. An unauthorised intrusion of an owner's airspace is a trespass but is restricted to such height as is necessary for the enjoyment of the land by the owner. Above that height, individual owners do not have specific proprietary rights, otherwise an infringement could be claimed on every occasion that a space probe came over a garden. Overflight by aircraft is governed by the Civil Aviation Act 1982 which prevents any claim in trespass or in nuisance against the operator provided that the appropriate delegated legislation has been complied with. The Rules of the Air Regulations 1991 are current in the United Kingdom. Aircraft are protected from actions so long as they fly at a reasonable height. The defence succeeded in *Bernstein* v *Skyviews and General Ltd [1978] QB 479*, where on the facts the defendants were not liable when they flew some hundreds of feet above the plaintiff's land with the object of taking photographs for commercial gain. If an overflight causes physical damage to property, for example by parts of the aircraft falling on to land, the owner is strictly liable for any damage or loss caused by the aircraft (*Southgate* v *Commonwealth of Australia [1987] 13 NSWLR 188*).

Remedies

(a) Damages

This will be the plaintiff's primary remedy. The tort is actionable *per se*, but if no loss occurs the courts will ignore the trespass if it is purely trivial. In such a case, damages would be nominal.

(b) Injunction

In an appropriate case, an injunction will be granted irrespective of whether damage has taken place. This could include construction operations, although in the *Richard Costain* case the operation of the injunction was suspended where the offending party offered a substantial sum as compensation for the trespass. Where approriate, damages can be awarded in lieu of an injunction.

(c) Recovery of Possession

A person dispossessed from his land may bring an action for recovery of the property. The plaintiff can claim compensation for depreciation of the premises and use of the land. This would include lost rents (Mesne Profits) and the costs of the action. In such circumstances an action for ejectment should be sought to obtain possession. Repossession on its own can be claimed under CCR Ord 26 (Green Book) or RSC Ord 113 (White Book), depending on whether the action is brought in the County Court or High Court.

(d) Self-help

The occupier may use reasonable force to eject a trespasser. The occupier must act carefully so as not to be in breach of the criminal law (*Protection from Eviction Act 1977* and *The Criminal Law Act 1977*).

Specific Defences to Trespass

(a) *'Volenti'*
     Consent of the occupier to be on the land, preferably in writing, would constitute a defence.

(b) As mentioned previously, certains officials have an automatic right to enter land.
(c) Public and private rights of way
The general public are entitled to exercise their rights over a highway, while those entitled to benefit from private rights of way (see Chapter 4, section 4.12) may gain access to them.
(d) Necessity
It may be that a person committed a trespass to prevent a greater wrong occurring, such as saving someone from injury or extinguishing a fire.

3.7   Nuisance

Nuisance comes in two main varieties: public and private. In tort, private nuisance is the major category encountered, while a public nuisance is a criminal offence which causes inconvenience or danger to the public at large. Environmental legislation allows local authorities to proceed quickly where a nuisance type situation is likely to affect the health of people in a particular locality (see Chapter 5, section 5.8).

3.8   Private Nuisance

A private nuisance is essentially an indirect interference with a person's use or enjoyment of land. It is a tort which protects a person from interference with the land which he occupies. The creator of the nuisance is responsible for it, while the effects of a nuisance may be felt by a number of successive occupiers. The nuisance may consist of the defendant allowing some item to enter the plaintiff's property, or probably more commonly by an activity taking place on the plaintiff's land affecting the defendant on his land. To succeed in a nuisance, action can be a struggle because a number of requirements have to be satisfied before being successful. The law attempts to strike a balance between allowing persons to use their land as they wish and the rights of persons not to be affected by their neighbours' actions. A number of requirements have been formulated to determine whether or not a particular set of circumstance is likely to result in a successful action.

(a) Indirect Interference

This may take many forms. Dirt, smells and noise are common situations that have been litigated. Sewerage, fumes and vibrations causing structural damage to houses have all constituted interference. Allowing a dilapidated wall to fall on to a neighbour's land has constituted a nuisance (*Brew Bros*

Ltd v *Snax Ltd [1970] All ER 587* – see also Chapter 4) and allowing water to flow on to a neighbour's land because of a blocked drain (*Sedleigh-Denfield* v *O'Callaghan [1940] AC 880*). In *Lemmon* v *Webb [1894] 3 Ch 1* the defendant committed a nuisance where tree roots spreading from trees he had planted intruded on to neighbouring land. In *Laws* v *Florinplace Ltd [1981] 1 All ER 659* the operation of a sex shop in a residential area was deemed to be a nuisance.

(b) Damage

Although it is easier for an occupier of land to succeed in private nuisance if actual damage can be shown, any substantial interference with the enjoyment of land will suffice. If the plaintiff is relying on personal discomfort it must be material. It is not an essential of the tort that the act complained of should cause ill health. Even if there is no physical damage, the court can award compensation for annoyance and discomfort. There need be no decrease in property values (*Kennaway* v *Thompson [1980] 3 All ER 329*). If the nuisance is a continuing one the award of an injunction together with damages is an appropriate remedy (*Kennaway* v *Thompson* – see above).

(c) Unreasonableness of the Act

The essence of this tort is that it is a form of action against unreasonable behaviour. If a person uses his land in a reasonable way so as to cause no undue inconvenience to others, it is unlikely that the tort will have been committed. The law attempts to balance the interests of the occupier against those of the defendant. The longer the interference lasts and the greater its extent, the more likely it is that it will be a nuisance. Where building works of a temporary nature, such as conversions or demolition, are carried out with a reasonable degree of care, so as not to cause undue inconvenience to neighbouring properties, no tort is committed. This principle was applied in *Andrae* v *Selfridge & Co Ltd [1936] Ch 1* where hotel proprietors complained of building works taking place nearby.

When judging the standard of reasonableness, the following are of importance:

(d) Locality

Different standards apply in different localities. Occupiers in urban and industrial areas may have to put up with more discomfort than those in more residential areas. Where the plaintiff has suffered material injury to his property, locality is irrelevant. In *St Helens' Smelting Co* v *Tipping [1865] 11 HL Cas 642* vapours from the defendant's copper smelting works killed off the plaintiff's trees and crops. The plaintiff's action succeeded because location was no defence where actual damage occurred.

(e) Utility of the Act

It is no defence that the act complained of is for the benefit of the public at large. The courts have to balance private interests against public benefit. In *Adams* v *Ursell [1913] 1 Ch 269* an injunction was granted terminating the activities of a fried fish shop in a poor area, while in *Shelfer* v *City of London Electric Lighting Co [1895] 1 Ch 287* vibrations which caused damage to the plaintiff's house resulted in an injunction being granted to stop the building of a power station.

(f) Sensitivity

The law of nuisance fails to assist those who require more protection than the community in general because of undue sensitivity. The rule applies both to the individual and also where property is put to an abnormally sensitive use. In *Robinson* v *Kilvert [1889] 41 Ch 88* the plaintiff used the ground floor of his landlord's premises for storing brown paper. Because of the heat from the boiler, in the cellar of the premises, the paper became badly damaged. The court decided that the heat was not unreasonable and the damage was caused because of the sensitive brown paper. Consequently, the defendant was not liable.

(g) Duration

The act complained of must have an element of continuity before it can be actionable. There must be in existence some state of affairs which repeatedly affects the plaintiff's land. A single nuisance, such as an activity, is not sufficent unless the act is evidence of a dangerous situation which results from a continuing state of affairs. In *Midwood* v *Mayor Manchester Corporation [1905] 2 KB 597* the plaintiff recovered in nuisance for damages caused by a single escape of gas. In *Spicer* v *Smee [1946] 1 All ER 489* defective wiring in the defendant's bungalow caused a fire which spread to the plaintiff's property and liability in nuisance was imposed. Similarly in *British Celanese* v *Hunt [1969] 2 All 1252* strips of metal foil stored over a period of time on the defendant's land blew on to the plaintiff's land and caused damage. The defendants were held liable.

(h) Malice

Improper motive is not an essential ingredient of private nuisance but its existence may be evidence of unreasonable behaviour. In *Christie* v *Davy*

[1893] 1 Ch 316 the plaintiff used her home for frequent musical evenings. The defendant, who lived in the adjoining semi-detached house, became so exasperated with the playing that he retaliated by knocking on the wall, beating trays and shrieking. The defendant's actions amounted to a nuisance as it was made for the sole purpose of annoyance. In *Hollywood Silver Fox Farm Ltd* v *Emmett [1936] 2 KB 468*, the defendant sent his son to discharge a shotgun near to the plaintiff's land to interfere with the breeding of the plaintiff's foxes because of a dispute over a sign. This was an actionable nuisance and an injunction was granted to restrain him in the future. In *Khorasandijan* v *Bush [1993] 137 Sol Jor 88* harassment caused by unwanted telephone calls was deemed to be actionable as a private nuisance.

The Parties to the Action

The right to sue in private nuisance depends upon having a proprietary interest in the land. Therefore, any plaintiff must be an occupier. This will cover an owner occupier and where appropriate any tenant in occupation. Where a permanent injury has been caused to the property, a landlord may sue despite the fact that he is not in possession. In *Masters* v *Brent LBC [1978] 1 QB 451* an occupier of a dwelling house successfully claimed damages for harm caused by the roots of a neighbouring lime tree. The damage had been caused before and after the plaintiff acquired the property. He was entitled to the full cost of repair.

The person primarily liable for the nuisance is the creator who in most cases is the occupier of the land. Liability may be incurred even though actual occupation of the land has ceased and entry on to the land to abate the nuisance is not possible. An occupier must abate a known nuisance. In *Sedleigh-Denfield* v *O'Callaghan [1940] AC 880* (see above) trespassers laid a pipe on land occupied by the defendant. Because the pipe became blocked, adjoining land was flooded. There was evidence that the defendant's employees had cleared out the ditch where the pipe was situated. The defendants were liable because they ought to have known of the nuisance and taken appropriate steps to abate it. Where premises are leased, the tenant will primarily be liable. If the landlord creates the nuisance and then leases the property or authorises the tenant to commit or continue a nuisance, liability may be incurred. The authorisation may be express or implied or by acquiesence. In *Harris* v *James [1876] 45 LJQB 545* the landlord as well as the tenant were liable, as the former had authorised the commission of the nuisance.

Remedies

A plaintiff in an action based upon private nuisance will be looking for damages together with an injunction. The latter is particularly important if there is a chance of the nuisance recurring and causing further damage to the plaintiff. As it is an equitable remedy, an injunction will not be granted if it would cause undue hardship to the defendant. If the nuisance is a continuing one, the better view is that only in unusual circumstances should damages be awarded in lieu of an injunction. A plaintiff may stop the nuisance by remedying the cause. This is the process of self-help or abatement. The plaintiff must ensure that no unnecessary damage is caused and that no damage is inflicted on an innocent third party such as a tenant. Unless there is an emergency, the offending occupier should be informed and given a reasonable time to remedy the situation. If abatement is chosen, an occupier cannot subsequently bring an action for damages.

Specific Defences to Private Nuisance

The following are of relevance to an action based on private nuisance:

(a) The harm is trivial – the so-called *'De Minimis'* rule. If the injury is minor or transient in nature, it will not be actionable. If combined with other activities the circumstances would create a nuisance the defendant will be liable.

(b) Statutory Authority – this may be particularly appropriate where works are carried out by local authorities.

(c) *'Volenti non fit injuria'* – consent of the plaitiff is a defence, but consent will not be implied simply because a party came to the premises knowing that a nuisance had been committed.

(d) Prescription – if the nuisance has been in existence for 20 years or more and falls within the scope of the Prescription Act 1832, the right to commit a private nuisance may be valid. In *Sturges* v *Bridgman [1879] Ch 852* a doctor complained of noise and vibrations from a confectioner who had a business next door to his consulting rooms. The interference had existed for at least 20 years but had not come into existence until the doctor built his consulting room in his garden. As the nuisance had not been created until the damage was caused, the Prescription Act 1832 provided no defence.

3.9   Public Nuisance

Public nuisance is a criminal offence. It is defined as an unlawful act or omission which materially affects the reasonable comfort and convenience of a class of Her Majesty's subjects. Examples include private nuisance situations where a substantial category of the public or a neighbourhood is affected and a diverse set of activities where public rights have been affected, including obstructing the highway, selling food unfit for human consumption, keeping a disorderly house and constructing a golf course so that one of the holes is adjacent to the highway and therefore affecting the use of the right of passage. Public nuisance is not limited to interference with land. In order to prevent a multiplicity of actions, a plaintiff may only sue for damages if he can show that he has suffered a particular form of damage over and above that suffered by the public at large. Such extra damage is known as special damage and frequently takes the form of personal injuries.

In *Dollman* v *Hillman Ltd [1941] 1 All ER 355* a person recovered damages where he suffered injury because of fat left on the pavement outside a butcher's shop, while in *Castle* v *St Augustine's Links [1922] 38 TLR 615* a taxi driver who lost his eye when a golf ball struck the screen of his cab succeeded in claiming special damages. Where the matter is one of public interest, a private person may ask the Attorney-General to bring an action for an injunction to have the offending activity terminated. Such an action is known as a relator action.

Statutory nuisances are dealt with in Chapter 5.

3.10   Rylands *v* Fletcher

In this case the defendant mill owner employed independent contractors to build a reservoir on his land. This was for the purpose of supplying water to run his mill. Unknown to the defendant and the contractors, an old mine shaft lay underneath the land. When the reservoir was filled, the water escaped through the shafts and flooded the plaintiff's mine. The plaintiff sued for damage incurred. Although it was established that the defendant had not been negligent and that the contractors were competent, the defendant was held to be liable. The reason for the decision is stated as follows:

> A person who for his own purposes brings on his land and collects and keeps there anything likely to do mischief if it escapes must keep it at his peril, and if he does not do so, is *prima facie* answerable for all the damage which is the natural consequence of its escape (*[1868] LR 1 Exch 265. Per Blackburn J at 279*).

Essentials

Control of the Land

(a) The defendant may be an occupier, the owner who is in control of things on the land (*A-G* v *Corke [1933] Ch 89*) or a licensee.

(b) Accumulation and non-natural user

The item must not be 'naturally present on the land' (*Rylands* v *Fletcher ibid at 280*). The defendant must have brought on to his land some item which is likely to do mischief if it escapes. Consequently, it did not apply to an outcrop of overhanging rock which naturally existed on the land as in *Pontardawe RDC* v *Moore-Gwyn [1929] 1 Ch 656* or to natural lakes or the land itself. The use of the land by the defendant must be essentially non-natural, which is a question of fact in each case. In the *Cambridge Water Case* (*Cambridge Water Co Ltd* v *Eastern Counties Leather plc [1994] 1 All ER 593*) the House of Lords considered the storage of chemicals on industrial premises to be non-natural use.

(c) Mischief

The item causing the mischief has included oil, gas, electricity and water. A falling flagpole (*Shiffman* v *Grand Priory of Hospital of St John etc. [1936] 1 All ER 557*), a fairground chair (*Hale* v *Jennings Bros [1938] 1 All ER 579*) and caravan dwellers (*A-G* v *Corke* – see above) have come within the definition.

(d) Escape

There must be an escape from the place controlled or occupied by the defendant to other land. In *Read* v *J Lyon Co Ltd [1947] AC 156* a factory inspector was injured by an explosive shell in a munitions factory. The claim failed as there was no escape.

(e) Foresight and damage

Rylands v *Fletcher* has always been treated as a strict liability tort. In *Cambridge Water Co Ltd* v *Eastern Counties Leather* (see above) the Law Lords stressed the need for foreseeability of circumstances before liability could accrue, so that although negligent conduct was not a prerequisite of the tort, the defendant must know or ought to know of the consequences. The defendant can only be liable for damage of a variety which could have been foreseen. There is some doubt as to whether the tort extends to personal injuries but it probably protects persons who do not necessarily have an interest in the land. Purely economic losses are not recoverable (*Cattle* v *Stockton Waterworks Co [1875] LR 10 QB 453*).

Specific Defences to Rylands v *Fletcher*

(a) '*Volenti non fit injuria*'.

(b) Act of a stranger

If the escape was caused by the act of a stranger over whom the defendant had no control there will be no liability. This is a person acting without the authority of the occupier and not a servant of the defendant. In practice it will be a trespasser. In *Rikards* v *Lothian [1913] AC 263* the plaintiff's premises were flooded when an unidentified person left taps on in premises of which the defendant was a tenant.

(c) Statutory Authority.

(d) Default by the plaintiff.

(e) Act of God
Whether such a defence exists is questionable. It has application to an extraordinary occurrence or circumstances which could not have been foreseen or guarded against. In *Nichols* v *Marsland [1876] 2 Ex D 1* it was successfully pleaded in a destructive storm, but in the Scottish case of *Greenock Corpn* v *Caledonian Rlw Co [1917] AC 556* on similar facts, the courts refused to accept the defence.

3.11   Product Liability

As considered earlier (section 3.4), the principles laid down in *Donoghue* v *Stevenson* have come to the assistance of an injured party who suffers loss caused by a defendant's negligence where there is no privity of contract between the parties. The difficulties encountered in proving negligence have always been considerable in connection with faulty products, and in the 1980s legislation was enacted making manufacturers liable on the basis of strict liability in respect of certain defective products. In the United Kingdom the relevant legislation is the Consumer Protection Act 1987 which was enacted in response to Directive 85/374/EEC. The Act and the Directive do not affect existing remedies. They leave untouched claims in contract against the retailer of the product, any action in negligence and, where appropriate, any claim for breach of statutory duty.

(a) On Whom is Strict Liability Imposed?

Liability is imposed on the 'Producer'. This will include the manufacturer but will also cover coal and minerals which are 'won or abstracted' and not manufactured. If a product does not come within any of these former categories but essential characteristics of the product are attributable to an industrial or other process, as in the case of crops, it will also cover the person who carries out that process. Liability is imposed on any person who brand-names a product or holds himself out as being a producer. Moreover, liability is imposed on persons importing a product into the European

Community from outside. A mere supplier of goods who does not come within the scope of the previous categories will not be liable, but where a supplier fails to identify the producer in circumstances where a consumer suffers damage the supplier must name the producer within a reasonable time or incur personal liability. Where building materials are incorporated into a building, that will amount to a 'supply' (see *section 46 Consumer Protection Act 1987*).

(b) The Product

In the Act, 'Products' are defined as 'any goods or electricity' (*section 2 Consumer Protection Act 1987*). This includes component parts and certain raw materials. Buildings themselves do not come within the scope of the definition but building materials are included.

(c) The Defect

Section 3 of the Act provides that there is a defect in a product if the safety of that product is not as persons generally are entitled to expect. All the circumstances are to be taken into account but the Act does indicate the sort of factors which need to be taken into account, such as packaging and any instructions relating to use.

(d) The Damage

The Act only provides for claims in relation to personal injury and damage to private property. Small claims are excluded (less than £250) while no claim can be made in respect of damage to the defective product itself. Damage to business property and economic losses resulting from defective products are excluded.

(e) Who can sue under the Act?

The victim or his/her dependants, where appropriate, may sue under the Act. A successful plaintiff must show that the damage was caused wholly or partly by the defect in the product. Any contributory negligence on the plaintiff's part will be taken into account. The basic limitation period is 3 years from the date on which the injury or damage was suffered. As in latent defect cases, in the tort of negligence (see section 3.4) there is an option based on discoverability in that a claim may be made within three years of discovering the damage. The 3-year period may only be overridden, by a judge, in personal injury claims. If the 'discoverability' option is chosen, the 'longstop' is 10 years and no claim may be brought more than 10 years after the defendant supplied the product to another.

Defences

A number of general defences are provided by section 4 of the Act. These centre around the fact that there is no actual defect and the defendant is not a supplier. Another defence is that the defect is attributable to compliance with any statute or European Community rules prescribing how the product is made. More problematical is the 'development risks' defence to strict liability claims by consumers. Those manufacturers who can claim that the state of scientific and technical knowledge at the time the product was put on the market was not such that they could be expected to have discovered the relevant defect are exempt from liability.

4 The Law of Property

4.1 The Meaning of Property

Any discussion relating to buildings or land must concern itself with the legal status of different types of property. In most legal systems a distinction is made between land/buildings and other types of property. In Civil law systems, this distinction is between Immoveable property (land and buildings upon it) and Moveable property (everything else). This indicates the permanent nature of land and its unique status in contrast to other forms of property.

4.2 Real Property

The primary distinction in English law is between real property, or realty, which comprises freehold land and personal property, or personalty, which comprises all other forms of property. The greatest right which a person may have in land is to hold an estate. Since 1926 the law only recognises the existence of two estates in land: the freehold and the leasehold. There are historical reasons for the leasehold estate being classified as an item of personal property. In the early development of land law a real action protected a freehold estate in land. If a freeholder had land taken, the courts would allow an action *in rem* (*actio realis*) to recover the land itself from the person who had dispossessed him. Rights to other forms of property, including the leasehold, were limited to claiming compensation in respect of the property taken. Until the Thirteenth Century the leaseholder could not recover possession and it was not until 1499 that the land could be recovered in such circumstances by action.

Personal property is sometimes known as chattels. Personalty is divided into chattels real and chattels personal. Because of their relationship, akin to rights in land, leaseholds are referred to as chattels real while chattels personal comprise every other type of property. The latter are divided into choses in possession and choses in action. The former are rights over tangible

117

moveables which may be touched and enjoyed simply by physical possession, while the latter are items which may be owned but not touched. These have no physical existence but can be protected by taking an action in the courts. Examples include debts, copyrights, shares and money due under an insurance policy. Chattels personal are also known as corporeal chattels to distinguish them from incorporeal chattels which have no material existence as in the case of choses in action.

4.3   The Historical Background of English Land Law

The development of English land law is said to begin with the Norman conquest of 1066. At this date all land became vested in King William I. The basic rule today is that all land in England and Wales is owned by the Crown. Soon after coming to power the King made grants of land to his most senior followers and also to those English barons who submitted to his control. These senior followers to whom land was granted became known as holders or 'Tenants' of the land. These Tenants in Chief were themselves able to grant rights to others in respect of the whole or part of land they had received. Likewise, the recipients of land from the tenants in chief were able to make sub-grants to others. This system of granting rights over land, characterised by service to a sovereign or chief, was based on the feudal system and known as the process of subinfeudation.

(A) Tenure

In order to hold land, a tenant had to render services to his superior in the hierarchy. The terms upon which the land was held were of various kinds and the expression tenure indicated the conditions on which the land was held. The expression tenant is derived from tenure, meaning in general any holder of land. Nowadays tenant has a more specific meaning (see section 4.22).

There developed in this context two particular types of tenure:

(a) Free Tenure;
(b) Unfree Tenure.

(a) Free Tenures

These were for specified services. Once performed, the tenant was free to use the land as he desired. Examples included the following:

Knight Service
This required the tenant to supply horsemen to his lord for 40 days in each year.

Sergeanty
This was also a military tenure but the tenant had to perform some additional personal service to the King or a lord.

Socage
These were mainly agricultural services such as the provision of crops or livestock to a lord. Sometimes a small payment would be made instead.

Spiritual Tenure
Sometimes called Frankalmoign, this consisted of saying masses for the superior lord or the giving of alms.

(b) Unfree Tenures

These consisted of rendering services of a servile nature. Medieval serfs known as villeins held their land on this basis and because of the nature of the tenure they were not entitled to leave the land. The varieties of unfree tenure varied from manor to manor. Because a record was kept by the manorial court, these tenures became known as copyhold.

(B) Estates

This expression applies to the length of time for which a tenant was entitled to hold land. Nowadays two estates are recognised by the law:

(1) *Freehold estates*
    Where the duration of the estate is of indefinite length.
(2) *Leasehold estates*
    Where the duration of the estate is governed by a fixed period of time.

4.4   The Importance of Equity in English Land Law

Some further reference needs to be made to the contribution of the equitable jurisdiction of the English legal system to land law in England and Wales. As mentioned in Chapter 1, equity developed because of the deficiencies of the common law. These included the formalised writ system, procedural complexities and inadequate remedies. As a consequence of this, a set of separate and rival courts grew up alongside the common law courts, granting different remedies such as injunctions and specific performance. Equity was more flexible and recognised the existence of certain rights which the common law would not. The classic example of this was the trust, whereby the common law treated the trustee as being owner of the trust property, while equity took the view that the trust property is vested in the beneficiary. In the event of a conflict the equitable view prevails (*Supreme Court Act 1981 section 49*).

4.5 The 1925 Property Legislation

By the end of the Nineteenth Century, it had become apparent that English land law still had many traces of the feudal system in its operation and was not appropriate to the needs of an expanding industrial society. Many ancient doctrines still survived, especially relating to tenure, while different rules were in existence relating to real and personal property. The greatest problems concerned the transfer of land, which was complicated and cumbersome. Because of these difficulties a series of Acts were passed in 1925 bringing about important changes in the law. The underlying purpose was to simplify land law and thus make it cheaper and easier to transfer land and to abolish any remnants of the antiquated systems of tenure still existing. The main Acts enacted were as follows:

(1) Law of Property Act 1925;
(2) Land Registration Act 1925;
(3) Land Charges Act 1925;
(4) Administration of Estates Act 1925;
(5) Settled Land Act 1925.

4.6 Estates and Interests in Land

Two estates became established as the most important rights which can be enjoyed over land, namely the freehold and the leasehold. Other rights enjoyed by persons over land are known as interests. A legal interest is a right over land which before the Judicature Acts (1873–75) was only recognised by the Common Law Courts, while an equitable interest was one which before the Judicature Acts was recognised by the Courts of Equity only. If the common law refuses to recognise a particular set of circumstances as being legally valid equity, in certain circumstances, will perfect it and acknowledge its validity.

Estates in Land

The Law of Property Act 1925 is the most important of the Acts passed in 1925 and even now forms the basis of land law in England and Wales. Section 1 of the Act states that the only estates which are capable of existing or of being conveyed or created at law are:

(1) an estate in Fee Simple in Possession (freehold);
(2) a Term of Years Absolute (leasehold).

The above are the technical terms to describe the freehold and the leasehold. Before the 1925 legislation it was possible to have a number of other different types of estate but that is no longer the case. As far as the Fee Simple Absolute in Possession is concerned:

Fee – this means that the estate can be inherited
Simple – essentially the freeholder can pass the estate to anyone
Absolute – signifies that the grant will continue for ever
in Possession – denotes that the person who has the benefit of the estate is entitled to immediate possession of the land or, if the land has been let, is entitled to rent from the land

As far as the Term of Years Absolute is concerned, the position is simpler as there has only ever been one category of leasehold estate:

Term of Years – the estate is held for a minimum period of certain duration
Absolute – the estate is enjoyed absolutely even though it may be determined in various ways

Interests in Land

A person may have a right over land which does not amount to an estate but which must be recognised. Such an interest in land may be of a legal or an equitable nature. Section 1 of the Law of Property Act 1925 says that only five interests are capable of being recognised as legal interests. Of these five interests, only two (an easement or similar right over land and a charge by way of legal mortgage) are now of any practical importance.

4.7   Reversions and Remainders

It may be that a person is entitled to an interest or estate in land at a future date. These future rights in land, sometimes described as reversionary interests, are classed as reversions or remainders. A reversion arises where A has an estate in fee simple and grants to B an estate or interest of shorter duration than his own, such as a leasehold. A is said to have the fee simple in reversion as the land will revert to him when B's rights terminate. In such a case, A is said to hold the reversion to the lease.

Alternatively, if A grants his complete rights in the land by means of two successive transactions, such as to B for life and then to C in fee simple, the right to possession of the land is said to 'remain' away from A. Therefore C's interest is consequently known as a remainder and C is a remainderman.

4.8   The Freehold Estate

Since 1925 the only freehold estate recognised at law is the fee simple absolute in possession. For all practical purposes this estate gives rights in perpetuity over land and passes to its holder extensive powers over the land. Those other categories of freehold estate which were recognised before 1925 can now only exist as equitable interests. By its definition, the holder of the fee simple may transfer the estate to any person desired. At one time complicated rules applied in respect of the language which had to be used to transfer a fee simple. These were known as words of purchase and words of limitation. Nowadays it is suffcient to indicate in the conveyance, or other document, that the property has passed from one person to another.

Natural Rights of a Freeholder

As a characteristic of ownership, a freeholder enjoys certain natural rights which arise from possession of the fee simple. The major rights are as follows:

(a) Right of Support

This means that a landowner is entitled to such support from his neighbour's land as is necessary to keep the landowner's soil at its natural level. In *Redland Bricks Ltd* v *Morris [1969] 2 All ER 576* excavations by a brick company resulted in the plaintiff's market garden slipping on to the defendant's land owing to lack of support. The right of support does not apply in the case of support for buildings which operates as an easement (see section 4.12).

(b) Rights of Alienation

A freeholder may dispose of his holding in land to any person he wishes. This applies to part or the whole of the land. Alienation may take place by will or by deed.

(c) Enjoyment

A freeholder has extensive rights of enjoyment and, subject to what is mentioned in the next paragraph, may 'waste' (alter the nature of) the land if desired.

Restrictions on a Freeholder's Rights

(a) Rights of Others

A freeholder takes the estate subject to any rights of way over the land and rights of tenants under leases. A restrictive covenant (see section 4.14) may restrict the use to which the land can be put.

(b) Liability under the General Law

Liability may arise, particularly in tort and under the rules laid down by environmental law.

(c) Air Space and Minerals

Ownership rights extend up to the sky and down to the centre of the earth. There are restrictions on an individual's rights to extract coal, iron ore, petroleum and certain other minerals. Any interference with the air space of a freeholder will amount to a trespass, as was seen in Chapter 3. Civil aircraft are given an exemption by the Civil Aviation Act 1982 so long as they are flying at a reasonable height above the ground. These rules are laid down by the Civil Aviation Authority.

(d) Wild Animals

Wild animals living on a freeholder's land cannot be owned but the landowner does have the right to catch and appropriate such animals. As soon as animals are killed they fall into the ownership of the landowner, even if killed by trespassers.

(e) Water Rights

A landowner has rights at common law to draw percolating water from his land. A succession of Water Resources Acts have stated that water can only be taken for domestic purposes if a licence is granted by the appropriate authority, which in this case is now the Environmental Agency.

(f) Statutory Controls

These are probably the most important restrictions on the right of the freeholder to deal with his land as he pleases. Major examples include Town Planning legislation, powers of Compulsory Purchase and Housing law. Tenants of certain types of property are protected by (diminishing) provisions giving them security of tenure and in other cases the right to purchase the freehold.

4.9   The Enforceability of Legal and Equitable Interests

A legal interest which exists over land is enforceable against the world at large. Whoever acquires an estate in land, over which a legal interest exists, is bound by it and takes the land subject to it, irrespective of whether they know of it or not. In most cases, legal interests have to be made by a deed to be valid and consequently there is little difficulty in a purchaser becoming aware of the existence of that interest. An equitable interest is a personal right which may be enforced against the community at large, subject to one major exception. This is the so-called *bona fide* purchaser for value of the legal estate who has taken the estate without notice of the equitable interest and a person who claims through such a purchaser. This doctrine contains a number of expressions which are explained as follows.

(a) Bona fide

This means that the purchaser must act in good faith. Any fraud or under-hand practice will forfeit the privilege of the doctrine.

(b) Purchaser

This indicates a person who takes property.

(c) Value

Consideration must have been given for money or monies worth.

(d) Legal Estate

The purchaser must obtain a legal estate.

(e) Notice

A potential problem with this doctrine is that if its operation simply depended upon a purchaser actually finding out about the existence of any equitable interest over the property, purchasers would refrain from carrying out standard conveyancing processes, because if they did make the normal searches and enquiries they would find themselves bound by any equitable interests found. A number of different types of notice have been devised to tackle the problem:

(1) *Actual notice*

This is where the purchaser has actual knowledge of the existence of the right from any circumstances.

(2) *Constructive notice*

It is presumed that a purchaser will have notice of any equitable interests which would be revealed by the normal searches and investigations carried out in the conveyancing process. In the case of title deeds (the documents which indicate ownership) this would include any equitable interests registered on the title in the previous 15 years. Constructive notice is also presumed where an investigation of the title leads to circumstances being revealed which should lead the purchaser to further investigations.

(3) *Imputed notice*

Where a person employs a solicitor or other agent to act on his behalf, any notice received by the agent, acting in his capacity as agent, will be imputed to the purchaser.

(4) *Statutory notice*

Since 1925, registration of an interest in the Land Charges Department of the Land Registry has constituted statutory notice of the existence of that interest to any intending purchaser. Registration takes place under the Land Charges Act 1925 (now 1972). Such notice is equivalent to actual notice. Failure to register the interest renders it void against a purchaser. This process has done much to reduce the importance of the doctrine of notice in recent years. The system is not all-embracing. Certain equitable interests are not incapable of registration. Covenants to be found in leases and certain equitable interests created before 1925 are good examples. In such circumstances the other types of notice rules apply. Certain equitable interests may be overreached, in which case a purchaser of a legal estate may disregard them even if there is actual notice of their existence.

4.10 Fixtures

One important factor on a disposition of land and/or buildings is to determine whether a particular object is a fixture or a chattel. A fixture is an object which changes its nature from a chattel and becomes part of the land on which it is to be found. The fixture may be changed back to a chattel by separating it from the land. The distinction has a major practical consequence in that no stamp duty is payable when a chattel is transferred. Whether the transaction is a conventional sale of a freehold house, a sale to a purchaser by a bank or building society, or the granting of a lease, what is comprised in the transaction and what is retained by the grantor are crucial. The basic rule is that fixtures pass with the land but chattels do not. On a transfer of land, chattels may be removed but not fixtures which have become a constituent part of the land. In order to ascertain whether an object is a fixture or a chattel, the courts have evolved two tests:

Test 1: The Degree of Annexation

This is the primary test. Such a test is applied to show how permanently the object has been attached to the land. The greater the item is attached to the other real property by nailing, screwing, being set in concrete or similar, the more likely it is that it will be a fixture. Petrol pumps on a filling station forecourt were deemed to be fixtures in a dispute over their status (*Smith* v *City Petroleum Co Ltd [1940] 1 All ER 260*). If the article rests on the ground by its own weight, there is a presumption that it is a chattel. In *Holland* v *Hodgson [1872] LR 7 CP 328* Blackburn J illustrated this princi-ple, where he stated that a pile of stones stacked together in a yard would be considered as chattels but the same set of stones forming a wall would be part of the land. In *Royal Bank of Canada* v *Beyak [1981] 119 DLR 505* a mobile home was held to be a chattel. In *TSB* v *Botham [1994] 1 All 3R 272* electrical 'white goods' were slotted into standard holes in a fitted kitchen and, on appeal, they were held to be chattels.

Test 2: The Purpose of Annexation

This test is used if the first is difficult to apply, as is often the case in such disputes. In the event of a conflict between the two rules, this rule will prevail. The task here is to ascertain the object of the annexation and to ascertain whether the item has been fixed with the purpose of permanently improving the land. If it has, it will be a fixture. If, on the other hand, the reason for fixing the item to the real property is to increase enjoyment of it, or for security purposes, the item(s) could well remain as a chattel(s). Each situation depends very much on its own facts. Is the intention to improve the use of the land or enhance the chattel? In *Hamp* v *Bygrave [1983] 266 EG 720* items in a garden comprising a statue and a number of large urns were held to be fixtures, while display cases and tapestries have been held in a number of cases to be chattels (*Leigh* v *Taylor [1902] AC 157; Viscount Hill* v *Bullock [1897] 2 Ch 482*).

   In *Elitestone Ltd* v *Morris [1997] 2 All ER 513* the House of Lords had to decide whether a wooden bungalow resting on, but not attached to, con-crete pillars was a chattel. If so, the defendant's tenancy of the site could not be one of a dwelling house and he would not enjoy security of tenure under the Rent Act 1977. Overruling the Court of Appeal, the Law Lords took the view that the 'two fold' test was unhelpful in this case and that the matter needed to be considered on a more common sense basis. Deciding that the property was a fixture, the judges took the view that a house which was constructed in such a way that it could not be removed except by destruction could not have been intended to remain a chattel.

Removal of Fixtures

Fixtures pass with the land and chattels do not. On a sale of land, fixtures must be left for the fee simple owner. In certain cases special rules apply. By section 62 of the Law of Property Act 1925, when a freehold is transferred, fixtures pass automatically to the purchaser without express mention. Any fixtures attached to the demised premises, by a tenant, belong to the landlord but certain fixtures can be classed as 'tenant's fixtures' which may be removed by the tenant at the end of his lease. In *New Zealand Government Property Corporation* v *H M & S Ltd [1981] 1 All ER 759* the revised rent of the Haymarket Theatre in London was based upon the assumption that the tenant had the right to remove 'trade fixtures'. Similar principles apply to agricultural tenants protected by the Agriculture Act 1986 who must give the landlord the option to purchase the fixtures at the end of the lease.

4.11   Interests in Land

The expression 'Interest' in this context is used in its narrower sense to denote a third party right existing over land, as opposed to an estate in land. In its wider meaning, from the point of view of transferring land and buildings, the word can cover any proprietary right in land as opposed to a licence (see section 4.16).

4.12   Easements

An easement is a private right enjoyed by successive landowners over the land of another. Good examples include a right of way and a right to light through a window or other aperture. All sorts of rights have been recognised as easements. The use of a letter box, the right to enjoy a park, to store casks on a neighbour's land and to use part of a field as an airstrip are just a few examples. Easements may be legal or equitable interests, depending on their manner of creation. An easement has to be acquired. It does not exist naturally. As an easement is a private right, it needs to be distinguished from customary and public rights enjoyed by people in a particular locality and the community at large respectively (see section 4.16 and Chapter 5, section 5.4).

Characteristics

(1) *There must be a dominant and a servient tenement*
   This means that there must be a piece of land which benefits from the easement (the dominant tenement) and another area of land which has the burden of the interest over it (the servient tenement).
(2) *The easement must accommodate the dominant tenement*
   The interest must be to the advantage of the dominant tenement thereby improving the utility of the land or enhancing some aspect of it. A purely personal right, which does not benefit the land, will not constitute an easement. In *Moody* v *Steggles [1879] 12 Ch D 261* the owner of a public house successfully claimed an easement where a signboard had been hung over a neighbouring house. In *Hill* v *Tupper [1863] 2 H & C 121* the right to let out boats on a canal was deemed simply to be a personal right and was not beneficial to other land as such. Although the two properties must be near to each other, they need not necessarily be adjacent to each other.
(3) *The dominant and servient tenements must be owned or occupied by separate persons*
   The essence of an easement is that it operates as a right against the land of another. A person cannot have rights against himself. Where a person owns two adjacent pieces of land and habitually exercises rights over part of his own land which if that part were occupied by another would be an easement, that is said to be a quasi-easement.
(4) *The easement must lie in grant*
   An easement has to be granted in one form or another. The need for an easement to lie in grant combines a number of factors. The parties involved in the acquisition of the easement must be capable of giving the easement and receiving it (capable grantor and grantee), while the extent of the interest given must be definite. If the right is too vague, it will not constitute an easement (*Re: Ellenborough Park [1956] Ch 131*).

Acquisition of Easements

Apart from creation by statute, for example in the case of the former public utilities, an easement must be acquired by some form of grant. As a variation of this rule, an easement can sometimes come about by reservation.

(a) Express Grant (or Reservation)

This arises where the owner of the servient land grants to the other party the benefit of the easement in return for consideration. The transaction must be in the form of a deed to create a legal easement. A reservation arises where a landowner sells part of his land and wishes to retain an easement over the part sold for the benefit of the retained land. Again, a deed must be used to create a legal interest.

(b) Implied Grant (or Reservation)

Easements arise by implication where a freeholder is disposing of part of his land and retaining the rest. Certain rights arise by implication in favour of the grantee. Such an easement will be a legal interest.

(1) *Section 62 Law of Property Act 1925*
This provision transfers all the benefits attached to the land on a conveyance to a purchaser. The parties can exclude it by express intention.

(2) *The rule in* Wheeldon v Burrows [1879] 12 Ch 131
At common law, where a person sells part of his land the purchaser will obtain the benefit of any rights which the seller was enjoying over the land at the time of sale. The right must be necessary for the reasonable enjoyment of the land and also be continuous and apparent, which means that the right must be of a permanent nature and discoverable with relative ease. This rule only applies to easements and not to profits, but it does include dispositions by will and not just by deed.

(3) *Intended easements*
Where the parties obviously intend that the land disposed of to the grantee should have some specific and definite use, the law will give effect to the presumed intention of the parties and imply an intended easement (*Pwllbach Colliery v Woodman [1915] AC 634*). An intended easement can also arise by reservation as far as the grantor's retained land is concerned.

(4) *Easements of necessity*
Related to the intended easement is the easement of necessity. If an easement is essential to the use of the retained land, where other land is disposed of, the courts will not allow the retained land to be 'landlocked'. The easement is one of necessity and not convenience (*BOJ Properties v Allens Mobile Home Park Ltd [1980] 108 DLR 305*). Although rights of access prevail in this area other easements of necessity have been recognised. In *Wong v Beaumont Property Trust Ltd [1965] 1 QB 173* a ventilation duct attached to the outside wall of a Chinese restaurant came into this category.

(c) Prescription (Presumed Grant)

Where an activity has been enjoyed over the servient land for a period of time and certain conditions are satisfied, the existence of an easement will be presumed by long use. In theory, three forms of prescription exist:

(1) *Common Law*

User since Time Immemorial (1189) is required here, but in practice evidence of at least 20 years user would suffice, although the same criteria apply as in the case of establishing a local custom (see Chapter 1).

(2) *Lost Modern Grant*

If prescription at common law is not possible, the courts may operate a legal fiction known as the lost modern grant. This presumes where there is evidence of use for at least 20 years, that a grant has been made some time in the past but has been lost. This fiction revives the previously lost grant.

(3) *Prescription Act 1832*

This is the usual way of acquiring an easement by prescription. It provides that 20 years uninterrupted user as of right will create a valid easement unless it can be shown that the right was enjoyed by permission. After 40 years of uninterrupted use, the claim can only be defeated by showing that written consent to exercise the right was given.

Requirements to Establish the Easement

(a) Continuous

A degree of regularity is required in the exercise of the easement.

(b) Nec vi Nec clam Nec Precario

The easement must be enjoyed without force, secrecy and without anybody's permission. As a precaution against acquisition in this manner, payment is often demanded to show that permission has been sought and granted.

(c) Uninterrupted Use

The prescription periods must immediately precede the action. It is not sufficent to show that the right has been enjoyed for the qualifying period at some time in the past. An interruption will break the qualifying period. Interruptions of less than one year are disregarded.

Easements of Light

Easements of light have always been subject to different rules. The right to light does not arise naturally. Instead it has to be acquired through a window or other defined aperture in a building. Only one prescription period applies in this case: 20 years uninterrupted user. Consent in writing will defeat the claim, but user need not be as of right and proof of actual enjoyment of the light over the period is sufficent. Oral consent will not defeat the claim. A servient landowner may obstruct the passage of light to the dominant land by registering the obstruction as a local land charge with the local authority. The notice has effect for one year. This procedure, introduced by the Rights of Light Act 1959, and amended by the Local Land Charges Act 1975, replaced the unsightly practice of erecting hoardings to prevent any light reaching the dominant land. A person claiming a right of light may seek a declaration to that effect. A person is entitled to the amount of light which is sufficent according to the ordinary notions of mankind (*Colls* v *Home and Colonial Stores Ltd [1904] AC 179*) but that amount may vary depending upon the purpose for which the light is required (*Allen* v *Greenwood [1980] Ch 119*).

Extinguishing an Easement

This situation may come about in the following ways:

(1) *Statute*
    The Commons Registration Act 1965 is an example of this. The Act required registration of common rights in the appropriate local authority register, otherwise they became unexerciseable.

(2) *Release*
    This arises where the dominant owner gives up the easement. Release may be express or implied. A deed will be required in the case of a legal easement but equitable principles will perfect an informal release. Release may be implied from the circumstances and it is a question of fact whether a particular act or omission shows an intention to release. Simple non-user does not necessarily amount to an implied release (*Cook* v *Mayor of Bath [1868] LR 6 Ex 77; Moore* v *Rawson [1824] 3 B & C 332*).

(3) *Unity of Seisin*
    Where the dominant and servient properties fall into both the same ownership and possession, the easement will cease to exist.

Apart from the above methods it may be that an easement becomes extinguished by a significant alteration to either the dominant or servient properties, rendering the operation of an easement impossible.

4.13   Profits à Prendre

This is an interest in land which gives the right to take some item from the land of another. A right to cut and take timber or to catch fish comes into this category. A profit may be a legal or an equitable interest, depending upon the method of creation. Most of the rules relating to easements also apply to profits but there are differences. In the case of a profit there is no requirement to have a dominant tenement. This profit in gross may exist independently of the ownership of land, while a profit appurtenant is one which exists for the benefit of the dominant tenement. Another distinction is made between a several profit which is a right enjoyed by one person only, to the exclusion of all others, and a profit in common which is one enjoyed by many people. The rules as to acquisition by prescription under the Prescription Act 1832 are similar but the time periods are different. Instead of the two periods of 20 and 40 years, the periods are 30 and 60 years respectively.

4.14   Restrictive Covenants

A covenant is a contractual agreement which may be positive or negative in nature. For example, a covenant may be to pay rent or not to build on a particular piece of land respectively. Covenants can operate on the transfer of freeholds and between the parties to a lease. A restrictive covenant is a negative covenant which restricts the use to which land may be put. It arises when, on the sale of freehold land, the purchaser agrees to restrict the use of his land in order to benefit other land. The person who agrees to adhere to the restrictive covenant, who covenants not to use his land in a particular manner, is the covenantor, while the person who obtains the benefit of the undertaking is the covenantee. Such a covenant is an equitable interest and cannot exist at common law. Common examples include restricting a dwelling house from being used for business purposes and regulating the size of gates and walls on a housing estate.

Restrictive covenants are mutually enforceable between the contracting parties but problems as to their enforcement arise where either of the original parties to the restrictive covenant dispose of their legal estate. The issue is: to what extent is a restrictive covenant binding on successors in title of the original parties to the covenant? The problem does not arise in the case of a positive covenant. Such a covenant can never be binding on the successors in title of the original parties, although there are alternative methods of 'getting round' that problem. In the case of a restrictive covenant cumbersome rules still have to be applied to determine the extent to which the burden and the benefit of a restrictive covenant can 'run' with the land.

Burden of the Covenant

This is the obligation of having to adhere to the restrictive covenant. At common law the burden of the covenant does not pass with the land

(*Austerberry* v *Oldham Corporation [1885] 29 Ch 750*). In equity the burden will pass with the ownership of the land provided that:

(a) the covenant is 'negative' in substance;
(b) the parties intend that the covenant should run with the land;
(c) successors in title have notice of the covenant;
(d) the covenantee retains land capable of being benefited.

These rules were developed from *Tulk* v *Moxhay [1848] 18 LJ Ch 83* where the Plaintiff, who owned a major part of Leicester Square in London, sold the gardens in the Square and retained the surrounding land. Tulk's action against a successor of the purchaser succeeded, as the above conditions were satisfied. The covenant must be intended to bind successors in title of the covenantor. Land which is identifiable must be benefited by the covenant. In the case of a restrictive covenant there must be a dominant and a servient tenement. To protect a restrictive covenant which affects freehold land the interest must be registered as a land charge or as a notice in the Charges Register at the Land Registry where title to the land is registered (see section 4.19). Restrictive covenants in leases cannot be registered. Finally, as the plaintiff is seeking an equitable remedy, the plaintiff must not be in a position where such a remedy will be refused.

Benefit

Although the common law rule is that the benefit of a covenant can be assigned, subject to normal contractual principles, a successor in title of the original covenantee must show that the benefit of the land has been expressly or impliedly assigned to him or that it was originally annexed to the land, or it relates to land subject to a building scheme. The covenant must benefit land retained by the covenantee. According to *Federated Homes Ltd* v *Mill Lodge Properties Ltd [1980] 1 WLR 594*, Section 78 of the Law of Property Act 1925 will effect a valid annexation without the need for appropriate language in the relevant conveyance. If this is not the case, the benefit can be assigned at the same time as the transfer of the land.

Building Schemes

Where there is a building scheme (or scheme of development) restrictive covenants may be enforced by one purchaser or successors in title against other purchasers or their successors in title. If the requirements of the scheme are satisfied, the benefits and burdens of the covenant automatically pass to all purchasers in the area. The leading case is *Elliston* v *Reacher [1908] 2 Ch 374* which laid down certain rules for the application of such a scheme:

(a) the plaintiff and defendant must derive title from a common vendor;
(b) the estate must be laid out in a defined area;
(c) the restrictions must be intended by the vendor to be for the benefit of all the lots sold and the purchaser bought the plots on that basis.

Discharge and Modification of Restrictive Covenants

At common law a restrictive covenant will be discharged if the dominant and servient properties come under the ownership of the same person, while if the covenant has been abandoned the courts will not enforce it. A number of statutes provide for discharge of a restrictive covenant but the most important provision is under Section 84 of the Law of Property Act 1925, which provides for an application to the Lands Tribunal with appeal on a point of law to the Court of Appeal. Each case depends very much on its own facts and the tribunal may order that compensation be paid to any person entitled to the benefit of the covenant. The covenant must be attached to freehold land or to a lease originally granted for at least 40 years with 25 or more unexpired. There are four grounds upon which the application can be made:

(a) the covenant should be rendered obsolete because of a change in the character of the property or neighbourhood (*Re: Truman, Hanbury, Burton and Co Ltd's Application [1956] 1 QB 261*);
(b) the restriction impedes some reasonable use of the land or is contrary to the public interest (*Re: Osborns and Easton's application [1978] 38 P&CR 251*);
(c) the parties expressly or impliedly agree to its removal;
(d) the discharge or modification will not injure anyone entitled to the benefit.

Current planning policies of the relevant local authority should be taken into account but these are not conclusive.

4.15   Mortgages

A mortgage consists of a transfer of property by a borrower to a lender in return for a loan. The borrower is known as the mortgagor and the lender the mortgagee.

Legal Mortgages

By sections 85 and 86 of the Law of Property Act 1925 a legal mortgage can either be granted in respect of freehold land by:

(1) demise, or
(2) charge by deed expressed to be by way of legal mortgage (Legal Charge).

In the case of a leasehold such a mortgage is created either by sub-demise (sub-lease) or by legal charge.

In practice the legal charge method is used. The demise is a cumbersome method in that it involves a transfer of the estate to the lender until the mortgage is paid off, and then a subsequent transfer of the relevant property to the borrower. The legal charge does not involve this. Instead the borrower retains the estate in land, the form of deed is short and simple, while the lender has all the remedies in the event of default by the borrower that he would have had if the mortgage was made by demise. It is standard practice for a lender to retain the title deeds of the property while the mortgage exists. In the case of registered land, the appropriate details of the mortgage must be entered on the Land Certificate. The Land Certificate will be retained by the Land Registry and the lender will be issued with a Charge Certificate.

A mortgage requires payment of the *Principal* sum borrowed on a fixed date, while *Interest* is payable on the loan. Nowadays, the most common forms of legal mortgages are:

(1) instalment mortgages – regular repayments of principal and interest;
(2) morgages based on insurance policies – 'endowment' mortgages;
(3) morgages related to the stock market.

The Equity of Redemption

This is the right to pay the mortgage off when the money is due. Any provision in a mortgage which impedes the ability of the mortgagor to redeem will not be recognised. There should be no 'clog or fetter' on the equity of redemption. It is a proprietary interest in land and the parties to a mortgage cannot agree to prevent its exercise. When the borrower pays off the mortgage, the loan is said to be redeemed. In practice, by convention, the date of redemption, sometimes called the legal or contractual redemption date, will arise 6 months from the date of the loan, so that the mortgagee's powers arise virtually immediately. At common law, the borrower has no right to redeem at any other time and therefore will be relying on rights in equity to do so. The equity of redemption comprises a number of different factors. Although the courts cannot simply declare mortgage terms to be unenforceable because they are not reasonable, relief will be granted by equity in the case of mortgage provisions which are oppressive or fraudulent. A provision which prevents redemption completely will not be upheld. Postponement of the right to redeem may be valid so long as the mortgage as a whole is not oppressive, particularly if the parties are in an equal bargaining position

(*Knightsbridge Estates Trust Ltd* v *Byrne [1939] Ch 441*). If the right to redeem is merely illusory it will not be upheld, as in *Fairclough* v *Swan Brewery Co Ltd [1912] AC 565* where there was a provision only allowing redemption of the mortgage of a lease 6 weeks from the end of the term. The restraint of trade rules (*Esso Petroleum Co Ltd* v *Harper's Garage [Stourport] Ltd [1968] AC 269*) also apply to mortgages and where there is excessive restraint on the mortgagor's activities this could amount to a 'clog'. Another problem involves collateral advantages. The question here is the validity of a provision in a mortgage that the lender can obtain an additional advantage in addition to repayment of principal, interest and costs. If the lender obtains an advantage which ends on redemption, or is collateral to the main transaction, it seems that such a provision will be valid (*Multiservice Bookbinding Ltd* v *Marden [1979] Ch 84*) as long as it is not invalid or unconscionable. If the advantage is designed to last beyond the time when the mortgage will be redeemed it will not be valid (*Noakes & Co* v *Rice [1902] AC 24*).

The Rights of the Mortgagor and the Mortgagee

Mortgagor

1. To repay the mortgage debt.

2. Right to grant leases
   A mortgagor in possession can grant agricultural or occupational leases for up to 50 years. In the case of building leases the maximum period is 999 years. The lease must take effect within 12 months and the rent must be the market rate. Institutional lenders frequently exclude this provision in standard legal charges.

3. Accept surrenders of leases.

4. Compel a transfer to a nominee.

5. Bring actions without the consent of the mortgagee. For example, a claim for arrears of rent in the County Court.

6. Make copies of relevant title deeds.

7. Protection under the Consumer Credit Act 1974.

A court may set aside or reopen any credit agreement which is classed as 'extortionate'.

Mortgagee

1. To have possession of the title deeds.

2. Sue for the debt.

3. Possession of the mortgaged property

In theory, possession can be obtained by the mortgagee without any fault on the mortgagor's part (*Four Maids Ltd* v *Dudley Marshall Properties Ltd [1957] Ch 317*). In practice, possession is required before a mortgagee can exercise any power of sale, and if the lender does obtain possession he is liable for 'wilful default'. This means that he will be liable for any income due to the occupier had he acted as a prudent manager of the property. The courts and statute have laid down circumstances where the borrower can seek relief.

4. Sale

The lender's power of sale arises as soon as the contractual date of redemption has passed or, in the case of a repayment mortgage, when a payment is overdue. The power cannot be exercised until:

(a) at least 3 months' principal is due;
(b) 2 months' interest is in arrears; or
(c) there has been a breach of some other covenant in the mortgage deed.

The sale may be by auction or by private treaty. There is an obligation on the mortgagee to obtain the true market value of the property as at the date of sale (*Cuckmere Brick Co Ltd* v *Mutual Finance Ltd [1971] 115 SJ 288*), while a building society mortgagee has an obligation by statute (Building Societies Act 1986) to take care to obtain the best price reasonably obtainable. The society can sell when it considers appropriate and this may mean selling when the market is buoyant. Sales to oneself or related organisations are not allowed (*Cuckmere Brick Co Ltd* v *Mutual Finance Ltd* – see above).

5. Foreclosure

This amounts to a confiscation of the mortgagor's rights and is rarely sought nowadays. It puts an end to the borrower's equity of redemption. The remedy can be sought where there is no fault on the mortgagor's part as soon as the contractual date of redemption has passed. The mortgagor acquires the estate free from prior mortgagees. The process arises in two stages: *Decree nisi* and *Decree Absolute*, after which the mortgage will be foreclosed.

6. Receiver

The power to appoint a receiver and the exercise of his powers arise in the same circumstances as the power of sale. Such a process may be appropriate where the mortgagor has leased the property subject to the mortgage, or the market value of the premises is too low to make it worth while exercising the power of sale. The receiver is deemed to be the agent of the mortgagor and after appointment has power to intercept any income due to the property. There is an established order in which the receiver must distribute monies received in respect of the mortgaged property.

7. Leases
A mortgagee in possession has the same powers as a mortgagor to grant leases and accept surrenders of them.

Equitable Mortgages

These arise where the mortgagee receives an equitable interest in the mortgaged land. They can arise in the following circumstances:

(1) The deposit of title deeds or a Land Certificate as security for a loan. It seems that such a transaction must now be made in writing and in practice is made by a deed containing the terms of the mortgage.
(2) An agreement in writing to create a legal mortgage.
(3) Equitable charge, which arises where a person agrees that land is to be responsible for satisfying a financial obligation.
(4) Mortgage of an equitable interest.

Remedies

An equitable mortgagee has the right to sue for the debt and in theory can initiate foreclosure proceedings. A receiver may be appointed if the mortgage is made in the form of a deed.

Further Mortgages

It is possible to have more than one mortgage at the same time. Subsequent mortgages can be legal or equitable in nature, depending on the methods by which they were created. Where the mortgaged property is placed on the market and the property is not valuable enough to repay each of the mortgages, the rules as to priorities of mortgages may arise. Established practice is for the first mortgagee to have the title deeds while that mortgage will take priority over any other mortgage. Once the land is registered a mortgage protected on the register will defeat all later mortgages. A problem is that of tacking. Tacking of mortgages arises where a subsequent mortgagee insists on repaymernt of the loan before payment of a prior mortgage. Consolidation of mortgages will occur where a borrower enters into two different mortgages with the same mortgagee. In such circumstances the lender may refuse to permit the redemption of one without the other if certain conditions are satisfied. The Law of Property Act prohibits consolidation (*Law of Property Act 1925 section 93*) but banks and building society mortgagees frequently exclude the relevant section in the Act, thereby allowing themselves to consolidate.

4.16 Licences

A licence is simply a permission to do some act which would otherwise amount to a trespass. It does not amount to an interest in land, except in exceptional circumstances, nor does it constitute a proprietary right. Keeping to normal terminology, the licensor grants the permission and the licensee receives it. Problems relating to licences arise in connection with both freeholds and leaseholds. In this context we are concerned with freeholds only.

Problem

As a licence is a purely personal right between the parties and confers no interest in land on the licensee it is of little worth. Two problems have arisen in this context:

(1) To what extent can the licence be revoked?
(2) To what extent is a licence binding on a third party who acquires the freehold estate from the estate owner over which the licence is being exercised?

Categories

(a) Bare Licences

A bare licence arises where no consideration is given for the exercise of the right. It may be revoked at any time and is not binding upon the purchaser of the freehold estate. The licensee must be given a reasonable time to leave the premises (*Wood* v *Leadbitter [1855] 13 M & W 838*). Any licence not coming within the other categories is classed as a bare licence.

(b) Licence Coupled with an Interest

The interest will generally be a profit à prendre. The licence is needed to enter the land in the first place to exercise the interest. The licence may also be coupled with a chattel interest, such as a licence to enter land to remove cut timber which has been bought. As long as the interest continues, the licence cannot be revoked and is binding on a purchaser.

(c) Contractual Licence

A contractual licence is one which contains the essentials of a valid contract. Consideration must be given. Ordinary contractual principles will determine whether or not the revocation of a contractual licence amounts to a breach of contract. If it does, the licensee will be entitled to damages. If an equitable remedy is sought there must be compliance with the maxims of equity, while in some circumstances it is simply not practical to seek such an order; threatened eviction from a restaurant for example. The modern view is that a contractual licence is not binding on a third party (*Ashburn Anstalt v Arnold [1988] 2 All ER 147*).

(d) Licence Protected by an Estoppel

The doctrine has been extended to licences in cases where without an estoppel a party would only have a gratuitous licence revocable at will. The remedies available appear to vary depending upon the circumstances. Sometimes a proprietary right in land will be awarded (*Pascoe v Turner [1979] 1 WLR 431*), in other cases a sum of money equal to expenditure (*Dodsworth v Dodsworth [1973] EGD 233*), while in others an order protecting the licensee from revocation (*Inwards v Baker [1965] 2 QB 59*). Many of the cases are of a domestic nature but the concept can be applied wherever the circumstances satisfy the qualifying conditions. In *Crabb v Arun DC [1976] Ch 179* both parties agreed that Crabb could use a particular access to a road. Relying on this assurance by the local authority, he sold some land knowing that as a consequence he could only have access to his land by using the new access. Even so, the defendants closed off the access knowing of his position. The Court of Appeal restored the access to the plaintiff. A result similar to the licence protected by an estoppel situation can sometimes be reached on the basis of a constructive trust.

4.17   Co-ownership of Land and Buildings

This area of law is also known as concurrent interests in land. It arises where two or more persons are entitled to simultaneous enjoyment of the land. Where only one person is entitled to the estate, that person is known as the *Beneficial Owner*. Where more than one person holds the estate at any given time, they will either be a joint tenant or a tenant in common.

(1) Joint Tenancy

This arises where those who jointly hold the estate in land are in essence one person. Against all others, the joint tenants are in the position of a single owner. It arises whenever land is conveyed to two or more persons without words of severance, that is without words to indicate that they are to take the estate in distinct shares.

Characteristics

(a) *The right of survivorship*
On ceasing to be a joint tenant, that person's share will automatically pass to the other joint tenants irrespective of any indication to the contrary by will or intestacy.

(b) *The four unities*
The established view is that such a tenancy cannot exist unless there is unity of possession, interest, time and title existing between the parties holding the estate at the same time.

(2) Tenancy in Common

This arises where land is held by separate titles and there is no need for the shares to be equal. It is appropriate where the parties contribute differing amounts of capital to the purchase of the land. There is no right of survivorship and on death an individual share will pass to those entitled to the share by the will of the tenant in common, or if the tenant has died intestate subject to the intestacy rules.

4.18   Successive Interests in Land

The device of the trust has been used in English land law as a means of creating successive interests in land. This means being able to 'tie up' the land for the future. There are two methods of effecting this:

(a) The Strict Settlement

This is a device which creates a succession of beneficial interests in favour of a number of persons. Historically, it was a method of keeping large landed estates in the family unit but allowing dispositions of property to be made where appropriate. The Settled Land Act 1925 governs the law relating to strict settlements. The usual strict settlement was made on marriage or death. On marriage a husband would be given a life interest (tenant for life) and not the legal estate. Trustees would be appointed to manage the settlement. The consent of trustees is required before the tenant for life can carry out dispositions in connection with the estate. So far as its creation is concerned, a strict settlement can be created either *inter vivos* or by will. A trust instrument and a vesting deed are required.

(b) The Trust for Sale

These are governed by The Law of Property Act 1925. The trust for sale was a settlement used to secure a regular income for the beneficiaries. It is used, nowadays, to facilitate the transfer of land. Under a trust for sale, land is transferred to trustees on trust to sell and invest the proceeds for the benefit of specific beneficiaries. It can be created expressly or impliedly, and where land is conveyed to persons as joint tenants they hold it on a trust for sale.

4.19   Registration and Land Law

Registration in connection with the law of real property can cover a number of situations but usually encompasses the following:

(a) registration of interests (mainly equitable) over land and buildings;
(b) registration of local land charges;
(c) registration of title to land and buildings.

(a) The system of registering interests which exist over land is very much tied up with the *bona fide* purchaser rule (see section 4.9). Since 1926 it has been possible to register certain equitable interests, thereby constituting statutory notice to any intending purchaser of the existence of the right. This process assists those entitled to the benefit of the interest and purchasers in that:

(1) it enables purchasers to find out about the interest;
(2) the process protects that interest.

The process is known as Registration of Incumbrances or Registration of Land Charges. The Land Charges Act 1925 (now 1972) instituted a register in which many equitable interests (but not all) are capable of registration. It is also possible to register a puisne mortgage in this way. This is a legal mortgage which is not protected by a deposit of the relevant documents relating to the legal estate affected. Registration is deemed to constitute notice to all persons, while non-registration makes the interest void against a purchaser. A search should be made at the Land Charges Department of the Land Registry at Plymouth by the purchaser as part of the conveyancing process. Certain other registers are kept under the Land Charges Act, such as a register of pending actions and one relating to writs and orders affecting land. One problem with the system is that registration is against the name of the estate owner and not against the description of the property. This system of registration is now of little importance and only has application where the title to the land is still unregistered and needs to be effected with a first registration of title the next time that the land is sold. The system has always had shortcomings in that not every equitable interest is capable of registration and consequently cannot be investigated in this way.

(b) Local authorities are required to maintain a Local Land Charges Register. These charges are registered against the land itself. A personal search may be made but it is safer to have the search made by the staff of the relevant authority. Matters covered under this heading include planning issues, compulsory purchase orders, open cast coal mining information, listed buildings and light obstruction notices. Failure to register these charges does not affect enforceability.

(c) Registration of title to land and buildings is the system of actually registering the *Estates* in land themselves. The relevant law is to be found in the Land Registration Acts 1925–1988, while land registration rules which are frequently updated govern procedure.

What Can Be Registered?

Both Freeholds and Leaseholds are capable of registration. In the case of an initial grant of a lease, the grant must be for 21 years or more, or if there is an assignment there must be at least 21 years unexpired. The principal benefits of the system are as follows:

(1) it provides a central record of the property;
(2) the state guarantees title to the land;
(3) the conveyancing process is simpler.

Since 1990 the whole of England and Wales is an area of compulsory registration. If the land has not already been registered the next time that the freehold is transferred, or an appropriate leasehold is granted or assigned, application must be made for first registration of title to the land. As the Head Office of the Land Registry is unable to cope, on its own, with all applications for first registration of title, it has been established practice for many years for District Land Registries, acting under the auspices of the Central Registry, to deal with all pending registrations in a particular geographical area. At one time there were severe restrictions as to who could actually inspect the register but recently the process has become considerably more open.

The Land Certificate

This document is the equivalent of the title deeds in non-registered title conveyancing and it acts as a mirror of the register. Proof of title is the register and any intending purchaser will be bound by the register and any overriding interest (see section 4.19). It comprises three parts:

(1) Property Register

This gives a description of the land, the estate held and the title number. In the case of a leasehold it also contains relevant information relating to the terms of the lease.

(2) Proprietorship Register

This states the name(s) of the Registered Proprietor(s) together with the nature of the title and any Minor interests (see section 4.19) affecting the right of the proprietor to dispose of the land.

(3) Charges Register

This contains any burdens on the land. If there is a mortgage the Registered Charge, which is broadly the equivalent of a legal mortgage of unregistered land, is completed by entry of the chargee as proprietor of the charge, and a certificate of charge is issued to the chargee with the land certificate being deposited in the registry.

Whether freehold or leasehold, the estate must be given a class of title. The most common is *Absolute* title which can apply to both freeholds and leaseholds. This recognises that the estate is vested in its holder. In the case of freeholds, the registry may grant a *Possessory* title. In such a case no guarantee is given in respect of the title prior to the date of first registration. Unusually a freehold may be given a *Qualified* title in which case the title is granted subject to some condition. *Good Leasehold* only applies to leaseholds and is fairly common. This recognises the validity of the lease in question but does not guarantee the freehold from which the lease has been granted. Upgrading of title is common on subsequent dispositions of land where title is less than absolute.

Overriding Interests

There are certain interests which do not appear on the Land Certificate but which bind the proprietor and any purchaser of registered land. A list of these interests is set out in Section 70 of the LRA 1925. Important examples include any rights acquired by a squatter under the Limitation Acts, local land charges, short leases not capable of registration and, where the title to the land is less than absolute, any interests excepted from the effects of registration.

Minor Interests

These are interests existing over land with a registered title which do not come within the category of overriding interests. They mainly comprise those interests which in non-registered land would be covered by the Land Charges Act 1972 and the doctrine of notice together with any beneficial interests which exist under a trust. Such interests must be protected by an entry on the register, which varies in nature depending upon the type of interest to be protected. The entry will take the form of a Notice, Caution, Restriction or Inhibition.

Indemnity and Rectification of the Register

Rectification of the register may take place where there has been a mistake, fraud or error, and the Registrar considers that it is appropriate to order rectification. An indemnity may be paid where a person suffers loss unless the applicant has contributed to it by his loss or lack of proper care.

4.20   Access to Neighbouring Land

There has never existed any general rule of access whereby a landowner may lawfully enter neighbouring land to carry out necessary works on his own land. The enactment of legislation to remedy this problem was put foward by The Law Commission in 1985 (Law Com no 151). The relevant Act is the Access to Neighbouring Land Act 1992. Under the Act a person may obtain an order for access to neighbouring land in order to carry out works which are reasonably necessary for the preservation of his own land. This is particularly relevant in the case of repairs to a wall or to a roof. The court has a discretionary power to make an 'access order' on the application of the person who wishes to carry out the relevant works. The right of access is limited to the carrying out of 'basic preservation works'. The right is not a permanent one and is intended to be a 'one off'. The Act applies to repairs only and not to alterations. The application is made to the County Court and is registrable as a notice if the land has a registered title.

4.21   Party Walls

This is a difficult term to define but is basically a wall adjoining houses or land which belongs to two different owners. The common use of the wall by the adjoining owners is the characteristic of the concept. The usual problem with party walls is to ascertain where the boundary lies. The Party Walls Act 1996, which came into force in July 1997, gives certain rights in connection with 'party walls' and 'party structures'. The most common type of party wall dispute relates to the central walls which separate the properties in terraced and semi-detached houses. A 'party structure' is a structure such as a partition which separates buildings which are approached by different entrances. There are common law rights to carry out work on a party wall, notwithstanding that part of the wall is owned by the party who does not wish to carry out works or to have them carried out by the other party.

In London these rights have long been codified by the London Building Acts, but the new Act extends the provisions to the remainder of England and Wales. The Act, in essence, debars each owner from dealing with their half of the party wall without informing their neighbour. The works covered include repair, rebuilding or even demolition, but the instigator of the changes is liable to safeguard the position of the adjoining owner and may have to pay compensation. There is a somewhat complicated set of procedures to be followed as far as serving notices is concerned. The dispute mechanism operates through a simple resolution procedure normally involving construction based surveyors.

4.22   The Leasehold Estate

The leasehold estate is an alternative method of holding land from the free-hold and is encountered in many forms. It is a contractual arrangement and the usual essentials of a valid contract must be present for the transaction to be valid. It can involve, for example, a private individual paying a weekly rent for living accommodation, a farmer working a farm which is let to him by the freeholder, a company leasing an office block for the purposes of its business, or a letting of a retail unit in a shopping centre.

4.23   Background to Leaseholds

The leasehold estate arises where a person possessing an estate in real property grants a lesser estate in land to another for a fixed period of time. The Law of Property Act 1925 recognised the *Term of Years Absolute* as an estate in land. The leasehold has always been treated as an item of personal property and is categorised as *Chattels Real*. Whereas the estate in land is known as the *Leasehold,* the document which creates the leasehold is called a *Lease.* The grantor of the lease is known as a *Lessor* while the person to whom it is granted is known as a *Lessee.* As a general rule, a lease must be made in the form of a deed to be valid, while the lease will contain covenants setting out the contractual obligations of the parties. The property which is the subject of the lease is known as the *Demised Premises.* Unlike freeholds, a lease can either be an *Initial Grant* which arises on the first grant of the lease to the lessee, or it can be taken on *Assignment* where a lease already exists.

As in the case of a freehold, it is common for the parties to initially agree the contents of the lease in a contract before the actual deed is entered into. This is known as an *Agreement for a Lease*. At the end of the period for which the lease is entered into, the demised premises will revert back to the lessor. As mentioned earlier (see section 4.7) the *Reversion* is the right in the demised property which remains with the lessor during the continuance of the lease. The expressions *Landlord* and *Tenant* are used to indicate the owners for the time being of the reversion and the lease. An *Assignment* of a lease must be distinguished from a *Sub-Lease*. The latter involves the lessee retaining the lease but granting a lease of the whole or part of the demised premises to another. This transaction is sometimes known as an *Under Lease* and must be for at least one day less than the grant of the original lease. Leases from which sub-leases are granted are known as *Head Leases*.

4.24   Essential Elements of a Valid Leasehold

Before a valid leasehold can be created it is necessary to satisfy three requirements:

(a) compliance with the appropriate formalities;
(b) the letting must be for a fixed term;
(c) the occupier must have exclusive possession of the demised premises.

(a) Formalities

The law of landlord and tenant makes a distinction between fixed term leases and periodic tenancies. A fixed term lease arises where the parties fix the maximum duration of the term in advance, such as 3, 7 or 21 years. A periodic tenancy arises where the tenant enters into possession of the demised premises and the letting continues until it is determined by either party. Section 52 Law of Property Act 1925 requires a fixed term lease to be in the form of a deed to create or transfer the legal estate. As an exception, by section 54 of the Law of Property Act 1925 a fixed term lease for 3 years or less will be valid so long as:

(a) it starts from the date of the grant (takes effect in possession);
(b) is at a full rent.

In the case of a periodic tenancy there is no requirement for a deed to be entered into. Such lettings are created by an express tenancy agreement or by implication from the circumstances. In some circumstances (albeit fairly limited nowadays), a periodic tenancy may arise by statute, thereby giving the tenant security of tenure of the demised property.

A problem which can arise is where the parties attempt to create a fixed term lease for a period of more than 3 years but no deed is entered into. Such a transaction will not be recognised at common law but such an arrangement will be recognised in equity so long as certain conditions are satisfied. For an equitable lease to arise, the following must be satisfied:

(1) there must be evidence of a contract which satisfies the requirements of section 2 Law of Property (Miscellaneous Provisions) Act 1989; and
(2) the court must be prepared to grant specific performance to the agreement for the lease. A tenant who has not acted properly in connection with the transaction and who does not satisfy the 'maxims of equity' would not obtain the benefit of the transaction.

This recognition of the equitable lease is known by the leading case of *Walsh* v *Lonsdale [1882] 21 Ch 9* where it was held that a tenant who is in possession of the demised premises, holding under a contract for a lease of which specific performance would be granted, occupies the same position as if a formal lease had been granted. Although the existence of an equitable lease recognises that the parties are in the position of landlord and tenant towards each other, there are problems with the concept especially as far as third parties are concerned. In particular, the occupier only has an equitable interest in the property and not an estate in land. The enforceability of such a right will be governed by the workings of the Land Charges Act 1972 and the Land Registration Act 1925. An equitable lease does not come within the scope of a 'conveyance' in section 62 of Law of Property Act 1925, and an equitable tenant cannot claim the advantages covered by that section, while an equitable tenant might find himself at a disadvantage in that the 'usual covenants' (see section 4.25) which automatically require a tenant to carry out repairs where there is solely an agreement for a lease may result in forfeiture proceedings being brought against a tenant where there is only a contract and not an executed lease.

(b) Fixed Term

It is established law that the duration of the term of a lease must be certain. Where the transaction initially contains an agreement for a lease, such contract is void unless some definite time for commencement is expressly stated or inferred (*Harvey* v *Pratt [1965] 1 WKR 1025*). If the parties enter into an executed lease, the term will commence immediately unless there is an express provision giving some other date. In the case of a fixed term, any time period can be chosen as long as the maximum duration is certain or capable of being rendered certain. In *Brillant* v *Michaels [1945] 1 All ER 121* the plaintiff entered into an agreement to take the tenancy of a flat when it fell vacant. The agreement was held to be void for uncertainty, as was the case in *Lace* v *Chantler [1944] KB 568*, where a purported letting was entered into in 1940 'for the duration of the war'. A similar result was reached in *Prudential Assurance Co Ltd* v *London Residuary Board [1992] AC 386,* where a letting was to continue 'until the land was required by the London County Council for road widening'. In this case a yearly tenancy had been created as the tenant had entered into possession and paid a yearly rent. It is not uncommon for fixed term leases to commence some time after the agreement for the lease has been entered into. This is known as a future or reversionary lease. By section 149 Law of Property Act 1925, a term may not take effect more than 21 years after the agreement to enter into it has taken place. If a lease takes effect immediately it is said to take effect in possession. As far as periodic tenancies are concerned, they do not offend the certainty requirement because the period when rent is due and payable is certain, while they can also be rendered certain by the giving of the appropriate notice to quit. The parties can choose any time period for their letting, but a week, a month and a year are probably the most common time periods. Either party may determine the letting as agreed between themselves. The normal practice is that a letting is determinable on giving a least one full period of notice to expire at the end of the tenancy. This rule is subject to considerable statutory modification. For example, a weekly residential tenant must be given at least 4 weeks' notice (*Protection from Eviction Act 1977*), while a yearly tenant must be given at least 6 months' notice. A landlord has a statutory duty to provide a rent book for a weekly tenant, giving relevant information relating to the letting.

A Tenancy at Will arises where there is a tenancy, but the landlord or tenant is entitled to terminate the letting at any time. If a tenancy at will is created expressly, in writing, it needs careful drafting to be enforceable as such a letting. A Tenancy at Will can also arise where a purchaser of land enters into possession before completion of the transaction. Such a tenancy is outside the scope of the Landlord and Tenant Act 1954 Part 2 (see section 4.28) which gives security of tenure to business tenants. Another type of tenancy is the Tenancy at Sufferance, where a tenant *holds over* (stays in possession) at the end of a lease. *Perpetually Renewable Leases* (where the lease contains a provision allowing the tenant to renew the letting on the same terms as before) have never been liked by the courts and are now covered by section 145 Law of Property Act 1925, which converts such leases into 2000 year terms.

(c) Exclusive Possession

It is not possible for a tenancy to arise unless the occupier has exclusive possession of the demised premises in addition to the other requirements. This is the right to exclude all other persons from the land, including the freeholder. The right to exclusive possession will not automatically be lost by the tenant because the lease reserves the freeholder's right to come on to the subject premises to view the state of repair or similar. If exclusive possession is not present, the occupier of the land will almost certainly have a licence and not a lease. This is a simple permission which is not worth a great deal. In particular, it will almost certainly mean that the holder will not have the benefit of any of the statutory provisions which give benefits, such as security of tenure or compensation for improvements to the demised premises.

It has always been of the greatest importance to ascertain whether or not a letting of real property is a lease or licence. The leading case is *Street* v *Mountford [1985] AC 809,* where it was decided that, if the occupier has exclusive possession, a tenancy arises irrespective of the intentions of the parties. The only circumstances which would negative such a conclusion would be if there was no intention to create legal relations between the parties or the occupier was in possession but referable to some other type of legal relationship rather than a lease. The courts will look at the transaction as a whole, disregarding any pretence or sham. In *Street* the so-called 'licence' to occupy a furnished room at the top of a building was held to be a lease. In *Aslan* v *Murphy [no 1] [1990] 1 WLR 766* a 'licence' to occupy a small room, which deemed to exclude any right to exclusive possession and allowed the licensor to use the room, was held to be a lease. It may be that if the property owner provides services for the occupier a licence will arise. In *Marchant* v *Charters [1977] 1 WLR 1181,* a letting of a bed sitting room was held to be a licence where the licensor had the rooms cleaned daily and provided bed linen, while in *Abbeyfield [Harpenden] Society* v *Woods [1968] 1 WLR 374* the Court of Appeal decided that a room in an old people's home was a licence. An obligation to provide services does not necessarily imply a licence. This would only arise if the provision of such services required unrestricted access by the owner or his employees.

4.25   Covenants in Leases

The terms of a lease are referred to as covenants. These are contractual stipulations and in most situations these provisions will be expressly agreed between the parties. If there are no express covenants dealing with such matters, the common law will imply the following covenants into the lease.

(A) Implied Covenants

(a) By the Landlord

(1) *Quiet enjoyment*
   This means that the tenant is entitled to enjoy the property free from disturbance in title and free from substantial physical interference by the landlord. The covenant only operates between the landlord and tenant or persons who derive direct title from the same landlord. Examples of the covenant include *Owen* v *Gadd [1956] 2 QB 99,* where

scaffolding was erected which obstructed access to the premises; *Perera v Vandiyar [1953] 1 WLR 672,* where the landlord cut off essential services; *Kenny v Preen [1963] 1 QB 400,* where the landlord tried to drive the tenant out by persistent threats, and *Lavender v Betts [1942] 2 All ER 72,* where the doors and windows were removed by the landlord, making the property only habitable with considerable discomfort. A tenant is such cases will be seeking damages together with an injunction. The Protection From Eviction Act 1977 (as amended by The Housing Act 1988) renders it a criminal offence to threaten tenants, in addition to the civil aspects involved (see section 1 of the 1977 Act – offences include harassment and unlawful eviction).

(2) *Not to derogate from grant*

A landlord must not act inconsistently with the letting. It is not appropriate for a landlord to take away with one hand what he has granted with the other. If a landlord permits or allows adjoining premises to be used as a nuisance to the tenant or makes the demised premises unfit for the purpose for which the premises were let, there is a breach of this covenant. The leading case is *Aldin v Latimer, Clark, Muirhead [1894] 2 Ch 437,* where the landlord was held liable when, having let premises for the purposes of timber drying, he built on adjoining land and interrupted the flow of air to the tenant's premises. A similar conclusion was reached in *Grosvenor Hotel Co v Hamilton [1894] 2 QB 836,* where the landlord leased an old house to a tenant and then used machinery on adjoining land which caused the house to be unstable. A landlord is not liable under this covenant if nearby property is let for a similar purpose and as a consequence a tenant suffers financial loss. From *Newman v Real Estate Debenture Corporation Ltd [1940] 1 All ER 131* it appears that an express covenant to let the demised premises for residential purposes only may imply that any letting of part for business purposes is a derogation from grant.

(3) *Fitness*

The basic rule is *caveat emptor*. There is no general implied covenant at common law that the landlord guarantees fitness for user or fitness for habitation of the demised premises. The onus is on the tenant to ensure the condition or suitability of the premises.

Exceptions

(a) *'Smith v Marrable' [1843] 11 M & W 152*

This common law provision is to the effect that the landlord implies that, at the commencement of a lease of a furnished house, the demised premises are fit for human habitation.

(b) *Section 8 Landlord and Tenant Act 1985*

This section imposes on the landlord an obligation that residential premises will be fit for human habitation at the commencement of the letting and will continue to be so for the length of the term. Unfortunately, the provision is of little use because it only covers lettings where the rent does not exceed £80 per year in London and £52 elsewhere. As there has been no revision of these rental levels since 1957, there must be very few people covered by the provision. Moreover, the landlord must be notified of the defects, and it will not apply if the defects cannot be rendered fit at reasonable expense.

(c) *Section 11 Landlord and Tenant Act 1985*

This provision applies to 'short leases' of dwelling houses (including flats) of less than 7 years. It requires the landlord to keep the structure and exterior of the property in repair and also to keep the services in the property in working order. The landlord is only liable if he has notice of the defect but the provision cannot be 'contracted out' (excluded), except with the consent of the tenant and the approval of the court.

In addition, section 4 of the Defective Premises Act 1972 imposes on the landlord a duty to take reasonable care to prevent physical injury or damage to property which might be caused by the disrepair of the premises. The duty only applies where the landlord has responsibility for such matters.

(b) By the Tenant

(1) *To pay rent*

In those cases where the rent is not agreed between the parties expressly and it is obvious that the parties envisage a tenancy coming into being, it is implied that the landlord is entitled to a reasonable sum for the use and enjoyment of the land.

(2) *Rates and taxes*

Unless the lease provides to the contrary, such payments fall on the tenant.

(3) *Waste*

Waste consists of a tenant altering the nature of the premises. There are a number of varieties of waste depending upon its degree and whether or not it is an act or an omission. A tenant for a fixed term is liable for voluntary and permissive waste. This means that the premises must be kept in proper repair and the tenant will be liable for causing damage or failing to maintain the demised premises. A periodic tenant is liable for voluntary waste only, but must maintain the property in a 'tenant like manner' *(Warren v Keen [1954] 1 QB 15)*.

(B) 'Usual Covenants'

If the parties to an agreement for a lease agree the bare essentials such as rent, length of term etc. but the agreement contains no other express provisions, it is an implied term of the agreement that the lease will contain the 'usual covenants'. They are similar to the implied covenants with the addition of a forfeiture clause for breach of the tenant's covenants, and an undertaking by the tenant to repair the demised premises also allowing the landlord to enter the premises to view the state of repair. Additional covenants can also be usual depending upon the type of premises, the purpose for which they are let and the geographical location *(Flexman v Corbett [1930] 1 Ch 672; Chester v Buckingham Travel Ltd [1981] 1 All ER 386)*.

(C) Express Covenants

Modern day leases tend to centre around express covenants dealing specifically with the obligations of the parties. It is proposed to look at a number of covenants which are commonly found in leases.

(a) Rent

This is the consideration given by the tenant for exclusive possession of the demised premises. The amount must be certain or capable of being ascertained with certainty. Rent is payable in arrears unless it is indicated to the contrary in the lease, as is common. A rack rent is the full annual value of the premises at the start of the lease. A ground rent is a smaller figure where the difference has been capitalised as a premium by the landlord at the beginning of the lease. Many long leases which qualify for enfranchisement, under the Leasehold Reform Act 1967, were granted in this manner. The destruction of the demised premises, or other events preventing the tenant from enjoying the property, do not extinguish the liability of the tenant to pay rent. This concept is derived from the absolute nature of contractual obligations. In *Paradine v Jane [1647] Alleyn 26* a tenant was held liable to pay 3 years' arrears of rent to his landlord, despite the fact that his cottage had been set on fire by soldiers and become uninhabitable during the civil war. It was established in *National Carriers v Panalpina [Northern] Ltd [1981] AC 675* (see also Chapter 2) that the doctrine of frustration can apply to leases in appropriate circumstances.

Remedies of the Landlord for Non-payment of Rent by the Tenant

(1) *Action for arrears*
By section 19 Limitation Act 1980, the action must be brought within 6 years from the date it fell due, otherwise it will be statute barred.

(2) *Distress*
This is a remedy which allows a landlord to recover rent by seizing goods found on the premises to pay off rent arrears. It does not require the landlord to proceed through the judicial process. If within 5 days of the goods being seized the rent remains unpaid, the goods may be sold to pay off rent arrears. The landlord may distrain himself. If he does not, he must employ a certificated bailiff and a company landlord must always do so by statute. There are considerable problems involved in executing this process, not least being the validity of the distress and also privileged goods. These are items which are exempt from the process and include loose money, perishable goods, clothing, tools of the tenant's trade and fixtures. Third parties with goods on the demised premises are partially protected by the Law of Distress Amendment Act 1908 (see *Salford Van Hire [Contracts] Ltd* v *Bocholt Developments Ltd [1995] 2 EGLR 50* for an illustration of the problems relating to distress and third party goods).

(3) *Forfeiture*
This is the right of the landlord to bring the lease to an end and re-enter the demised premises. It is sometimes called a proviso for re-entry. The courts tend to lean against such clauses and insist that forfeiture is not normally an option for the landlord unless the lease contains a forfeiture clause permitting the landlord to instigate this procedure on the happening of a particular event(s). If the landlord exercises forfeiture, he can in theory either:

(i)　re-enter on to the demised premises;
(ii) commence possession proceedings against the tenant.

For all practical purposes, especially where the property is a residential one which is occupied, only (ii) above is an option and the landlord must bring proceedings for possession. In practice, where the premises are let as a dwelling it is unlawful to enforce forfeiture, other than by court proceedings, while any person is lawfully residing on the premises. This right of re-entry, as it is sometimes called, may be held to be reserved if the tenant's covenants are expressed in the form of conditions. Before that can be the case, expressions such as 'upon condition that' or 'provided always' need to be used. More commonly, it will arise upon the happening of an event giving rise to forfeiture.

At common law a landlord had to make a formal demand of the tenant for any monies owing, but the majority of forfeiture clauses dispense with the need for the landlord to make the demand. If at least 6 months' rent is in arrears, the Common Law Procedure Act 1852 saves the landlord from making such a demand. There is no requirement in forfeiture proceedings for non-payment of rent that the landlord serve a notice on the tenant under section 146 of the Law of Property Act 1925. Forfeiture of the lease brings the landlord/tenant relationship between the parties to an end and any underleases are also determined (see section 4.27). A tenant can apply for relief to the High Court or County Court depending upon where the proceedings were commenced. This must be sought and granted before the order is enforced.

(b) Rent Review

It is common practice, in leases of commercial premises, for the lease to provide that the level of rent payable by the tenant be reviewed at prescribed intervals to counteract the effects of inflation. On review, if the reviewed rent is a higher figure than the current level of rent, the rent provision will be replaced by the higher sum. If not, the former sum will be payable. In practice the vast majority of such clauses have been 'upwards only' not allowing for the revision of the rent below the initial rent payable. The form of these clauses and the review periods vary from lease to lease. Five years is a common period but it is not unusual to find shorter periods. One issue which has been of importance in rent review cases for many years is whether or not a landlord will lose his right to a review of the rent if the timetable stated in the rent review clause is not adhered to. The House of Lords' decision in *United Scientific Holdings* v *Burnley BC* (see *Metrolands Investments Ltd* v *J H Dewhurst Ltd [1986] 3 All ER 659*) held that there is a strong presumption that time is not of the essence in such circumstances and late service of the appropriate documentation will not deprive the landlord of his right to a review. In *United Scientific Holdings* the landlord served the appropriate notice 2 months after the last date for service under the rent review timetable but was entitled to a review. Time will only be of the essence if the lease provides expressly to that effect, if there is some indication in the lease that time is of the essence or there is some indication from the surrounding circumstances that time must be of the essence, because the rent review procedures are clearly interrelated to some other issue such as exercising a break clause or an option under the lease.

(c) Repair

Most leases contain express repairing covenants imposing obligations on the landlord, tenant or both parties. If there is no such covenant then, subject to the law of waste and the limited circumstances in which a landlord impliedly agrees to repair (see earlier in this section), neither party is liable for repairs. Repairing covenants come in many forms and are literally construed. Often these covenants contain an exception for 'fair wear and tear' exonerating the tenant from disrepair which has accrued by normal use and the elements. However repairs may be required to prevent the consequences originally flowing from fair wear and tear producing disrepair which wear and tear would not produce. Landlords may seek to recover the cost of repairing obligations from the tenant by means of a service charge (see below). Repair means the replacement of subsisting parts of the premises but not actual improvements to the property itself otherwise a landlord could end up with a building quite different from that originally let. In *Brew Brothers* v *Snax Ltd [1970] 1 All ER 587* a covenant imposing an obligation to put new and different foundations into a property was deemed not to be a repairing covenant, while in *Lurcott* v *Wakely [1911] 1 KB 905* a wall of a house had fallen into such a state that it needed rebuilding. This was considered to be a repair. The standard of repair required will vary from covenant to covenant, but the general rule was stated in *Proudfoot* v *Hart [1890] 25 QBD 42* as being such repair, as having regard to the age, character and locality of the property, would make it reasonably fit for the occupation of a reasonably minded tenant of the class who would be likely to take it. The standard of repair required by a repairing covenant is construed by the standard prevailing at the commencement of the lease and not the end (see *Calthorpe* v *McOscar [1924] 1 KB 716*).

Remedies

Landlord's Remedy for Tenant's Breach of Repairing Covenant

The landlord's claim will be for

(1) damages for breach of covenant; and/or
(2) forfeiture.

Damages

This will be the cost of repairs. At common law, if an action was brought by the landlord after the lease had ended, the amount recoverable was based on the tenant's covenant to yield up the property in repair. By section 18 Landlord and Tenant Act 1927, the amount recoverable by the landlord must not exceed the diminution in value of the reversion. A landlord who has reserved the right to do so in the lease can effect the repairs and charge the tenant for them. One particular statutory provision is of importance here. This is the Leasehold Property (Repairs) Act 1938, which has application where the landlord is proceeding for damages or forfeiture and the lease was originally granted for 7 years or more and has at least 3 years remaining on it. In such a case the landlord cannot proceed without first serving on the tenant a notice in prescribed form that complies with section 146 Law of Property Act 1925. Such a notice will contain the following:

(1) the nature of the breach alleged;
(2) a requirement for the tenant to remedy the breach (if capable of being remedied) – see *Expert Clothing Services and Sales* v *Hillgate House [1985] 2 All ER 998*;
(3) a requirement for the lessee to pay compensation in money for the breach (if the landlord requires it).

In circumstances where the 1938 Act applies, the landlord's notice must inform the tenant of his right to serve a counter notice within 28 days, claiming the benefit of the Act. The landlord will only be able to proceed further if he obtains leave from the court, which will only be granted in fairly narrow circumstances as follows:

(1) the value of the reversion has been diminished;
(2) immediate repair to the demised premises is required;
(3) repair is necessary to protect another occupier;
(4) the cost of immediate repair is small compared with that which is likely in the future;
(5) it is just and equitable to grant leave.

Tenant's Remedies for Landlord's Breach of Repairing Covenant

Liability will depend on the specific wording of the covenant. The landlord's liability will not arise until he has notice of the defect or knowlege of it. Most leases will have an express provision whereby the landlord may enter the premises to view the state of repair. Costs incurred in carrying out repairs are debts and not damages.

(1) *Damages*
This will represent such compensation as will restore the tenant to the original position had he not suffered the wrong complained of. It will be the difference between the premises in their present state and the premises if the landlord had carried out his obligations. It includes the cost of alternative accommodation and any repairs paid for by the tenant. It can also include compensation for living in unpleasant surroundings. The tenant may commence proceedings in the civil courts, or instead may withhold rent and then if sued may set off the landlord's claim in respect of non-payment.

(2) *Specific performance*
This may be appropriate in the case of a clear breach. The maxims of equity will apply. This remedy is not available to a landlord where the tenant is in default (*Hill* v *Barclay [1816] 16 Ves 402*).

(3) *Self-help*
The tenant must give the landlord notice. At common law, a tenant who carries out repairs may recoup himself out of future rents for the money spent. It only applies to such proportion of the tenant's expenditure as is reasonable (see generally *Lee-Parker* v *Izzet [1971] 2 All ER 800*).

(d) Alterations and Improvements

It is common to insert in a lease an express covenant which prohibits alterations to the demised premises. An alteration is a change in the actual fabric of the demised premises, such as converting a house into flats or subdividing existing rooms (*Viscount Chelsea* v *Muscatt [1990] 2 EGLR 48*). This amounts to a change in the form, structure or constitution of the building. A change in appearance, on its own, will not suffice if it does not affect the fabric. Covenants prohibiting alterations/improvements may be either absolute or qualified. An absolute covenant is a complete prohibition. A qualified one is where the landlord's consent is required before the appropriate changes can be made. Any improvement to the demised premises will normally be treated as an alteration and be covered by the appropriate statutory provisions relating to alterations. In *Woolworth & Co* v *Lambert [1937] Ch 37*, where a tenant wished to convert two shops held under separate leases into one shop, it was confirmed that an improvement need not necessarily add to the value of the demised premises. The question as to whether or not an improvement has been carried out has to be considered from the tenant's point of view and not that of the landlord. The operation of covenants relating to alterations is governed by section 19[2] of the Landlord and Tenant Act 1927.

If the covenant is absolute, section 19[2] does not apply and if the covenant is broken, the landlord may forfeit the lease or compel the tenant to reinstate the premises unless he has waived his rights (*Viscount Chelsea* v *Muscatt* – see above). If the covenant is qualified, it is deemed to be subject to a proviso that consent should not be unduly withheld. If the covenant is qualified but the alteration is not an improvement, section 19[2] does not apply. In such a case the tenant can only make the changes if the landlord gives consent. Where there is a qualified covenant and the alteration is an improvement, consent must not be unreasonably withheld. The onus of proving that the landlord has unreasonably refused consent is on the tenant. In such circumstances, the landlord can demand payment of a reasonable sum in respect of any lessening in the value of the premises or neighbouring premises belonging to the landlord and, where the improvement does not add to the letting value of the demised premises, an undertaking to reinstate the premises to their former condition at the end of the lease. See generally *Central Estates [Belgravia] Ltd* v *Woolgar [1972] 3 All ER 610*.

(e) User

If there are no restrictions as to use in the lease, the tenant may use the premises as desired, subject to the general law and in particular compliance with planning restrictions and Building Regulations. Nowadays, use covenants tend to restrict the premises to a particular use or prohibit certain specific uses. Often such covenants are linked to a covenant whereby the tenant cannot apply for planning permission without the landlord's consent. Section 19[3] of the Landlord and Tenant Act 1927 applies to user covenants. If the covenant is absolute, the Act does not apply nor does it apply if the covenant is a qualified one and the change of use involves structural alterations to the demised premises. If structural alterations are not involved, the landlord cannot charge a fee for giving his consent if the covenant is a qualified one, but there is no proviso that consent must not be unreasonably withheld.

(f) Assignment/Sub-letting

An assignment of a lease, which takes place when the tenant transfers his rights in the demised premises to another tenant for the remainder of the term of the lease, must be distinguished from a sub or under letting, which arises where a tenant of the demised premises retains the estate in land but lets the whole or part of the premises to another tenant. In such circumstances the sub-letting must be for a period less that the initial grant. Where a tenant attempts to sub-let for a period equal to or more than the unexpired term of the tenant's lease, this operates as an assignment of the lease.

Formalities

For an effective assignment to come about, the assignment must be made in the form of a deed. This rule applies equally to fixed term leases of 3 years of less which come within the scope of section 54[2] Law of Property Act 1925 and also to periodic tenancies. The formalities required in connection with a sub-letting are the same as in the case of the initial grant of a lease. This can include a periodic tenant granting a sub-lease for a specific term of years (see section 4.24).

Absolute and Qualified Covenants

If the lease is silent as to assignment and/or sub-letting, a tenant is free to effect these dispositions. Most contemporary commercial leases deal with the issue by inserting provisions in the lease, restricting such transactions in an attempt to ensure that undesirable tenants do not obtain use of the demised premises. Much depends upon the wording of the covenant, which will be construed according to the *contra proferentam* principle. If the assignment is an involuntary one, which takes place through operation of law, such as the death or bankruptcy of a tenant, this will not amount to the breach of a covenant against assignment. If the covenant is an absolute one, but the tenant disposes of his estate, the transaction will be effective to vest the legal estate in the new tenant or sub-tenant as appropriate but, so long as there is a forfeiture clause in the lease, the landlord will have the right to instigate forfeiture proceedings. Any landlord may waive his rights and allow alienation to take effect. The notice under section 146 of the Law of Property Act 1925 has to be served on the new tenant.

If the covenant is a qualified one, a number of statutory provisions govern the giving of consent by the landlord. By section 144 of the Law of Property Act 1925, a landlord cannot demand payment for giving his consent nor can he refuse consent on the grounds of colour, race, nationality or gender of the proposed tenant. Section 19[1] of the Landlord and Tenant Act 1927 states that in the case of a qualified covenant, consent to assign or sub-let must not be unreasonably withheld (note the changes made by section 1a of this provision by the Landlord and Tenant (Covenants) Act 1995). Section 19 [1] is frequently expressly stated in the lease. Irrespective of whether the landlord's actions are reasonable or not, the tenant must first ask the landlord for consent. If the landlord then refuses the tenant, either the tenant seeks a declaration, or takes a chance and goes ahead with the assignment/sub-letting. There is a considerable amount of case law dealing with what is reasonable and what is not in these circumstances.

The two factors of concern to the landlord should be the 'quality' of the proposed tenant and the proposed use of the premises. In *Parker v Boggon [1947] KB 346* there was deemed to be an unreasonable withholding of consent because the proposed assignee had diplomatic immunity against legal proceedings, while in *Bates v Donaldson [1896] 2 QB 241* the landlord refused consent because he wanted the demised premises for himself. Examples of reasonable refusals are *Pimms v Tallow Chandlers [1964] 2 QB 547* where the proposed assignee wanted to exploit the lease to obtain participation in the landlord's future development of the property and *Lee v K Carter [1949] 1 KB 85* where an assignment would allow the assignee to have Rent Act protection of the property not available to the assignor (see section 4.28). A very useful provision which comes to the aid of tenants is to be found in the Landlord and Tenant Act 1988. This provides that a landlord must act promptly with any application for consent, and sets out a timetable for the matter to be dealt with. Failure to adhere to this could result in an action for damages for breach of statutory duty. One device which assists landlords in assignment/sub-letting cases is the use of a so-called *'Bocardo'* clause (*Bocardo Sa v S & M Hotels Ltd*

[1979] 3 All ER 737). This is where the lease provides that the tenant must offer to surrender the tenancy as a precondition to any dealing, whether assignment or sub-letting. If the landlord does not approve of the identity of the proposed assignee, he can accept a surrender of the lease. Such a provision is not invalidated by section 19[1] of the 1927 Act.

(g) Options

An option is a right or opportunity which a tenant may exercise under a lease. Obvious examples are options to renew the lease, to determine the letting or to purchase the landlord's reversion. An option is a privilege and is usually dependent upon the tenant complying with all the covenants in the lease. Where a tenant failed to observe a covenant to repaint the demised premises at regular intervals, the option to renew the lease was lost (see *West Country Cleaners [Falmouth] Ltd* v *Saly [1966] 3 All ER 210*). If the breach is spent, the option might not be lost, as in *Bass Holdings Ltd* v *Morton Music Ltd [1987] 3 WLR 543* where the tenant had twice withheld rent in the past but owed none at the end of the lease.

(h) Service Charges

These are commonly found in lettings of flats. They cover items such as heating, lighting and other services provided by the landlord. To prevent the problem of overcharging, the Landlord and Tenant Acts 1985 and 1987 have limited the landlord's right to recover only reasonable sums incurred, and to require the landlord to prepare estimates and necessary details. In certain cases, tenants must be consulted.

4.26   Enforceability of Covenants in Leases

An established rule in connection with leases has been that by means of privity of contract, an original tenant may be sued for a sum of money due under a lease which has long since been assigned. In a lease the relationship of landlord and tenant exists between the owner of the freehold reversion for the time being and the owner of the lease for the time being. Where the parties hold the demised premises directly as landlord and tenant, there is said to be privity of estate between them. Where privity of estate exists, the landlord is liable to the tenant on those covenants that 'touch and concern' the land and vice versa. In practice, all covenants regularly found in leases come into this category. These are the covenants that regulate the position between landlord and tenant.

The Landlord and Tenant [Covenants] Act 1995 applies to leases commencing after January 1st 1996. In future, the landlord will not be able to sue the original tenant in respect of default by an assignee. All covenants entered into by landlord and tenant will pass to assignees, except personal ones. As a safeguard, a landlord can prescribe in advance either the circumstances in which he will consent to an assignment or any conditions to which consent shall be subject. This is made clear by the new section 1a of the Landlord and Tenant Act 1927 section 19. If consent is subsequently refused on the pre-scribed ground or is given subject to a prescribed condition, the landlord shall not be regarded as having unreasonably withheld consent.

4.27   Termination of Leases at Common Law

(a) Effluxion of Time

A fixed term lease will automatically determine at the end of the stipulated period. No notice is required at common law. Various statutes give qualify-ing tenants the right to a new lease or to remain in possession of the demised premises (see section 4.28).

(b) Break Clause

Fixed term commercial leases may allow either party to terminate the letting at a particular time or on the happening of a particular event. Such a provision is a privilege and there must be exact compliance with the clause to obtain the benefit of it.

(c) Notice to Quit

This is the conventional method by which a periodic tenancy is determined. Unless the parties have agreed to the contrary, a period of notice equal in length to the duration of the tenancy must be served unless it is a statutory exception to the normal rules. The notice served by either party must expire at the end of a period of the tenancy.

(d) Service Tenancies

A letting of accommodation granted on the basis that the tenant is employed by the landlord will cease when the employment of the tenant ceases.

(e) Merger

If the leaseholder acquires the reversion to the lease, the estates will merge and the letting will come to an end at common law.

(f) Surrender

This arises where the tenant gives up his interest in the demised premises to his immediate landlord. The surrender may be express, in which case a formal deed will be used, or it can arise by operation of law where the tenant does some act which is inconsistent with the continued existence of the tenancy and the landlord concurs. The giving up of possession by the tenant and the return of the keys to the landlord is a classic example.

(g) Frustration

In theory, at least, the doctrine does apply to leases, although in the *Panalpina* case (see Chapter 3), where the only access road to the demised premises was closed by the local authority for 18 months, the House of Lords took the view that this was insufficent to frustrate a 10 year fixed term lease.

(h) Disclaimer

This tends to occur where the tenant is bankrupt or, in the case of a company tenant, the organisation is in the process of winding up. If the lease is unsaleable or likely to give rise to a liability to pay more money, the trustee or liquidator, as appropriate, will generally wish to disclaim.

(i) Forfeiture

Reference has been made earlier to the circumstances where a landlord is entitled to forfeit a lease (*Central Estates [Belgravia]* v *Woolgar [1972] 3 All ER 610*). Such a right of entry is only implied into a lease where the 'usual covenants' apply in the case of an open contract. In all other cases, before the right of re-entry can be exercised the lease must expressly contain a forfeiture clause. If the landlord (or more likely his agent) does some unequivocal act which acknowledges the continuation of the tenancy, where he is aware of the breach by the tenant he will have 'waived' his right to forfeit. The landlord must have knowledge of the breach. An unqualified demand for rent falling due after the date of the breach will be an implied waiver (*Blackstone Ltd* v *Burnetts [West End] Ltd [1973] 3 All ER 782*).

4.28   The Major Statutory Provisions Affecting Leaseholds

General

One particular characteristic of the law of Landlord and Tenant in the Twentieth Century has been the additional 'gloss' of detailed statutory provisions which have modified the common law rules where the tenant satisfies certain qualifying conditions. These provisions have provided tenants with security of tenure (the right to a new lease or to stay in possession of the demised premises at the end of the lease), regulation of rent in respect of certain residential lettings and compensation for improvements to the demised premises. These rights emerged initially with agricultural lettings in the Nineteenth Century but spread in the Twentieth Century to include residential and business leases. Since the early 1980s their importance has been substantially diminished as political developments have led to the erosion, to a very large extent, of these benefits.

(a) Business Tenancies

Tenants of business premises may be entitled to:

(1) security of tenure (Landlord and Tenant Act 1954 part 2);
(2) compensation for improvements (Landlord and Tenant Act 1954 part 3).

Security of Tenure

Part 2 of the 1954 Act gives a *prima faciae* right to the grant of a new tenancy to a tenant who occupies premises for the purposes of a business or for that and other purposes. Part 2 is based on the notion that a business tenant stands to lose any goodwill which has been built up and much of the value of the equipment/stock if forced to leave at the end of the term. The Act reflects that the process of renewal should not in the majority of cases require court procedure to be followed.

Qualifying conditions
Before an occupier can obtain the advantage of part 2, the following must be satisfied:

(1) There must be a tenancy. The letting may be a fixed term or periodic tenancy. Licences and tenancies at will are excluded.
(2) The tenant must be in occupation. This is a question of fact and degree. There must be at least a thread of continuity. A sub-tenant can obtain the advantage of the Act.
(3) The tenant must occupy the premises for the purposes of a business. This covers a wide range of activities and has included any trade, occupation or profession in the ordinary meaning of those words. A mere casual user is not enough nor is an activity which does not realise a commercial profit. A tennis club, a hospital and a laboratory have been deemed to come within the definition (*Addiscombe Garden Estates* v *Crabbe [1958] 1 QB 513; Hills [Patents] Ltd* v *University College Hospital [1956] 1 QB 90*).

Exceptions to the Act
If the business is being operated on an illegal or immoral basis the Act will not apply. A tenant who has been in breach of covenant will not obtain the benefit of the legislation unless the landlord has acquiesced in its continuance. There are also certain tenancies which are expressly excluded from the Act:

1. *Residential lettings*
    These are excluded from part 2 of the Act. If any business user is simply incidental to the residential user and the letting is governed by residential statutory provisions, the relevant residential code will apply (Rent Act 1977 or Housing Act 1988). If the premises were initially let for residential purposes and then a significant business user came about, the tenancy is brought into part 2 of the 1954 Act.

2. *Agricultural holdings*
    This includes a letting under the Agricultural Holdings Act 1986 and a Farm Business Tenancy under the Agricultural Tenancies Act 1995.

3. *Mining leases*
    These are specifically excluded from the legislation. In *O'Callaghan* v *Elliot [1966] 1 QB 601* a tenant who had the right to extract sand and gravel fell outside the scope of the Act.

4. *Licensed premises*
    Until 1989, public houses selling alcohol were excluded from the provisions of part 2. Premises which had a licence to sell alcohol but that sale was ancillary to some other purpose, such as a club, came within the scope of the Act. Licensed premises now come completely within the scope of the legislation.

5. *Tenancy at will*
    An appropriately drafted tenancy at will of business premises is excluded from the benefits of the Act.

6. *Service tenancies*
    To be excluded, the lease must be created by an instrument in writing which states the purpose for which the tenancy was granted.

7. *Short tenancies*
    Tenancies for 6 months or less are excluded from the Act unless the letting can be extended for more than 6 months or the tenant and any predecessor in title have been in possession carrying on a business for at least 12 months.

8. *'Contracting out' provisions*
    On a joint application by the parties, before the initial grant of the lease, the parties may enter into an agreement that part 2 shall not apply. Such an agreement has to be sanctioned by the County Court.

Notices to Quit and Time Periods

Business Tenancies to which the Act applies do not come to an end by Notice to quit given by the landlord or by effluxion of time. They must be terminated in accordance with the Act. A relevant letting will continue after the relevant term date until one of the following takes place:

(1) landlord serves notice under section 25 of the Act;
(2) tenant serves notice under section 26 of the Act;
(3) tenant gives notice to terminate a tenancy under section 27 of the Act and indicates that he does not want a new one.

A tenant who gives a valid notice to quit to the landlord, surrenders the lease or has the lease forfeited will not have any rights of continuation by part 2 of the Act.

The Court Application and the New Tenancy

In the vast majority of cases, agreement is reached without the need for the court's intervention. In the event of a failure to reach agreement, a court application may proceed. The new tenancy will be as agreed between the parties or, if the court determines it, the period that it thinks reasonable. The statutory lease will be for a maximum term of 14 years.

Terms of the new tenancy
If these cannot be agreed, they will be fixed by the court. Apart from length and rent, regard must be had to the terms of the current tenancy and 'all relevant circumstances'. In practice, the court will follow the terms of the current tenancy unless there is a good reason for not doing so. The decision in *O'May* v *City of London Real Property Co Ltd [1983] 2 AC 726* enshrines this principle. The rent will be that which the parties could command if let in the open market but disregarding:

(a) any effect on the rent of the fact that the tenant or his predecessors in title have been in occupation;
(b) any goodwill attaching to the holding on account of the tenant's business;
(c) any improvements made under the current tenancy.

Surveyors will give evidence as to rentals based on comparables. Provisions exist for fixing an interim rent.

Grounds of Opposition

These are governed by section 30 of the 1954 Act and are as follows:

(1) *Repair, section [30] 1a*
This is a discretionary ground and it must be a serious breach.

(2) *Rent, section [30] 1b*
The delay in paying rent must be persistent and it is not enough to show that there are arrears outstanding. This is also a discretionary ground (see *Hurstfell Ltd* v *Leicester Square Property Co [1988] 37 EG 109*).

(3) *Other substantial breaches of covenant, section [30] 1c*
This discretionary ground is based on fact and the landlord's interest must be shown to be prejudiced. Illegal user could well come into this category, as could breaches of an enforcement notice (see Chapter 5, section 5.7) which would be likely to continue in the event of a new letting.

(4) *Suitable alternative accommodation offered by the landlord, section [30] 1d*
The accommodation must be just as good as that at the present. This is a mandatory ground and if the landlord establishes it, the ground of opposition will be sustained.

(5) *Dispositions of the whole estate, section [30] 1e*
In this case the tenant is, in relation to the landlord, a sub-tenant of part of the property originally let and the landlord can realise a better rent by reletting the property as a whole. The total rents must be substantially higher and all the lettings involved must terminate at the same time.

(6) *Landlord requires possession to demolish or reconstruct the premises, section [30] 1f*
This is the most litigated of the grounds and requires several ingredients to be present to succeed. The landlord must show the relevant intention and that the works cannot be carried out without obtaining possession of the building. In practice, the landlord must show that the scheme is commercially viable and he has the means to carry it through together with the necessary statutory consents (planning permission/building regulations approval etc.). The landlord must also show that he could not reasonably carry out his work of demolition or reconstruction without obtaining possession of the holding. If the landlord has reserved a right under the lease to enter the premises and carry out works/improvements, it is unlikely that the court will uphold the ground of opposition (see *Betty's Cafes Ltd* v *Phillips Furnishing Stores Ltd [1959] AC 20; Heath* v *Drown [1973] AC 498*).

(7) *Landlord intends to use for own business/residence, section [30] 1g*
As in the case of ground 6 above, the burden is on the landlord to establish the necessary intention at the time of the hearing. It is possible to occupy through an agent or manager. Occupation must be for

more than a minimal period and it will assist the landlord if he gives an undertaking to the court that he will occupy. By section 30[2] of the Act, the landlord cannot rely upon this ground if his own interest has been purchased or created less than 5 years before 'the termination of the current tenancy'.

Compensation Provisions

Grounds 1, 2 and 3 are discretionary, and even if proved by the landlord, the court has a final discretion to determine whether or not a new tenancy be granted. Ground 4 operates within narrow limits. If a tenant is unable to obtain a new tenancy because the landlord can establish grounds 5, 6 or 7 he is entitled to compensation for disturbance. The amount payable is the rateable value of the premises. If the business has been carried on at the premises, whether by himself or a predecessor for more than 14 years, the compensation will be twice the rateable value of the premises.

Compensation for Improvements

Part 1 of the Landlord and Tenant Act 1927, as amended by the Landlord and Tenant Act 1954, governs compensation to a tenant for improvements carried out to the demised premises. The premises must be used for trade, business or professional purposes. Agricultural holdings, mining leases and service tenancies are specifically excluded. The improvements must add to the letting value of the holding at the termination of the tenancy. It does not apply to fixtures which the tenant is by law entitled to remove, or to improvements which a tenant is contractually bound to carry out.

The tenant must inform the landlord of his proposals and give relevant details. If the landlord objects, the tenant needs a certificate from the County Court indicating that the improvement is a proper one. The certificate will not be given if the landlord proves he has offered to carry out the improvements himself. The tenant must have completed the improvement within the time agreed with the landlord or as fixed by the court, while the claim for compensation must be made within 3 months of the act determining the tenancy.

(b) Residential Lettings

Introduction

From 1915 to 1977, legislation was enacted which gave qualifying residential tenants in the private sector a number of benefits. These included imposing controls over the maximum amount of rent charged, giving tenants security of tenure of the demised premises and allowing the tenancy to be passed on to a statutory tenant at the end of the term. From 1980 onwards a distinct change of policy emerged. Beginning with the Housing Act 1980 and developed by the Housing Act 1988, it became impossible to let in the private residential sector on the basis of the Rent Acts. Regulation of rent and security of tenure at the end of the letting became relics from the past. From 1989 it has only been possible to create assured or assured shorthold tenancies in this sector, while since the Housing Act 1996 assured tenancies have for all practical purposes become assured shorthold lettings (see below).

Rent Acts

The Rent Act 1977 was the last in a series of Acts allowing qualifying tenants to be 'protected' in relation to:

(1) Security of tenure – the right is to hold over in possession of the house or flat as a 'statutory tenant' at the end of the fixed term or where notice is given by the landlord under a periodic tenancy.
(2) Registration of a 'fair rent' which will become the maximum rent recoverable under the letting.

Tenants enjoying Rent Act protection before 1989 are still subject to that legislation. Such lettings are still of significance and will be into the Twenty First Century. To obtain the benefit of the legislation, the occupier had to be a tenant of premises let as a separate dwelling, paying a rent of at least two-thirds the rateable value of the premises. After the tenant's original contractual tenancy comes to an end, a statutory tenancy arises in favour of the occupying tenant. On the death of the tenant, the letting may be passed on to a surviving spouse or member of the family. The Housing Act 1988 abolished the right of a family member to succeed to the tenancy but preserves the right of a spouse to have the tenancy passed on to them, even if the original tenant dies after 1989. There are a number of mandatory and discretionary grounds for possession of the demised premises.

Housing Acts (mainly Housing Act 1988)

Residential lettings in the private sector centre around:

(1) Assured Shorthold Tenancies;
(2) Assured Tenancies.

(1) *Assured Shorthold Tenancies*
These are fixed term tenancies, now of any length, where the landlord can recover possession at the end of the tenancy and the rent which is

agreed with the tenant is recoverable. There is no security of tenure. If the tenant does consider the rent excessive, an application can be made to a Rent Assessment Committee to modify it.

(2) *Assured Tenancies*

The Housing Act 1988 created a new type of tenancy known as an 'Assured Tenancy'. This enabled the landlord to recover a market rent but gave some security of tenure to the tenant. An assured tenant may only be removed if the landlord can prove a statutory ground for possession. These are more numerous than the Rent Act grounds. Since the enactment of part 3 of the Housing Act 1996, any assured tenancy is to be an assured shorthold tenancy unless the parties otherwise agree. The consequence of this is that, under the current housing legislation, security of tenure is all but abolished.

Leasehold Enfranchisement

The Leasehold Reform Act 1967 allows a tenant holding under a long lease and at a low rent either to purchase the freehold (enfranchisement) or to the grant of an extended lease for a period of 50 years. The Act was passed to circumvent the problems caused to leaseholders where the original tenant had entered into the lease paying a premium and a ground rent to the landlord. At the end of the lease, a tenant could easily end up with little in the way of a saleable asset. To obtain the benefit of the Act, the tenant must have a long tenancy granted originally for a term exceeding 21 years and be paying a rent of less than two-thirds of the Rateable Value. The lease must be of a house which the tenant occupies as a main residence. This means residence for the last 3 years or for periods amounting to 3 years in the last 10 years. The freehold price will be as agreed between the parties, or as reached by the Leasehold Valuation Panel if the price cannot be agreed. The basis of the valuation for the purchase of the freehold is that the leaseholder is morally entitled to the ownership of the builing while the freeholder has similar rights to the ownership of the land. Tenants of flats have been given similar rights by the Housing and Urban Development Act 1993. In that case the benefit is either enfranchisement or an extended lease of 90 years to the existing term which is renewable.

(c) Agricultural Tenancies

For approximately the last 50 years, tenant farmers have been governed by the philosophy enshrined in the Agricultural Holdings Act 1948 (AHA). The AHA gave tenant farmers security of tenure for life so long as they worked the land properly and were financially sound. The Act also allowed tenants to claim compensation for improvements to the demised premises. In 1976 the Agriculture (Miscellaneous Provisions) Act extended lifetime security of tenure to two generations of successors. This Act was repealed in 1984 but tenancies granted between 1977 and 1984 are still subject to the 1984 Act provisions.

Under the AHAs, where succession to the lease is sought a surviving close relative (usually spouse) must apply to the Agricultural Lands Tribunal (ALT) within 3 months of the death of the former tenant. The applicant must show that for 5 out of the last 7 years their main income has been derived from agriculture. The last Agricultural Holdings Act was enacted in 1986 which, by and large, reverted back to the 1948 Act provisions. The AHAs have given security of tenure to tenancies of 2 years or more, in which case they continue from year to year, and to lettings for less than 1 year which are allowed to operate as yearly tenancies. Both types of tenancy continue indefinitely until terminated by notice to quit from the landlord. At least 12 months' notice must be given to the tenant who has a right to serve a counter notice within a month. The landlord's notice cannot take effect unless the landlord obtains the consent of the Agricultural Lands Tribunal. Consent will only be granted if one of a number of specific grounds is made out, and even then the ALT can refuse the landlord's notice if it considers it 'just and reasonable' in the circumstances.

The Agricultural Tenancies Act 1995

This Act created the concept of the 'Farm Business Tenancy'. The Act applies to agricultural lettings entered into after September 1st 1995. It is not possible now to create a letting which comes under the 1986 Act.

Under the Act the letting must be primarily agricultural but as long as that situation remains it will allow a tenant to diversify without the problem arising as to whether it is a business or agricultural tenancy. No security of tenure is given to the tenant. The letting continues on a year-to-year basis until notice is given. The landlord must still give the tenant at least 12 months' written notice. The parties can agree to have break clauses as in a commercial tenancy. They can also agree rent reviews. If they do not either party can demand a rent review every 3 years. The Agriculture (Maintenence, Repair and Insurance of Fixed Equipment) Regulations 1973, as amended, contain detailed provisions apportioning legal responsibility between landlord and tenant as regards building and other fixed equipment. These regulations do not apply to the new tenancies unless the parties specifically agree to incorporate them. This is a major difference between tenancies under this Act and the Agricultural Holdings legislation.

4.29   The Conveyancing Process

The major object of the 1925 property legislation was to try to simplify the process by which land is transferred. In England and Wales there have been two systems of conveyancing in operation since 1925:

1. *Where the title to the land is registered*
    The Land Registration Act 1925 introduced a national system of registration of land. By this Act, geographical areas of England and Wales were made, from time to time, areas of compulsory registration. The consequence of this designation was that the next occasion on which a freehold or long lease was transferred to a new purchaser, application had to be made by the new owner for registration of title. The process of registering the title is effected through the Land Registry in Plymouth but, because of the large number of applications involved, District Land Registries are to be found in most parts of England and Wales, dealing with applications for first registration of title. If the Land Registry is satisfied as to who owns the property it issues a Land Certificate. Once issued, the state, through the Registry, guarantees title (ownership) of the land/buildings in the name of the proprietors of the property on the Certificate.

2. *Where title to land is unregistered*
    In this case it is necessary for the purchaser to 'investigate title'. The consequence of that is having to prove that the vendor owns the estate, which is done by examining the previous documents of title relating to the property (title deeds). The current requirement is that the purchaser must check that the chain of ownership is at least satisfactory for the last 15 years. This is known as showing a good root of title. The 15 year period is the minimum which needs to be investigated. It may be considerably longer if there has been no transfer of the property for many years. The Registration of Title Order 1989 has now made all land in England and Wales within an area of compulsory registration. Therefore, all properties are now subject to the registered title system. The obligation to go through the process of first registration only arises on the first sale of the freehold or the grant of an appropriate lease. Consequently, it will be many years before each estate in land has a Land Certificate covering it. There have been recent initiatives to speed up the system (*Land Registry Rules 1997*).

5 Aspects of Public Law

5.1 Background

Those who work in areas related to landed property and the construction industry need to have an understanding of Public law. Public law is concerned with the state, public bodies, and the relationship between individuals and these organisations. One significant aspect is administrative law which attempts to regulate and control the government agencies which administer the legislative process. This is an expanding area of law which deals with applications for judicial review. This is a process whereby the courts scrutinise the manner in which a public body has acted when coming to an administrative decision. Such cases have increased significantly in recent years. This is law which is essentially statute based. Some aspects are products of the Nineteenth Century which have been developed into a more modern format, while others are of recent origin. Growing awareness of the problems which beset a highly industrialised society together with increased public interest in environmental matters have put these areas of law in the public eye more than ever before.

5.2 Local Government in England and Wales

Certain powers and responsibilities have been delegated by central government to local authorities. This is government on a regional basis formulated by a pattern of elected bodies for defined areas which are given responsibility for the provision of services and regulating administrative processes. Such authorities are corporate bodies whose powers are derived from statute. The essence of local government is that elected members formulate the policies in a particular subject area and these policies are carried out by officers of the authority who are given powers of decision making. Over the last 20 years there have been considerable attempts to reduce the influence of local government by central government appointing government agencies to take over responsibilities in areas which were previously in the domain of the authorities. Nevertheless, large areas of responsibility, such as housing, education, the town planning system and building control, are in the hands of local authorities, and their powers and importance should not be underestimated. The present system of local government in England and Wales dates from April 1st 1974 when the Local Government Act 1972 became effective. This Act set up a two-tier system which recognised the County as the major administrative unit. Within the County areas, District Councils (sometimes called Borough Councils) were designated with responsibility for much day-to-day work, such as applications for planning permission and approvals under the Building Regulations.

As the 1972 Act was originally envisaged, six of the English County areas were designated as Metropolitan Counties. These comprised the large conurbations of the West Midlands, Greater Manchester, Tyne and Wear, South Yorkshire, West Yorkshire and Merseyside. The Districts within these counties are designated Metropolitan Districts. These were set up with constitutions similar to those of other Districts but with extended functions. The Local Government Act 1985 abolished the Metropolitan County Councils, leaving their District equivalents as the only tier of local government in these areas. Also abolished by the 1985 Act was the Greater London Council. Local government in London is administered by the 32 London Borough Councils which since 1986 have been the only tier of government in the London area, creating a similar predicament to the Metropolitan areas in the regions. In London, there has been considerable criticism that there is no co-ordinating authority having overall control. It appears that the capital will soon have its own mayor, similar to other capitals in Europe.

Local authority business is conducted through meetings and rules are laid down as to their calling and conduct. Much work is delegated to committees who specialise in a particular matter, such as planning or housing. Membership of committees is fixed by the authority. There are two major types of control. The most effective, which come directly from central government, are financial in nature and relate to restrictions on borrowing and the withholding of grants. In certain situations the courts will interfere with the decision of a local authority which is wrong and rectify it. This used to be effected by the use of orders of the High Court, known as Prerogative Orders, but in recent years these procedures have been considerably developed by new statutory provisions and High Court rules which allow an 'aggrieved person' to make an application for a judicial review. This process allows an applicant to claim a declaration followed by an injunction in addition to a claim for damages. Leave of the court is required before the case can be brought, while the Divisional Court, which decides the case, is only concerned to see that the authority, or relevant public body under scrutiny, has come to its decision in a proper manner. It is not concerned with the actual merits of the case. In recent times many changes have taken place in the manner in which such government conducts its business. This has come about to a large extent because of changes in financing. Good examples include the restrictions on public sector housing projects and strict guidelines laid down as to the operation of 'direct labour' organisations.

The process initiated in London and the Metropolitan areas of having one tier of local government, on a unitary authority basis, spread in the late 1990s to Non-Metropolitan areas. The Local Government Commission for England began a process, in 1992, of investigating geographical areas of England and Wales and making recommendations as to the future of regional government in those areas. The process has now been extended to the whole of England and Wales. The result has been a tendency towards creating Unitary authorities but not in every case. In many areas the *status quo* of a two-tier system has been kept. In some areas the County Council has been abolished and its functions replaced by existing District Councils. Cleveland County Council is an example. In some instances an existing District Council has been given unitary status, while the other Districts in the same Non-Metropolitan area have retained their previous status and the status of the County Council has been retained. The city of Stoke-on-Trent comes into this category. In Wales, the two-tier system has been replaced by 21 Unitary Councils. Impending constitutional changes in England and Wales with the creation of a Welsh assembly will probably not affect the structure of local government significantly in the short term.

5.3   The Privatisation of Public Utilities

A significant development in the latter part of the Twentieth Century, which began in the 1980s and was developed in the 1990s, has been the denationalisation and privatisation of the former public utilities in the United Kingdom. As a consequence, the former statutory undertakers responsible for provision of services such as gas, electricity, water, sanitation and telecommunications etc. have now been replaced by large companies who are supposed to trade in the same way as any other large public company. Because of their special position, whereby a number of these organisations have a virtual complete monopoly, as in the case of water and gas provision, 'watchdog' bodies have been set up to monitor the duties and operation of the supply companies. Criticism has been made that the 'regulators', such as OFGAS (gas), OFWAT (water) etc. do not have enough powers and have too 'cosy' a relationship with their respective industries.

5.4   Highway Law

A highway is a strip of land over which the public at large has the right to pass and repass. It is a public right of way and as long as it satisfies the characteristics of a highway, it may encompass all types of passage from the least used footpath to the busiest road. The law relating to highways is mainly statute based but some common law provisions do apply. The principal Act is the Highways Act 1980. It is a highly practical subject whose principles are frequently invoked when construction works are being carried out or disputes arise in connection with liability in respect of repair and upkeep of rights of way. Responsibility for the upkeep of highways rests with the relevant 'Highway Authority' (HA) which is the County Council, Unitary Authority or Central Government itself (Highways Agency).

Creation of Highways

A highway may be created by

(a) Common law;
(b) Statute.

A new right of passage will be created by statute. Creation on a common law basis only becomes an issue where a right of way is being claimed as a highway, and consequently for public use, while others are claiming that it is a private right of way.

(a) Common Law

Three essentials are required:

1. *Dedication*
    There must be evidence that the landlowner intended to make over to the public a right of passage over his land (*animus dedicandi*). Dedication may be express or implied. If express, there will normally be a deed of dedication embodying an agreement entered into by the landowner with the highway authority providing for compensation to the freehold owner. Dedication will be implied if 20 years' open and uninterrupted user as of right can be proved. Implied dedication can be prevented by taking appropriate action, such as appropriate notices on the land; 'private property', 'no public right of way' or the highway authority is informed that the way does not have the status of a highway and sufficent reasons are put foward. The onus of proving lack of intention is on the person who seeks to deny rights to the public over the way.

2. *Fee Simple Owner*

The person dedicating the way must be the freeholder. This is because the person granting the right must be able to do so indefinitely.

3. *Acceptance*

There must be acceptance of the right of passage by the public at large. If the right of passage is limited to particular groups or classes of the population, such as one-legged men born in Birmingham, it will not be a highway. Dedication may exist subject to restrictions as to the method of user, such as 'pedestrians only' or 'cyclists only'.

(b) Statute

Legislation may bring about the creation of a highway. The Highways Act 1980 has particular importance here, regulating the several statutory methods involved.

Adoption, Maintenence and Repair

(A) *The vast majority of highways are 'maintainable at public expense'.* In such circumstances, it is the duty of the appropriate authority to maintain, repair and remove obstructions. This includes the following:

(a) Highways constructed before 1836 (the date on which the Highways Act 1835 came into operation). These are now known as 'ancient highways'.

(b) Those adopted under the procedure laid down in the 1835 Act or subsequent legislation.

Adoption means that the responsibility for the way has been taken over in terms of paving and providing sewers etc. It will take place in one of three circumstances:

(1) Section 36 of the Highways Act 1980 where the way was constructed by the highway authority or its predecessors.

(2) Section 37 of the Highways Act 1980 where the authority certifies that a newly dedicated way has been made up in a satisfactory manner.

(3) Section 38 of the Highways Act 1980 by agreement between a developer and the authority, in which case the road becomes adopted on completion of any stipulated works.

(B) *Highways maintainable by the Department of Transport.* Trunk roads come into this category. In practice, local highway authorities carry out the work on an agency basis.

(C) *Highways which are the responsibility of private individuals*. Obligations in this respect tend to arise by long user where a particular body or individual has carried out repairs in 'living memory'. Sometimes the obligation to repair passes with the land so that those in possession take over these obligations.

(D) *Highways for which no one is responsible for repair*. These 'Private Streets' are the responsibility of no one so far as ordinary repairs are concerned. Those persons whose property fronts on to the street (frontagers) may be liable for emergency repairs. Highway authorities have statutory powers to require the making up of private streets, in which case an authority can decide to carry out works and charge the cost to the frontagers. The procedure can be laborious and protracted, involving estimates and apportionment of cost on the basis of frontage to the street to be notified to owners of premises.

Accidents and the Highway Authority

Common Law

At common law, a highway authority owes a duty of care to prevent injury to the public when carrying out works of improvement or repair (*Haley* v *London Electricity Board [1965] AC 778*).

Statute

Although it has long been recognised that the highway authority is liable to a plaintiff who suffers injury on account of the authority's *Misfeasance* (negligently carrying out repairs or wrongfully maintaining the way), at one time they were not liable for *Nonfeasance* (where a person was injured because the authority had failed to carry out repairs which needed to be executed). Section 58 Highways Act 1980 provides a defence to such actions if it can be shown that the highway authority has taken such care as was reasonably required in the circumstances. This would take into account, *inter alia*, the character of the way, the amount of traffic expected to use it, the standard of repair and maintenance which a reasonable person would expect, whether the authority could be expected to know that the way was dangerous and whether any notices were displayed on the highway. A common sense attitude is taken in such cases. In *Whitting* v *Hillingdon LBC [1970] 114 Sol Jor 247* the highway authority was not liable where the plaintiff fell over a tree stump at the edge of a footpath. The path was inspected regularly and the defendants could not be expected to search for every conceivable danger.

Extinguishment and Diversion of Highways

It is a fundamental rule of highway law that 'once a highway always a highway'. Once dedicated, it can only be stopped or diverted by the exercise of statutory powers.

Normal Procedure

This is by application to the Magistrates Court by the highway authority, either because the way is unnecessary or the diversion will make it nearer or more convenient to the public. The application is made under section 116 of the Highways Act 1980. If the application is brought on behalf of a private individual, such as a developer, that person is responsible for the costs incurred. All interested parties must be informed and have the right to be heard in the Magistrates Court.

Rights in Relation to the Highway

The public
The right to use the highway is limited to passing and repassing over the highway. If these rights are exceeded, a person may find themselves a trespasser. The rule is to be interpreted in a reasonable manner, which would include such matters as properly parking a vehicle on the way for delivery purposes (*Rodgers* v *Ministry of Transport [1951] 1 All ER 634*).

Adjoining owners
The highway authority has rights over the 'skin' of the way but it is presumed that the owners of the land on each side of the way own the soil to the middle of the road. Statute has restricted many of the rights of private individuals in these matters, while giving public authorities extended powers to provide amenities and public services.

By section 154 Highways Act 1980, the highway authority can require a landowner to cut back trees and shrubs overhanging a highway and have dangerous trees or shrubs felled if they are likely to fall on to the highway (see also *The Hedgerow Regulations 1997* in this context).

Projections
An owner of land adjoining a highway is liable for injuries caused by the collapse of a natural projection (such as a tree) if he knew of the defect or ought to have known of it (*Brown* v *Flower [1947] 177 LT 281; Caminer* v *Northern and London Investment Trust [1951] AC 88*). In the case of an artificial projection (such as a lamp or hoarding) liability is strict (*Tarry* v *Ashton [1876] 1 QB 314*).

Interference with the highway

The rights of the public to pass and repass over the highway are protected by both the criminal law and the civil law. At common law, certain offences developed in relation to highways. These have been extended by the creation of statutory offences relating to such matters as digging up the highway, narrowing the way by erecting scaffolding and allowing structures adjoing a highway to become dangerous. These offences are to be found in the Highways Act 1980 (sections 131 to 137). Civil liability is based on the tort of nuisance.

Obstruction

In the tort of nuisance, unlawful interference with the highway can result in a civil action for damages, an injunction or both. To succeed, a plaintiff must show that the restriction is unreasonable in extent and duration, and not a temporary hindrance. In some cases the highway authority will issue licences (temporary permissions) to allow works to be carried out.

5.5   Provision of Sewers and Drains

This area of law used to come within the scope of Public Health legislation. Nowadays, it is better to deal with it in connection with Highway matters. The law is to be found in the Water Industry Act 1991 (WIA). Section 219 of that Act makes a distinction between sewers and drains:

Drains are pipes used for the drainage of one building or of any buildings or yards appurtenant to buildings within the same curtilage.

Sewers includes all sewers and drains used for the drainage of buildings and yards apurtenant to buildings.

Drains are a private responsibility but sewers may be public or private. Most sewers are public sewers and there is a duty on sewerage undertakers to provide such public sewers as are necessary for draining the area effectually. An occupier of premises in a sewerage undertaker's area has a right of connection to a public sewer. Similar rules apply to the owner of a private sewer within the sewerage undertaker's area.

5.6   Building Regulations

Background

The general purpose of the Building Regulations is to ensure that buildings are constructed so as to be safe and not a danger to the health and safety of occupants. They originate from the Public Health Act 1875 which enabled local authorities to make bye-laws for regulating the construction of buildings. These provisions were repealed and extended and eventually became based on model bye-laws issued by Central Government. In 1965 the first set of Building Regulations was issued. The current Regulations are the Building Regulations 1991, with subsequent amendments, derived from the Building Act 1984. The Regulations now include the inner London area which was previously subject to the London Building Acts 1930–78. A separate system of building control applies in Scotland and Northern Ireland.

Purpose and Nature of the Regulations

The Building Act 1984 empowers Building Regulations to be made for the following purposes:

(a) to secure the health, safety, welfare and convenience of people in or about buildings who may be affected by buildings or matters connected with buildings;
(b) to further the conservation of fuel and power;
(c) to prevent waste, undue consumption, misuse or contamination of water.

The 'Requirements' of the Regulations are as follows and are set out in Schedule 1:

A Structure
B Fire safety
C Site preparation and resistance to moisture
D Toxic substances
E Resistance to the passage of sound
F Ventilation
G Hygiene
H Drainage and waste disposal
J Heat producing appliances
K Stairways, ramps and guards
L Conservation of fuel and power
M Access and facilities for disabled people
N Glazing materials and protection.

One major characteristic of the current Regulations is that they are much shorter and simpler than their predecessors. They impose less detailed control and are drafted in such a way that rigid enforcement is discouraged. Technical detail to support the Regulations is to be found in a series of 'approved documents' and a number of other non-statutory guides and notes. These refer to Codes of Practice, British Standards and similar matters. Their use gives flexibility to the system as they can be altered and updated with relative ease on account of their non-statutory nature. Although use of the approved documents is not mandatory, and will not result in any civil or criminal proceedings being incurred, they can be relied upon in legal proceedings where breach of the Regulations is alleged.

Obtaining Approval under the Regulations

There is a duty upon persons undertaking works which come within the scope of the Regulations to submit plans together with specifications and particulars. The Regulations apply to the initial erection of a building, an extension and any material alteration or change of use. Temporary buildings, those not open to the public and agricultural buildings are exempt. The Building Act 1984 introduced a system of 'approved inspectors', as an alternative to the local authority system, whereby a suitably qualified individual could give a private certification of approval or compliance with the Regulations. This system has not been a success and standard practice is to adhere to the system operated exclusively by the relevant local authorities. The applicant may either submit a 'building notice' to the local authority or submit 'Full Plans'. The latter is the established method of obtaining approval. If plans are submitted which satisfy the Regulations, the plans must be passed. Plans can be passed subject to conditions. The decision of the authority must be given within 5 weeks of the application while this period may be extended to 8 weeks with the agreement of the parties. If works are not commenced within 3 years of the deposit of plans, the authority is entitled to declare the plans as having no effect. Those undertaking building works must indicate the stage that the work has reached. Consequently, notice must be given before the commencement of the works and after completion. The authority may at any time check to see that the Regulations are being complied with.

Contravention is dealt with in the magistrates court. In addition to any fine payable, penalties are imposed for each day the default continues after conviction. Within 12 months of the completion of unauthorised works, the relevant authority may require the owner to alter or pull down the works which infringe the regulations. In default, the authority may do the works themselves and charge the cost to the owner. In appropriate circumstances an injunction may be sought. As far as civil liability is concerned, the 1970s and early 1980s saw numerous cases before the courts where building contractors and local authorities were sued in negligence for breach of the Regulations based on the case of *Anns* v *Merton LBC* (see Chapter 3, section 3.4). Liability in this area of the law is now covered by *Murphy* v *Brentwood BC* (also see Chapter 3, section 3.4) which for all practical purposes decided that there is no claim in negligence in respect of a defective building caused by breach of a Regulation if there is no injury to property or person. Such claims are treated as being claims for economic losses which the law in these circumstances now denies. Section 38 of the Building Act 1984 imposes general civil liability for breach of a duty imposed by the Building Regulations but this section has yet to become law.

5.7 Planning Law

The first comprehensive planning Act in England and Wales dates from 1947. The first attempt to give England and Wales a systematic planning law system was in 1909 but it was not until after the Second World War that an organised system of planning law emerged. The other two areas of law concerned with the living conditions of the population developed much earlier. Both Public Health and Housing legislation were developed to quite a sophisticated degree in the Nineteenth Century, but these are areas of law which have tended to relate to what is happening to individual properties and not to concern themselves with the community and landscape *en bloc*. The law places on a landowner an obligation to obtain planning permission before a building may be erected or the use of land is substantially altered. The current major enactment is the Town and Country Planning Act 1990, while legislation relating to conservation of historic buildings is to be found in the Planning (Listed Buildings and Conservation Areas) Act 1990. Planning law is essentially statutory in nature and delegated legislation plays a significant role in the planning process.

Relatively few planning disputes reach the court system. This is because the process is essentially an administrative one. Day-to-day responsibility for planning matters is entrusted to local government. The local planning authority decides whether planning permission should be granted or not, and in doing so is guided by the law, but more importantly policy is dictated by the current thinking on such matters of the government of the day. This policy is shaped by the Department of the Environment which is the government body responsible for planning matters. Appeals are made to the relevant minister (Secretary of State at the DOE) whose decision does not form any precedent for future matters. Planning matters only tend to reach the courts if the local planning authority or the minister has made a mistake as to the manner in which they have come to a decision. Local planning authorities are responsible for planning matters at a local level. This has mainly been the District Councils but with the growth of Unitary Authorities it may be the County Councils in some areas. In Inner and Outer London, the London Boroughs have appropriate reponsibility.

Development Plans

The Development Plan is central to the planning system and constitutes a blue-print for policies in that area. Since the 1947 Act, planning authorities have been required to produce these plans to show their planning intentions for the future. The plan has two main parts: the structure plan, prepared by the County Councils or Unitary Authority where appropriate, formulates policies and general proposals, while local plans need to be prepared by District or Unitary Authorities. All Metropolitan authorities have been directed to make Unitary development plans, although at the time of writing (November 1997) only one has been made. These statutory plans must be taken into account in any development control decision. In recent years, development plans have gained in importance. Any determination under the planning legislation has to be 'in accordance with the development plan unless material considerations indicate otherwise' (see section 54A Town and Country Planning Act 1990). Notice should be taken of Planning Policy Guidance Notes (PPGS) and Minerals Planning Guidance Notes (MPGS). These are published to provide concise and practical guidance on planning policies, while advice on legislation and procedures is to be found in Departmental Circulars.

The Need for Planning Permission

The key word in the planning system is development. If an activity on land amounts to development the consequence is that planning permission is required, while if the activity does not amount to development then no planning permission is required. 'Development' is defined in the Town and Country Planning Act 1990 as 'the carrying out of building, engineering, mining or other operations in, on, over or under land, or the making of any material change in the use of any buildings or other land'. It therefore comprises:

(1) Operations;
(2) Material change of use.

In most cases, operations development is straightfoward. If a building is being erected on land this will be operations development, although technically engineering works and mining activities come within the scope of the Act. To constitute operations there must be a change in the physical character of the land. Material change of use is a more difficult concept. Material change means a substantial change and it is quite possible to have a change of use which does not amount to development. Whether the change is material is a question of fact and degree for the Local Planning Authority. An intensification of use may amount to a material change (*Brooks and Burton* v *DOE [1977] 1 WLR 1094*). A potential developer may seek a determination under section 64 of TCPA 1990, from the Local Planning Authority, as to whether a particular activity constitutes development within the Act. A appeal may be made against the authority's decision to the DOE with a further appeal to the High Court.

The Act also states that there are certain activities which do not amount to development and consequently do not need planning permission. These are:

(1) Internal works.
(2) Repairs to the highway.
(3) Repairs to public services such as sewers.
(4) Use of a building within the boundary of a house which is incidental to its enjoyment. This must not involve the erection of any new structure, simply an alteration to an existing one.
(5)   Use of land for agricultural or forestry purposes.
(6) A change of use within a specified use class.

The subject of Use Classes has been dealt with by statutory instrument since the immediate post-war legislation. The Use Classes Order (*Town and Country Planning (Use Classes) Order 1987 SI 764*) puts certain uses into classes, with the result that a change of use from one to another within the same Use Class will not be development. Therefore there is no need to seek planning permission. So, a change from one type of office use to another type of office use or from one type of shop use to another shop use will not attract the need for planning permission. It should be remembered that as far as the above are concerned, it may still be necessary to obtain consent under the Building Regulations or because the building is a listed building.

Permitted Development

Certain activities on land are considered to amount to development but are not important enough to warrant the need for permission. These classes of development are to be found in the current General Permitted Development Order (*Town and Country Planning [General Permitted Development Order] 1995*). No express consent is required from the Local Planning Authority because planning permission is deemed to be automatically granted. The GPDO also deals with the procedures for publicity, consultation and determination of applications for planning permission. A well known example of the operation of the GPDO is in part 1, which permits extension to a dwelling house provided certain restrictions relating to cubic content, ground area, height and distance from the highway/boundary of the property are not exceeded.

The Application Itself

The application is made to the Local Planning Authority with the appropriate fee. The form should be accompanied by plans and drawings indicating the location and form of development. If the applicant is not the estate owner, a certificate stating the applicant's legal interest in the land and, where appropriate, that notice has been given to the owner must also be submitted. In the case of operations development, an intending developer may wish to test the likelihood of whether or not the authority will allow a consent. In such a case an outline application may be made, indicating the proposed development with an appropriate site plan. Any permission granted will be subject to a subsequent approval of 'reserved matters', such as landscaping or access which are not referred to in the application. The application may be refused, granted or granted subject to conditions. If the final course is chosen, the conditions must relate to the proposed development and must not be inserted for an underhand purpose (*Newbury DC* v *DOE [1980] AC 578*). Unless the parties agree to an extension, the planning authority has 8 weeks in which to come to a decision. If permission is granted, the development which is authorised must be started within 5 years of obtaining consent. Applicants for major projects must now consider the environmental aspects and whether or not the application is subject to an 'Environmental assessment statement'.

Appeals

Where a planning authority refuses an application or imposes conditions upon the consent, the applicant may appeal to the Secretary of State at the DOE. Notice of appeal must be given within 6 months. Most appeals are dealt with on the basis of written representations made by the parties, but if either side requests it the issue must be dealt with by public local enquiry before a Planning Inspector from the Department. A final appeal, on a point of law, may be made to the High Court. If planning permission has been refused or granted subject to conditions and the owner of the land can show that the land is incapable of reasonably beneficial use in its existing state, the owner may serve a purchase notice on the planning authority requiring them to buy the land at market value (sections 137–148 of the 1990 Act).

Enforcement

In the case of 'a breach of planning control' the Local Planning Authority has a discretion to issue an enforcement notice on the owners and occupiers of the land and any other person who the authority considers is materially affected by the notice. If the breach occurs in a Conservation Area, or the building is listed, a Listed Building Enforcement Notice may be issued. The notice must specify the breach complained of, the steps to be taken to remedy the breach, the date upon which the notice will take effect and the period for compliance with the notice. Breach of planning control on its own is not a criminal offence but failure to comply with a valid enforcement notice is. The notice must be served within 4 years of the breach complained of and in other cases within 10 years of the breach.

To avoid the use of delaying tactics, the planning authority may serve a stop notice requiring the offending development to be curtailed. There is no right of appeal in respect of this notice but any appeal against the enforcement notice must be made to the Secretary of State at the DOE. There is a further right of appeal on a point of law to the High Court. In the event of non-compliance with the notice, the planning authority may enter the land and carry out the steps required by the enforcement notice and recover any expenses due. Although enforcement notices are still the main weapon available to the planning authority, a number of alternative procedures have been devised to cover specific situations instead of relying on the enforcement notice in every case. In particular, a Planning Contravention Notice can be served where there is a suspected breach of planning control, and similarly a Breach of Condition Notice is applicable in breach of condition cases.

Buildings of Special Architectural or Historic Interest

Such buildings are now governed by separate legislation. The Planning (Listed Buildings and Conservation Areas) Act 1990 is applicable. There is an obligation upon the minister to compile a list of buildings of special architectural or historic interest. In this respect the government department works closely with local planning authorities and English Heritage. Once a building is listed, before any alteration or extension can take place, the applicant must obtain a Listed Building Consent. Failure to obtain such a consent may lead to a Listed Building Enforcement Notice being served on the person responsible.

5.8   Compulsory Purchase

In the United Kingdom, compulsory acquisition of land can only be carried out if there is a power of acquisition granted by law. Therefore, there is a need for statutory powers. In the late Eighteenth and early Nineteenth Centuries, powers were frequently sought, from Parliament, by private companies to enable them to provide services such as canals and later the railways. At that time the only method available of obtaining compulsory powers was to promote a private bill. The Lands Clauses Consolidation Act 1845 improved the situation by incorporating into one Act the types of provisions previously inserted into each separate Act by providing a code of law covering all questions relating to the exercise of powers of compulsory acquisition. This Code of compulsory purchase powers could therefore be incorporated into other legislation by reference. These provisions are consolidated in the Compulsory Purchase Act 1965. Nowadays, the normal acquiring bodies are government departments and agencies and local authorities. A variety of legislation deals with the acquisition process and the activating of compulsory powers. Sometimes land is acquired by agreement, in which case the transaction is similar to ordinary conveyancing procedures while there may be a confirmed compulsory purchase order (CPO) in the background. The basis of compensation is market value. Section 5 of the Land Compensation Act 1961 lays down a number of rules relating to the value of land, while retaining the right of the claimant to additional compensation for disturbance and other matters suffered in consequence of the land being taken.

The 'Six Rules'

1. No allowance is to be made on account of the acquisition being compulsory.

2. The value of the land shall be taken to be the amount which it might be expected to realise if sold on the open market by a willing seller. This rule is the proper basis of valuation. Such a seller is a free agent. He is not 'a person willing to sell his property without reserve for any price he can obtain for it'.

3. Where the land is specially suited or adaptable for a particular purpose, this shall not be taken into account, if the purpose is one to which the land could be applied only in pursuance of a statutory power or for which there is no market apart from the special needs of a particular purchaser or the requirements of any authority possessing compulsory purchase powers.

4. Where the value of the land is increased by reason of the use thereof or of any premises thereon in a manner which could be constrained by a court or is contrary to law or detrimental to the health of the inmates or to public health, the amount of that increase would not be taken into account.

5. Where the land is used for a purpose of a kind for which there is no general demand or market, compensation may be assessed on the basis of the reasonable cost of reinstatement if the Lands Tribunal is satisfied that reinstatement in some other place is *bona fide* intended.

This equivalent reinstatement rule is applicable where the claimant owns property for which there is no ready market. In such a case an assessment on market value basis would be unjust. Therefore the cost of acquiring property elsewhere for a specific purpose is allowed. There must be a *bona fide* intention to rebuild elsewhere while the cost of reinstatement must not be disproportionately high.

6. This relates back to rule 2 and states that the provisions of rule 2 shall not affect the assessment of compensation for disturbance or other matters not directly based on the valuation of land.

Additional rules deal with market increases and decreases. Those which are not genuine are to be disregarded, while an increase in the value of an owner's adjoining land which is not taken by the authority must be 'set off' against compensation if it results from the compulsory acquisition. Certain assumptions are also made by the Act in respect of planning permission (*Land Compensation Act 1961 section 16*).

Extra Claims

In addition to market value compensation, a claim may be made for disturbance. This is to compensate the claimant for having to vacate the premises. Any loss which relates to the compulsory acquisition can be recovered so long as the loss is not too remote and is the direct consequence of the compulsory acquisition. In *Harvey* v *Crawley Development Corporation [1957] 1 QB 485* the plaintiff made an additional claim for disturbance and expenses arising out of an abortive purchase of a new house and the actual purchase of her new home. The claim was successful.

Disturbance compensation may be assessed on the basis of total extinguishment. This only applies if the claimant is over 60 years of age, occupies business premises within an appropriate limit for rating purposes and does not wish to relocate the business elsewhere. The claimant is required to undertake that he will not dispose of the goodwill or re-engage in a similar business within the area. Also, he must adhere to the limits imposed by the authority (*section 60 Land Compensation Act 1973*).

Where part of the plaintiff's land is taken, a claim may be made for injurious affection. This may take a number of forms. A severance payment is claimed where the value of the claimant's land which remains after compulsory acquisition is so reduced that its new value, taking compensation paid for the land into account, is lower than the total value before the land was severed. A good example of severance would occur where farmland is severed on the construction of a new highway. Injurious affection proper greatly resembles private nuisance. The claim is made where after compulsory acquisition of part of the claimant's land, the land which remains is reduced in value because of works which are carried out on the land taken. This may cause noise, dust, loss of privacy or similar discomfort. Compensation will be equal to the diminution in the value of the land. Where no land has been taken from the claimant and he is prejudicially affected by what is done on neighbouring land, more difficulty arises. Before such a claim can be successful, the conditions laid down in *Metropolitan Board of Works* v *McCarthy [1874] 31 LT 182* have to be satisfied. These are as follows:

(a) The action giving rise to the depreciation of the claimant's land must be authorised by statute.

(b) The cause of depreciation must be actionable at law but for the statutory authority.

(c) Compensation can only be claimed for depreciation of rights in land.

(d) The loss must be caused by the 'execution of works' and not by the use of the land after the acquiring authority has carried out those works.

Because of the narrow basis upon which such a claim could be brought the Land Compensation Act 1973 was enacted. This gave owners a right to compensation for depreciation to their land caused by the use as distinct from the execution of the works (*Part 1 Land Compensation Act 1973*).

5.9 Environmental Law

What is it?

This expression applies to a number of areas of law which have relevance to the environment in which we live. Water, air, waste, the atmosphere and noise are typical examples. The law on these topics is derived primarily from Public Health legislation. The Public Health Acts 1875, 1936, 1961 dealt with matters such as sewers and drains, clean air, water supply, refuse collection and statutory nuisances. Similarly, until the 1960s the Building Regulations were derived from Public Health legislation. Planning law helped to lay the foundations of environmental law in England and Wales. In fact, until the late 1980s it was the only comprehensive body of law actually concerned with the natural environment.

A major piece of legislation is the Environmental Protection Act 1990 (EPA) which has brought into being a sophisticated overall system of pollution control. The Environmental Act 1995 is the most recent example of major legislation in this area.

Who has responsibility?

A wide range of authorities have responsibility. At central government level, the Department of the Environment is the relevant authority. At a local level, in non-unitary areas, the obligations vary from County to District while many 'Next Steps' agencies have environmental responsibilities. Another important factor is the role of EC law in environmental matters.

(a) Nuisance

Before the development of environmental law on an integrated basis, plaintiffs seeking to bring claims in many of these areas of law were reduced to relying on the common law remedy of a claim based on nuisance. This was, and is, a cumbersome, expensive and slow process. The solution lay in putting the most common nuisances in statutory form, having the system operated by local authorities, and instigating criminal penalties. Where a nuisance could be dealt with by this process it became known as a 'statutory nuisance'. Although originally conceived in the 1840s, for many years the law was to be found in the Public Health Act 1936. The current law is to be found in part 3 of the Environmental Protection Act 1990 (EPA). Section 79 of the Act states which circumstances can give rise to a statutory nuisance:

(1) premises in such a state as to be prejudicial to health or a nuisance;
(2) smoke emitted from premises so as to be prejudicial to health or a nuisance;
(3) fumes or gases emitted from premises which are private dwellings so as to be prejudicial to health or a nuisance;
(4) dust, steam, smell or other effluvia arising on industrial, trade or business premises and being prejudicial to health or a nuisance;
(5) any accumulation or deposit which is prejudicial to health or a nuisance;
(6) an animal kept in such a place or manner as to be prejudicial to health or a nuisance;
(7) noise emitted from premises so as to be prejudicial to health or a nuisance;
(8) any other matter declared by any enactment to be a statutory nuisance;
(9) noise that is prejudicial to health or a nuisance caused by a vehicle, machinery or equipment in a street.

'Prejudicial to health or a nuisance'

Before any of the above situations can be classed as statutory nuisances, the circumstances complained of must be 'prejudicial to health or a nuisance'. At one time the courts interpreted this as being any personal discomfort or temporary inconvenience (*Betts v Penge UDC [1942] 2 KB 154*), but more recent case law seems to indicate that the act complained of must either be a nuisance, in the common law sense, or an actual threat to the health of persons affected by it (*Coventry City Council v Cartwright [1975] 1 WLR 543; NCB v Thorne [1976] 1 WLR 543*).

Abatement

By section 79 of the EPA 1990, every local authority has a duty to inspect its areas for statutory nuisances and to take steps to abate them. This also includes investigating complaints from local residents relating to such matters. Where appropriate, the authority must serve an 'abatement notice' on the person responsible for the nuisance, and in some circumstances the owner of the subject property. The notice must state the steps to be taken to abate the nuisance and the penalties for non-compliance. An appeal against the notice can be made to a Magistrates Court within 21 days. In limited circumstances it is a defence to show that the best practicable means were used to prevent or counteract the nuisance, and in the case of the noise nuisances that the party had a consent from the local authority in respect of the noise under the Control of Pollution Act 1974. It is an offence not to comply with an abatement notice. The party in default can be fined up to £5000, while if the offence is committed on industrial, trade or business premises up to the sum of £20,000. Additional daily fines as high as £200 can be imposed for each day that the offending party is in default. The local authority may itself abate the nuisance if the nuisance is not remedied and recover the cost from the person responsible. Section 82 of EPA 1990 gives a private individual the opportunity to instigate statutory nuisance proceedings. The 'person aggrieved' must make a complaint to a magistrates court and, if satisfied that the nuisance exists, the local authority will take over the proceedings and seek an abatement order.

(b) Noise

In addition to the provisions relating to noise in connection with statutory nuisances, to be found in the EPA 1990, there are other provisions relating to noise in connection with construction sites, plant and machinery and new buildings. These provisions are to be found in the Control of Pollution Act 1974. As far as construction works are concerned, the level of noise is monitored by a consent which must be obtained from the local authority. Such an authority may also designate an area as a Noise Abatement Zone, in which case the noise emanating from the area must be registered in a 'Noise Level Register'.

(c) Water

Water based pollution was based on Rivers and Public Health legislation until 1989 when the Water Act was enacted. In 1991 this Act was replaced by five other Acts and subsequently the Environmental Act 1995. These Acts lay down stringent controls on the right to abstract water from a watercourse or from the ground other than for domestic purposes. Similar stringent rules apply in respect of what can be put into water and also regarding sewerage and trade effluent. The new Environmental Agency (EA) has replaced the regulatory and operational functions formerly undertaken by the National Rivers Authority (NRA).

(d) Contaminated Land

Derelict land only tends to appear to be a problem when the land is being considered for development. This ignores the health and safety and environmental problems that can be caused by land being in a contaminated state. The policy adopted towards contaminated land has traditionally been 'end-use'. Grants available under the Derelict Land Act 1982 have been aimed at ensuring that redevelopment of derelict land costs the same amount as if the development had taken place on a green field site. The Environmental Act 1995 seeks to provide a comprehensive statutory code for tackling contaminated land problems. Local authorities are required to inspect their areas in order to identify such land. If the land is found to be contaminated, the authority must notify the Environmental Agency, the landowner and any other relevant persons having responsibility. The worst contaminated land is classified as 'special' and comes under the direct control of the Agency. In other cases the 'enforcing authority' is the District Council, or in Unitary areas the appropriate authority.

The appropriate enforcing authority must serve a 'remediation notice' on the 'appropriate person', specifying what that person has to do to minimise environmental damage. It appears likely that the authority will frequently serve instead a 'remediation declaration'. This will be appropriate where there is nothing that the notice could usefully require the recipient to do, steps are in hand for remedying the contamination or the authority has power already to carry out the remediation work. The declaration should indicate why the notice has not been served. There is an appeal procedure against the notice to a magistrates court within 21 days. If the notice was served by the Environmental Agency, an appeal will lie to the Secretary of State at the DOE. Regulations have yet to be published dealing with the grounds of appeal. Non-compliance with the notice can result in criminal penalties. If prosecution in the magistrates court is likely to be ineffective, application can be made for an injunction in the High Court. Non-compliance can also result in the use of default powers by the enforcing authority.

Outstanding costs may be charged on the land to which it relates, but only if the landowner actually knowingly permitted or caused the contamination to occur. To charge land with outstanding remediation costs, an authority must first serve a charging notice on the person responsible. The consequence will be that if payment is not made, the authority may sell the land and recover its costs. Again, there are full rights of appeal, this time to the County Court. Once the Act is in force, each enforcing authority will be required to maintain a public register of remediation notices, statements and declarations. Part 2 of the 1995 Act has yet to become law.

6 Property, Construction and the Commercial Environment

6.1 Business Organisations

There are three main methods of carrying on a business in England and Wales. Either as:

(1) A Sole Trader;
(2) In Partnership;
(3) Forming a Limited Company.

Sole Trader

A sole trading position is adopted where only one person is entitled to a share of the profits in an organisation. This may arise in an operation run entirely by one person or where the proprietor of the business employs a number of people. Those who carry on a business in this manner will normally do so because of personal preference. Its principal advantage is almost certainly that of control. A sole trader will have virtually complete control over the organisation subject to the rights of creditors and the Inland Revenue. Such a person will take any profits which the business provides while the business can be run with a considerable degree of privacy. The formalities required are few. On the other hand if the business does incur losses there is nobody else to bear those losses, while the ability to raise money and to generate large sums of capital is a problem. In the professions it is difficult for a sole practitioner to find the time to carry out the work to earn fees, combine that work with management of a practice and take part in professional development. As a consequence many sole practitioners have tried to build niche practices in their respective areas of expertise or ended up amalgamating with others.

Partnerships

Traditionally, partnerships were chosen as a method of carrying on business if there was a restriction on forming a company, as was the case in many professions. In recent years those restrictions have been lifted to a large extent, but even so many professional practices appear to prefer to keep partnership status unless they are of considerable size. Business partnerships, as opposed to those in the professions, are rare because there is seldom any advantage in forming a commercially based firm as opposed to a professional one.

Law and Form

The law is governed by the Partnership Act 1890. The major characteristic of a partnership is that there is in existence the common intention between the partners to carry on a business with a view to making a profit. It will not arise simply because the parties are co-owners of property. It is an unincorporated association. A partnership is valid even though entered into by word of mouth with no formalities. For practical reasons, partners enter into a partnership agreement or articles of association of their firm. This will deal with matters such as the nature of the business, capital, profit and losses, partnership property, holding of meetings etc. The most important aspect of the agreement is that it overrides the basic terms stated in the 1890 Act, thereby being able to cover the position of each individual partner. This agreement is not open to public inspection nor are the accounts of the firm.

Relationship with Other Partners

Each partner owes a duty of good faith to the other partners. Each partner has implied authority to bind the firm by transactions entered into in the ordinary course of business. Partnerships operate on an agency basis. Each partner is entitled to take part in the management of the firm and is entitled to inspect the partnership books. Decisions are made on a show of hands in the majority of cases, but unanimity is required in the case of major changes such as the admission of a new partner. Partners are jointly liable on a contractual basis. The firm may be sued *en bloc* or individual partners may have proceedings brought against them. In tort, partners are jointly and severally liable. The estate of a deceased partner and a retired partner is liable for debts incurred by the firm while a partner. The partnership relationship is brought to an end by dissolution of the firm. This may be effected without a court order and will usually be effected by mutual agreement or by operation of law.

Limited Partnerships

Although common in most European countries, limited partnerships have never been popular in England and Wales owing to the ease of creating limited companies. The concept is governed by the Limited Partnerships Act 1907. If at least one member of the firm incurs complete liability for all partnership debts, the liability of the other members may be limited. There must be one or more general partners who are fully liable for the whole of the debts of the firm, and one or more limited partners whose liability is limited to a specified amount which is contributed when entering the partnership.

Companies

A company is an incorporated body which exists as a legal person quite distinct from its members. Its assets belong to the company and not to its members. Unlike a partnership, it has perpetual succession which means that it is unaffected by changes in the membership of the company or alterations to its structure. Companies are creatures of statute and the current law is to be found in the Companies Acts 1985. The Companies Act 1989 introduced new provisions relating to company accounts. The vast majority of companies are limited companies, which means they possess limited liability. This means that in the event of the company being limited by shares (the main type), if the company cannot satisfy its debts the liability of its shareholders is limited to the extent of their shareholding. Such companies can be identified by the word Limited at the end of the company name or the abbreviation Ltd. If the company is a public one (see below), its limited liability is indicated by the letters 'plc' at the end of the company name. Non-profit-making companies sometimes form themselves as companies limited by guarantee, while a handful of companies operate on the basis of unlimited liability primarily because they are not obliged to file accounts.

Operating the Company

Whatever the category of company, most are private companies. When a private company is formed, the proprietors of the company become members who purchase shares in the company. These shares represent the financial stake of the members. Such a company will tend to have a nominal capital which is issued by dividing the sum into shares of £1 each or similar. The nominal capital of the company may have little relationship to the actual financial state of the organisation. Private companies are often family businesses which tend to be small to medium sized organisations, although there are instances of large family businesses remaining as private companies, where the owners wish to retain as much control as possible. In the case of private companies, the members will also be the managers of the company. There are restrictions on the rights of members of private companies to transfer shares and on the number of members that the company can have. A public company has no such limitations on its membership and transfer of shares. Shares of public companies are bought and sold on the stock exchange and are freely transferable. Such a company is designated by the letters 'plc' at the end of the company name. In the case of these companies, professional managers are invariably recruited to act as managers and directors of the organisation.

A company is formed by lodging a number of documents with the Registrar of Companies (based in Cardiff). The most important of these are the Memorandum of Association and the Articles of Association. The Memorandum sets out the objects of the company while the Articles give details of the internal organisation of the company, such as the names of the directors. Once formed, a Certificate of Incorporation is issued to the company which signifies its birth. After it has been created it will continue to exist despite changes in its organisation until it is wound up. In addition to raising capital, by issuing more shares, a company may borrow money like any other person. In the case of small companies this is often in the form of loans made in return for personal guarantees given by major shareholders. In the case of companies with substantial fixed assets, a loan may be secured by a debenture which is a charge over the company's property.

Companies operate through the wishes of their members at general meetings and through decisions of the board of directors. A director's principal duty is to the company while it is standard practice to make one director a managing director. Directors must carry out their duties with skill and care. Despite their limited liability, they can be held personally liable if the company is trading fraudulently and they know that the company is not going to be able to pay its debts. Companies must hold an annual general meeting to discuss matters such as the accounts and payment of a dividend. This is a periodic income paid to a shareholder by the company, usually representing the financial buoyancy of the company. Decisions at meetings are made in the form of resolutions.

Liquidation of Companies

If a company is to be dissolved it is said to be wound up or put into liquidation. Most winding ups are voluntary operations decided upon by the directors, but the process can also come about by court order where a creditor has presented a winding up petition to the court. If the company has financial problems it may be able to save itself by making voluntary arrangements or by going into full liquidation. Directors of the company make a proposal for such an arrangement. This may amount to a composition of the company's debts or a scheme of arrangement of the company's affairs. The insolvency practitioner appointed under the Insolvency Act 1986 (normally Chartered

Accountants) will be appointed to act as supervisor. If the company is unlikely to be able to pay its debts, an alternative may be an Administration Order. This is made through the court system and the order will be made either because it is considered that the company's future can be secured or to give time for the organisation to make a voluntary arrangement. While the order is in force there can be no order made for liquidation.

Where liquidation of the company becomes necessary the liquidator takes control of the company's property. The powers of the board are taken over and the liquidator is required to call in all assets, realise them, and distribute the proceeds to the appropriate creditors so far as is possible. The liquidator will be particularly concerned with transactions of the company made immediately before liquidation to try to ensure that any disposals made with the intent of defeating creditors are traced. If so, they could well be rendered void. Once the liquidator has paid the costs and expenses of the liquidation, he must pay off the creditors who have submitted formal proof of their debt. Preferential creditors include VAT, PAYE and National Insurance Contributions, amounts secured by floating charges come next, while ordinary unsecured creditors are next in line. If there are surplus funds after distribution to the creditors, these are distributed to the members of the company according to their interests and rights.

6.2   Health and Safety at Work

Before 1974 the health and safety of people at work was governed by a number of stautory provisions. Those in the construction industry were governed by the Factories Act 1961 which was enforced by the Factories Inspectorate. In the 1970s it was realised that more emphasis was being placed on attempting to secure compensation for those injured at work instead of trying to prevent accidents. Consequently, a committee was set up under Lord Robens to inquire into the problem and to make recommendations. The result was The Health and Safety at Work Act 1974 and subsequent amendments to that Act.

The 1974 Act

The Act replaced existing legislation and introduced, in addition, a system of Regulations and Codes of Practice. The operation of the Act is in the hands of the Health and Safety Executive (HSE), while enforcement is the responsibility of Health and Safety inspectors. The Health and Safety Commission (HSC) has the overall duty of achieving the objectives of the legislation. The Commission can order investigations or inquiries into accidents.

Duties

Employers must ensure, as far as is reasonably practicable:

(1) the health, safety and welfare of employees at work;
(2) other persons are not exposed to health and safety risks;
(3) that premises are safe and without risk to health.

Inspectors

Inspectors have extensive rights to enter premises to make investigations and require the production of documents and information. An Improvement Notice may be served where a particular practice is required to be remedied, while in serious cases a Prohibition Notice may be served if there is a risk of serious personal injury.

The Act lays down criminal penalties. It does not confer any civil right of action but does not alter existing ones. Day-to-day operations in the construction industry, both in building and civil engineering work, are governed by the Construction Regulations.

6.3   Construction Regulations

General

When the Health and Safety at Work Act 1974 was enacted, the Construction Regulations that were in force were not repealed but were made to take effect under that Act. The major Regulations which were relevant were as follows:

1. The Construction (Lifting Operations) Regulations 1961.
2. The Construction (General Provisions) Regulations 1961.
3. The Construction (Working Place) Regulations 1966.
4. The Construction (Health and Welfare) Regulations 1966.

In 1992 the Management of Health and Safety at Work Regulations were issued. These and the Workplace (Health Safety and Welfare) Regulations 1992 are the best known of the six sets, known as the 'Six Pack' which came into effect on January 1st 1993. These are derived from a 1989 EC Framework Directive [89]391/EEC. They address a wide variety of basic health, safety and welfare issues such as ventilation, heating, seating and welfare facilities.

The Construction (Health, Safety and Welfare) Regulations 1996

These came into force in September 1996. Essentially, they consolidate, simplify and modernise the 1960s Regulations discussed above. There is now a single set of Regulations applying to most construction work and this has reduced the number of Regulations from 90 to 30. There are some detailed requirements in the schedules but as a general rule they lay down goals to be aimed for.

Duties under the Regulations

The main obligations are imposed on the self-employed, employers and those who control the way in which construction work is carried out. Employees also have a duty to perform their work in a safe manner. In this way the Regulations exemplify the philosophy behind the Health and Safety at Work Act 1974. In such matters everybody has a duty to co-operate with others and report deficiencies to those in control.

The Extent of the Duties

These are mainly the same as in previous Regulations. There have been updates to cover:

(1) safe means of access to and from work;
(2) preventing people falling from heights;
(3) preventing accidental collapse of structures;
(4) preventing risk from underground cables and other services;
(5) giving training in respect of work that could cause injury;
(6) providing welfare facilities.

New provisions have been made in respect of:

(1) providing safe traffic routes;
(2) preventing and controlling emergencies such as fire and explosions.

6.4   The Construction (Design and Management) Regulations 1994

What are these?

These Regulations are derived from the Health and Safety at Work Act 1974 but are based on the Temporary/Mobile Construction Sites Directive. This Directive came into effect in March 1995. The Regulations impose legal obligations on behalf of the construction team, instead of simply trying to avoid unsafe situations. They relate to all construction work. Property development and maintenence work are included.

How do the Regulations work?

There is an obligation to appoint two individuals: a Planning Supervisor (PS) and a Principal Contractor (PC). This is done by the client or the developer. Excluded from the Regulations are projects which are for private domestic clients, are 'in house' or are small projects where the construction phase lasts 30 days or less, occupies 500 person days or less, or employs fewer than 5 persons at one time. The Principal Contractor may be the same person as the Planning Supervisor (PS).

The Planning Supervisor

The PS must notify the Health and Safety Executive (HSE) of the project. Such a person is responsible for compliance with the design requirements. In addition, there is an obligation to advise the client in respect of the competence of the parties involved so far as health and safety matters are concerned. Adequate information must be given regarding potential hazards associated with design, and the PS must ensure that the health and safety plan has been prepared.

The Principal Contractor (PC)

The PC is responsible for co-ordinating work on the project, relevant information, compliance with the health and safety plan, and liaison with the PS. The health and safety plan is in two parts, governing pre-construction and the actual construction stage. Other contractors must co-operate with the PC and give him/her relevant information.

Enforcement

The Regulations are enforceable under the 1974 Act by the HSE, providing for criminal penalties in the event of non-compliance. There is an approved code of practice. A breach of a safety regulation is governed by the criminal law in the same way as the Health and Safety at Work Act 1974. A person who suffers physical injury through a breach of the Regulations can bring a claim for breach of statutory duty, if the Regulations were intended to protect such persons, there is an appropriate loss and the loss was suffered because of the breach (see Chapter 3, section 3.5).

6.5   Insurance

As in other aspects of life, insurance cover is a common feature of property and construction matters. A contract of insurance is one whereby the *Insurer* undertakes to pay a sum of money to the *Insured* on the happening of a particular event. The consideration for the contract is known as the *Premium*.

The Concept of Indemnity

A distinction is made between life assurance and insurance policies based on the concept of indemnity. Indemnity insurance involves the insurer agreeing to compensate the insured on the happening of a particular event. In such circumstances the insured can recover the loss suffered. In the case of life assurance, the event on which the agreement is based will eventually take place (death or attaining a particular age), while in the case of indemnity based insurance the insurer is guarding against a fortuitous event such as theft or fire.

Insurable Interest

An essential ingredient of every insurance contract is that the insured have an insurable interest. This is some foreseeable loss or liability.

The Contract of Insurance

When completing the proposal form, the insured will have made an offer to the insurer. To effect a contract this needs to be accepted by the insurer. The premium will be the consideration. The terms of the agreement are to be found in the insurance policy. The *contra proferentam* rule has application as regards interpretation of the policy, but in practice the policy will be in a standard form drawn up by the insurer. The provisions of The Unfair Contract Terms Act (UCTA) 1977 do not apply to contracts of insurance (see Chapter 2, section 2.7).

The Duty to Disclose

Insurance contracts are *Uberrimae Fidei* (of the utmost good faith). This requires disclosure of all facts that are material. Non-disclosure of a material fact makes the policy voidable at the insurer's option.

Insurance in Connection with Land and Construction Projects

It is standard practice to insure buildings in respect of loss and their contents. In the case of a construction project, insurance is required in respect of the works themselves and also in respect of third party claims. It is common for building contractors to enter into a so-caled CAR policy (Contractors 'All Risks'), which will give some risk of cover in connection with design work, while the professionals involved in the industry, such as architects, surveyors and engineers, will take out PI (professional indemnity).

6.6 Facilities Management

Facilities Management is concerned with the process of managing buildings and what happens inside them. This is linked with the idea of making the best use of buildings on a scientific basis. It is a relatively recent concept which owes much of its progress to the development of space planning and systems furniture in office based activities. It is far wider in scope than office based activities and it can cover essentially any type of building. The growth of information technology has had a considerable impact on its development. It does have its own professional body. This is the International Facilities Management Federation (IFMA).

A body of law is growing, mainly encompassing delegated legislation, which affects premises and workplaces. Much of it is health and safety linked. For example, a new set of Fire Regulations is expected to become law in 1998. They will apply to premises already holding fire certificates but not those issued under the Fire Precautions Act 1971. Licensed premises will not be exempt. In July 1997, the Lifts Regulations 1997 came into force. These govern the installation process together with maintenence and safe use of the lift system.

6.7 Disability Discrimination

The Disability Discrimination Act 1995 makes it unlawful for any employer to discriminate against a disabled person in recruitment procedures and employment practices. It also deals with discrimination in the fields of property and consumer rights. A disabled person is 'anyone who has a physical or mental impairment which has a substantial and long term adverse effect on his ability to carry out normal day to day activities'. There is no obligation to make immediate changes where there are no disabled employees.

Employment Aspects

An employer will discriminate if he treats a disabled person less favourably than he would treat a person without such a disability. This is unless he can show that the less favourable treatment was materially and substantially justifiable. Codes of Practice and delegated legislation will govern the operation of the Act.

An employer must make reasonable adjustments to working arrangements and the workplace itself to eliminate any discrimination. Five criteria are laid down which will assess whether or not the adjustments are reasonable. Any possible disruption to an employer will be taken into account. An aggrieved person who considers that they have been discriminated against may make a complaint to an industrial tribunal. The tribunal has the following options:

(1) to make a declaration as to the rights of the parties;
(2) order the employer to pay compensation to the employee;
(3) make a recommendation for changes that the employer should make within a specified period.

Service Providers

The Act also deals with discrimination in the areas of access to goods, services and also the disposal and management of premises. The essence of the discrimination alleged must be less favourable treatment. It is unlawful for a service provider to discriminate against a disabled person in respect of the former matters. This is where they are provided for other members of the public or provided for the disabled on different terms or to a different standard. These aspects are to be enforced in the County Court.

6.8   Competition Law

One fundamental characteristic of European Community law since its inception has been the promotion of the free movement of goods and services. The EC has pursued a strong competition policy since the Treaty of Rome in 1957. In each member state, competition policy is administered and enforced by national laws assisted by the European Commission. The Commission plays a major role in competition policy. Organisations need to comply with EC and national rules. Articles 85 and 86 of the European Treaty prohibit restrictive agreements and the abuse of a dominant position. The former is mainly concerned with the effects on trade of various restrictive practices, while the latter is concerned with monopolist situations. Under Article 85, exemption under the Treaty is only granted in individual cases if the Commission has been notified of the agreement concerned and a number of conditions are met. If an undertaking wishes to obtain official information that an agreement is not prohibited, it can apply for negative clearance. Because such clearance can only be given by the Commission, the practice has arisen of issuing 'comfort letters' which constitute an opinion that the agreement does not infringe Article 85. The Commission has the central role of enforcing the Community's competition policy and has wide powers to investigate and impose fines.

   In domestic law, agreements which are in restraint of trade are subject to both common law rules (*Esso Petroleum Co Ltd* v *Harper's Garage*

[Stourport] Ltd [1967] 1 All ER 699) and statutory provisions. These include the Fair Trading Act 1973 and the Competition Acts 1980 and 1998. Under the 1973 Act, a monopoly reference may be made to the Monopolies and Mergers Commission by the Director General of Fair Trading. Under the 1998 Act, much of the 1980 Act will disappear and a Competition Commission will replace the Monopolies and Mergers Commission. In practice the 1998 Act introduces a regime into the UK which applies already under EC competition law. In addition to a ban on abuses of dominant position and a general prohibition on anti-competitive agreements, there is a right to fine businesses up to 10 per cent of turnover for breach of the rules. Under the 1998 Act, the Office of Fair Trading (OFT) has much wider investigatory powers. In September 1990, Council Regulation 4064/89, known as the Merger regulation, came into force. It applies to mergers involving enterprises with an aggregate worldwide turnover of more than 5 billion ecu and where the aggregate community turnover of at least two of the enterprises concerned is more than 250 billion ecu. Unless they are primarily within one member state, such mergers are subject to examination by the European Commission (*Esso Petroleum Co Ltd* v *Harper's Garage [Stourport] Ltd* – see above).

6.9 Freedom of Establishment and Provision of Services

Articles 52 to 66 EC are concerned with the freedom of establishment and the freedom to provide services. The right of establishment is a necessary prerequisite to providing a service on a permanent basis in another member state. It applies to organisations and private individuals. The extent to which a person who has professional skills has rights of establishment depends on recognition of professional qualifications and the harmonisation of domestic systems of law in that respect. As long ago as 1962 the Council adopted a programme on the freedom of establishment. Developments in this area have moved at a slow pace, with national governments failing to respond. The principle of equal treatment has not always been suffcient to ensure that the would-be immigrant is able to practise a profession in another member state. The Commission has attempted to tackle the problem by providing separate Directives for each profession. The architectural profession has benefited from such a Directive. Other construction and property based professions in the United Kingdom have found difficulty in taking advantage of these provisions because of the lack of similarity between these professions and those in other member states. One significant development which has helped has been the principle of non-discrimination. In *Patrick* v *Ministre des Affaires Culturelles [1977] ECR 3409* a British architect who was qualified to work in France succeeded in not being debarred from carrying on his professional activities in the other country. The adoption of the Mutual Recognition Directive (89/48), which gives mutual recognition to 'Diplomas' obtained in other member states, may also increase an immigrant's chances of recognition.

The freedom to provide services is also connected with a person's right to visit a member state to provide those services. Articles 59 and 60 EC provide for the removal of restrictions on the freedom to provide services on the basis of Directive 73/148. This has been interpreted also as the right to be a recipient of services (*Luisi & Carbone* v *Ministro del Tesoro [1984] ECR 377*). The concept has been extended specifically to the situation where a student moves to a member state to undertake a vocational course. In such circumstances the student, spouse and dependants have the right to reside in the other state until the end of the course (Directive 93/96).

6.10   Import and Procurement Restrictions

Article 30 EC purports to eliminate quotas by prohibiting quantitative restrictions on imports between member states. This has been considered to include any measure which is a 'total or partial' (*Liseria Luigi Geddo* v *Ente Nazionale Risi [1973] 22/73*) restraint on imports. Some countries use import licence requirements to protect their own domestic industries and markets. The requirement of such a licence is a breach of Article 30 EC. Directive 70/50 passed by the Commission dealt with the question of 'measures having equivalent effect' to quantitative restrictions. This has been interpreted widely and has been considered to cover measures applicable to imports and domestic goods alike. Such measures include regulations designed to enforce minimum standards in respect of size, weight, quality, price and similar matters. The rules would also apply to certification and inspection requirements which ensure that goods conform to these standards. Article 30 EC is aimed at precluding the isolation of national markets and inducing competition. Any form of domestic preference will harm that objective. In *Commission* v *Ireland [1988] Case 45/87* (see also *Cassis de Dijon [Case 120/78]*), a tenderer who offered to use pipes which were manufactured in Spain when seeking to win the Dundalk Water Supply contract in Ireland complained to the Commission when his tender was rejected because the pipes did not have an Irish specification. When proceedings were brought against the Irish Government, by the Commission, the defendants were held to be in breach of their obligations under Article 30. In the United Kingdom a number of Regulations have implemented European Council Directives dealing with the procurement process. They have application to works contracts exceeding 5 million ecu let by a utility or public body (*Public Works Regulations 1991*).

Index